Inside ABC

Inside ABC

American Broadcasting Company's Rise to Power

by

STERLING QUINLAN

Illustrated with photographs

HASTINGS HOUSE · PUBLISHERS
New York NY 10016

Library of Congress Cataloging in Publication Data

Quinlan, Sterling.   Inside ABC.

   Bibliography: p.
   Includes index.
   1. American Broadcasting Company—History.   I. Title.
HE8689.8.Q54   1979   384.54'06'573   79-14049
ISBN 0-8038-6765-4

Published simultaneously in Canada by
Saunders of Toronto, Ltd., Markham, Ontario

Printed in the United States of America

Mary

Contents

Acknowledgment ix

Before Fading to Black xi

Part One
BEGINNINGS

1 A Marriage of Convenience 3

2 Adjourn? We Never Adjourn! 29

3 Shootout at 66th Corral 48

4 High Jinks, Hardball, and Mavericks 67

Part Two
CRISIS TIME

5 Minefields and ITT 87

6 Autonomy Has Been Overemphasized—Harold Geneen 98

7 That Phantom Department Called Justice 103

8 Two Years Down the Drain 114

Part Three
THE TURNING POINT

9 That Crazy Radio Idea 121

10 An Offer You Can't Refuse 133

11 Howard Hughes and His Takeover Machine   142
12 Mayhem In The Executive Suite   153

Part Four
GETTING THE ACT TOGETHER

13 Welcome to the Seventies   169
14 "All Humans Have Taken Nature For Granted"   184
15 Who's On First?   195
16 Derailed   206
17 Miracle on Sixth Avenue   216
18 A Flash in the Pan?   224

Part Five
ABC TODAY

19 Debits and Credits   237
20 News—ABC's Mega-Problem   245
21 Silverman Syndrome   256
22 A Company at the Crossroads   261
23 Dilemma of the Tube   265

Bibliography   277
Index   282

Photographs follow pages 78 and 202.

Acknowledgment

In addition to acknowledging thanks to all those patient souls who sat through long interviews (some of them several times), special thanks are due several persons whose cooperation made this book possible:

Lester Weinrott, of Chicago, served as my own "personal editor" on the manuscript as it was being written. His suggestions, counsel, and editorial assistance were of inestimable value.

Without the help of Roann Levinsohn of ABC, New York, the book would not be as factually accurate as it is. She unstintingly checked dates, names, events, provided files and suggested new sources of information.

Richard "Rick" Giacalone, Director of Still Photography for ABC provided the photographs used in the book. And Kitty Lynch, who operates ABC's research library, cheerfully turned over her facilities whenever they were needed. Without this excellent source this author would still be running down clippings from here, there, and everywhere.

Before Fading to Black

I thought this book would be about a company . . . a company I worked for, had disagreements with, ultimately left over the issue of autonomy; yet a company I have continued to admire out of some perverse sense of loyalty . . . no, that is not quite correct. I have admired ABC because of its *people*.

Therefore what began as a book about a company, ends up being a book about people:

—LEONARD GOLDENSON. The ultimate survivor. Tough and shrewd as they come, but with one vulnerable spot—his dedication to United Cerebral Palsy.

—ELTON RULE, who likes being President, but would not think twice about returning to his beloved California if the job ceased to be fun.

—EDWARD NOBLE, a philanthropist, yet a tightwad. A pixie who enjoyed adding to his legend as an eccentric.

—ROBERT KINTNER, a brilliant executive who became a pawn in the first power struggle.

—OLIVER TREYZ, a maverick in the classic ABC mold, who, had he grown in dimension, could have had it all.

—SIMON SIEGEL, whose inscrutable countenance was really a mask to conceal his sensitivity.

—THEODORE SHAKER, whose cold brilliance was cancelled by an enormous blind spot in dealing with people.

And many others: Fred Pierce, Fred Silverman, Richard O'Leary, Roone Arledge, James Duffy, Julie Barnathan, Tom Moore, Everett Erlick, John Campbell, Mike Mallardi, Jim Hagerty, Elmer Lower, Bill Sheehan—players on an unforgettable stage who stand out in mind as vividly as characters in a Chekhov play. Regardless of what they think of me, or I think of them, I wish them well.

As a company ABC has always been a haven for individualists, many of whom could not have succeeded as well at any other network. Some of the most interesting mavericks ever to ride the kilocycle range found a happy home there. Fear of failing was never ABC's problem because, until recently, one knew that at ABC you could not go down any further; you were already third among three and had only one way to go and that was up.

Innovation has been the mother of ABC's eventual success. Plus a shirt-sleeve kind of informality that has marked its essential style. As one industry watcher put metaphorically:

"CBS is like a beautiful girl from the finest finishing school, but in your heart you know she's a whore.

"NBC, with its amorphous, hydra-headed committee style of management over the years is like looking into a series of mirrors and getting back a series of reflections, none of which is alike.

"ABC is two guys bellying up to the Dorset bar at the end of a hard day. One says to the other, "Okay, what's the problem? I gotta catch the 7:10 train." They con the bartender into tossing for drinks. Four hours later the bartender is helping them solve the problem, and paying for most of the drinks."

ABC's past is as fascinating as its present. It is a star-crossed tale, the roots of which go back, not only to the origins of radio, but to the beginnings of the motion picture industry. One root goes back to Paramount Pictures and Adolph Zukor and Barney Balaban. The other goes to the beginnings of radio in 1926; to RCA and General David Sarnoff; to RCA's attempted monopoly of broadcasting through the ownership of the then two NBC networks, the "Red" and the "Blue."

Ironically both companies were spawned by the American bureaucracy, by the Department of Justice in 1949 and the Federal Communications Commission in 1943.

ABC has been lucky in its darkest hours. International Telephone and Telegraph almost took over the company in 1968. Howard Hughes tried and failed in 1969. ABC's success in the past few years has shaken its industry to its foundation. Heads have rolled at the other networks. For better or worse ABC has changed the viewing habits of the nation. ABC is not overly concerned with the fact that it is now the leader, or that it will not be the leader forever. Nevertheless, as positions change, there never again will be the wide gap that separated the three networks in the past.

How this company got to where it is today, how it operates today, and *why* it operates as it does today, is a story that should be of interest to all who ask: where are we today in communications? Are we victims of what we watch, or are we responsible for what we get?

The words "fade to black" are the last words a director utters before he closes a television program. To some who think our civilization has gone "tilt," or is on a collision course with disaster, the words "fade to black" may have ominous portent.

I happen to share that concern. The dilemma of the tube in our society is multi-faceted. Like cancer, it defies any simplistic solution. I cannot resist the urge to add my own thoughts to this growing dialogue.

We may have to color the problem "gray" before we "fade to black."

And ABC, the leading network at the end of this decade, must be as concerned as the rest of us. Maybe more so.

On a personal note I want to add that, in writing this book, ABC has given me the fullest possible cooperation. Files have been made available. Personnel at all levels have talked freely and openly. This is entirely my book about the company. No attempt has been made by anyone to change one word of substantive content. On the other hand I have been helped a great deal in the matter of accuracy of dates, statistics, sequence of events, etc., for which I am grateful.

It also should be noted that I was a member of the company's so-called inner circle in that I spent 17 years with the company— 11 as head of the company's Chicago television operations. The fact that I left the company as a result of irreconcilable differences does not change my opinion that ABC is uniquely colorful in the too-drab corporate world of today. Its *corpus*, to be sure, has some warts. No company has a monopoly on perfection. ABC has made its share of errors. But, by and large, it remains probably the most fascinating company in human terms in broadcasting today—a thesis that, as I have tried to develop it, has given this author a few laughs, some wistful nostalgia, and a lot of warm memories.

STERLING QUINLAN

Chicago, Illinois
April, 1979

Part One

Beginnings

1

A Marriage
of Convenience

IN THE WINTER of 1951 Leonard H. Goldenson, in his year-old
United Paramount Theatres headquarters in the Paramount
Building of New York City, received a phone call from a longtime
friend, Earl McClintock.

"Ed Noble, who owns ABC, is in financial trouble. Would
you be interested in ABC, Leonard?"

Goldenson, President of UPT, was not surprised. There had
been rumors about ABC's financial plight for months. He had to
believe the news was true because McClintock was also a close
friend of Noble's. Earl McClintock was head of the International
Division of Sterling Drug and had formerly served on the Board
of United Paramount's predecessor company, Paramount Pictures, Inc.

"I certainly am interested," said Goldenson. "When can we
meet?"

"I'll set up an appointment."

As soon as Goldenson hung up the phone his mind began to
turn. Acquiring ABC by merger would be an answer to his

3

dreams. United Paramount Theatres, Inc., virtually a corporate infant, had been set up slightly more than a year before—January 1, 1950. It had been created as a result of a government Consent Decree between Paramount Pictures and the U.S. Department of Justice. In it Paramount had agreed to separate its studio production facilities from its theatrical exhibition system. As a condition of the Consent Decree UPT was in the process of reducing its number of theatres from 1,500 to no more than 651 by the year 1952.[1] It was a monumental task, the largest and most complex job of reorganizing assets in the history of American business. The sale of so many theatres would bring in lots of cash and Goldenson knew where he wanted to put that cash—in the still almost virgin field of television. The year before he had tried to buy Dorothy Schiff's station in Los Angeles, and the *New York Daily News* station in New York City; but both attempts had met with no success. Dorothy Schiff, owner of the *New York Post*, knew that television was the hottest new game in the country; the few pioneering license holders who already were on the air were trying to get *more* stations, not sell the ones they had. Since WW II about 100 stations had taken the air and a number were under construction. To complicate matters, the Federal Communications Commission had "frozen" all license applications in 1948. But Leonard Goldenson was determined that, sooner or later, UPT would put all of its chips on television.

Rumors were rampant about ABC's cash bind. Still, ABC had pulled off a miracle of its own. Back in 1946 Robert Hinckley had ended a brilliant career in government service and had rejoined his old friend, Noble. Hinckley urged Noble to broaden his radio network into television. There was nothing startling about that, for the other radio networks and broadcast groups were planning to do the same thing. The competitors were interested in the lower VHF (Very High Frequency) channels of 2 through 6, but Hinckley had a better idea. Channel 7, he told ABC, was wide open in five of the six largest cities in the U.S. "Let's go after

---

[1] With approval of Department of Justice, final divestiture requirements were met in March, 1957.

those," Hinckley said. "We can get them without a contest." Frank Marx, ABC's engineering chief, agreed. Indeed, the higher channels might be better, said Marx. There were rumors about the Government eventually turning the lower portion of the 12-channel VHF spectrum over to the military. And so the rather threadbare third network, ABC, walked in where the bigger powers feared to tread and gained for itself an invaluable franchise in five of the country's largest cities—a franchise that, to this day, NBC and CBS have been unable to equal. In 1947 the licenses were granted, and a year later, three stations were launched in New York City, Chicago, and Detroit. In 1949 two more, San Francisco and Los Angeles went on the air. An incredible world record that deserves a place in the *Guinness Book of Records*.

However, Ed Noble soon discovered that television was a costly business. Even more costly was that of trying to develop a third network. The fourth network, actually, because a third television network, DuMont, was already operating.

A few days after his telephone call from McClintock, Goldenson, joined by his two top aides, Robert H. O'Brien and Walter Gross, and lawyer Ed Weisl, met with Noble in Noble's lavish suite in Waldorf Towers. Well wishes from colleagues preceded the visit:

"Be careful," they advised. "He's a smart old boy. When you shake hands with Noble count your fingers afterwards to see if you still have all five!"

The meeting went cordially enough. Chit chat. Sizing each other up. Noble had his "money man," Earl Anderson with him. It lasted about an hour. It took that long to pry out of the 69-year old self-made millionaire the most important information upon which any future negotiations would turn: the price.

The old man finally gave it to them with a smile. He wanted $25 million!

Goldenson's own smile froze. He was appalled. He was not a tall man and now he seemed to become perceptibly shorter. So did O'Brien, Gross and Weisl.

Yes, $25 million, Noble repeated, still smiling. He enjoyed giving surprises to people. That figure, he emphasized, was *not* negotiable. Other things were. But not the price. He had learned a long time ago, from the crusty old head of RCA, General David Sarnoff, that once you set a price you must stick with it.

Goldenson looked at O'Brien, and O'Brien looked at Weisl. All three could have used a few of Ed Noble's Life Saver peppermints, the candy product that had made Noble his first of many millions.

Based on the value of the assets, the price was plainly outrageous. ABC had earned the year before, in 1950, a paltry $84,605, because of television losses which were almost $2 million. In 1949 it had lost more than half a million dollars, with television losses amounting to $4½ million. In the very beginning, from the time Edward J. Noble had purchased the Blue Network from General Sarnoff, ABC's profits had been in the half to one-and-a-half million dollar range; but the coming of television changed all that.

"Ed, it's been a pleasure meeting with you," said Leonard Goldenson as he headed toward the door. "We'll let you know if we're interested in talking further."

As far as Goldenson was concerned, the meeting hadn't really been a pleasure at all. ABC, at its present book value was worth about $10 million. Fifteen at the most. Even if you tacked on five million for the dream of television and the future, you could not justify more than $20 million. He thought: if I brought Noble's figure to my Board of Directors they would think I had lost my mind. So Goldenson did what he thought was the smartest thing to do: he decided to let Ed Noble cool his heels. After a few weeks of silence—and a few more hundred thousand dollars down the drain—maybe then the candy king would come to his senses.

Yet this tactic did not make Goldenson entirely comfortable. What if another company came along and paid Noble such a ridiculous price? No question about it, television was hot. There might be other companies with enough imagination to see its potential. Losing an opportunity like ABC would be a blow since he had vowed to put all of UPT's fiscal eggs in the basket of the new technology. Yes, playing a waiting game definitely had its risks.

Ed Noble, on the other hand, thought he thoroughly understood Leonard Goldenson's game. He prided himself on knowing
every bargaining gambit in the book. If United Paramount
wanted to play a waiting game, let them do it at their own peril.
Hardly a day went by without some company expressing an interest in "helping ABC with its financial problems." To be sure,
losses were piling up, and though he was a wealthy man, he knew
he could not keep pouring money out at this rate. On the other
hand, television set sales were increasing dramatically every
month. Advertisers liked the medium. Stubborn resolution was
all that was needed to get over this hump; the kind of resolution
old General Sarnoff had taught Noble back in 1943 when Sarnoff
had stuck him with $8 million for the NBC Blue Network. Some
42 different companies (including, ironically enough, Paramount
Pictures) had dickered with Sarnoff, trying to get him down to a
lower price. Ed Noble remembered how he had tried, then had
backed off, playing the waiting game just as Goldenson was playing it now. But Sarnoff had stuck to his guns and forced Noble to
come up with the $8 million in cash.[2] So, thought Noble, Leon-
ard Goldenson and UPT could wait till hell froze over.

By now, at 69, Edward John Noble had earned enough
money, had achieved enough success, to be able to indulge in,
and enjoy, his eccentricities. Indeed, he took pleasure in springing them on friends and strangers. Noble had the benign country
bumpkin countenance of that famous old Hollywood character
actor, S. Z. Sakal; his square, cherubic face with its rosy cheeks,
blue eyes, and silver mane, made him a perfect candidate for
Santa Claus in Macy's window. On the other hand, he had a steel-

---

[2] Mr. James McGraw, President of McGraw-Hill Publishing Company was to
have been a purchaser along with Noble, but he dropped out at the last minute.
Time-Life, and Chester LaRoche, then joined Noble, each purchasing 12% of
the company. Later they sold their interest back to Noble. Mark Woods was
given the right to purchase 3% of the company, which he exercised. Among the
groups vying for the Blue Network were: American Type Founders Corporation;
Dillon, Read & Company; the Mellon family; Marshall Field; Paramount Publix
Corporation; and Thomas P. Durell.

What Noble got for his money was a network of 116 affiliates, and ownership of 2½ radio stations: WJZ, New York City; KGO, San Francisco; WENR,
Chicago, which shared a frequency with WLS, a farm oriented station.

trap mind and a cold, unforgiving heart—although, at the same time, his charitable contributions went far beyond those of most men of wealth.

Like most men of achievement, he was a man of contradictions. Yet Noble had something else going for him. Although he came from modest beginnings, his career fitting perfectly the American cliché of the "self-made man," the truth was that Ed Noble had never failed at anything he tried! Part of his legend was his uncanny ability to take losing situations and turn them around. Furthermore, he had an almost mystical belief in his ability always to come out on top in any financial deal.

On the personal side, he was, if not the biggest tightwad in New York City, at least a strong contender for such a dubious honor. No one ever remembered Ed Noble paying for a cab bill; only on rare occasions did he pick up luncheon tabs. In one burst of cost-cutting zeal he suggested to ABC President, Robert E. Kintner, that business phones be removed and pay phones installed. He knew about the legend that surrounded him and delighted in contributing to it at every opportunity.

Despite all this, he was a curiously likeable gentleman who chuckled at his own peccadilloes and knew that others were chuckling, too. If they were laughing *at* him, or *with* him, it made no difference to Noble. He knew that he was considered a "character." After you have made all the money a human being can require, what else was there to do, but become a "character"?

Yet there was no mistaking the fact that he was one of the country's outstanding success stories.

As a boy, Ed Noble had always had a fondness for peppermint lozenges. He bought them daily at the corner store in his small upstate New York home town of Gouverneur. In 1913, in Cleveland, he met Clarence A. Crane (father of the famous author, Hart Crane) and tried to interest the Cleveland candy maker in promoting his peppermint candies—called Life Savers— via car card advertising, a business in which Noble then worked.

Crane wanted no part of Noble's far-out promotion schemes. "If you think you're so good, why don't you promote them yourself?" he asked.

Noble did just that. He, and a boyhood friend, J. Roy Allen, scraped together $1,900 and bought Crane's stock and his "Life Savers" trademark. Noble returned to New York, rented a loft, bought some pans, kettles and sugar, and proceeded to make Life Savers at night while he worked days at his regular job with a car card advertising firm, Ward & Gow.

A problem, however, developed. The candy's flavor quickly evaporated in its poor cardboard wrapping. The mints took on the flavor of glue. So Noble invented a new container, along with a light cardboard shipping package that could be set up on counters as miniature display cases. Noble's success was assured. In 1928 he sold Life Savers for $22 million. The purchasing company, however, was merged into a large drug holding company which dissolved in 1933. In picking up the pieces afterward, Ed Noble acquired substantial amounts of stock in Sterling Drug, Vick Chemical, Bristol-Myers, and United Drug; not to mention the fact that he also *reacquired Life Savers!* Little wonder that he felt invincible.

In the early 'thirties Noble took up flying and became, also, an accomplished autogyro pilot. This interest in aviation led him to Washington where, in 1938, he became the first Chairman of the Civil Aeronautics Authority. After that he was appointed Under Secretary of Commerce, a position he relinquished in 1940 when he decided to campaign for Wendell Willkie.

Though he never carried cash, thereby adding to his reputation for being a tightwad, Ed Noble lived in lavish style. The thousand-acre estate he had bought from George C. Boldt, owner of the Hotel Waldorf-Astoria, had its own airport, golf course, tennis courts, swimming pool, and hunting grounds. In addition to this estate which was located in the Thousand Islands area of the St. Lawrence River, he owned a home in Greenwich, Connecticut.

Between Ed Noble and Leonard Goldenson there were virtually no similarities. For one, Goldenson was only 46, compared to Noble's 69. Goldenson had an ingratiating smile and a charm that belied his inner toughness. He listened well. Too well, some said. Goldenson often appeared almost too anxious to please. He disliked confrontations. He preferred having someone else be his tough guy.

Yet this was largely a facade. Very few knew how tough he could be, or how determined he was once he set a course of action.

The theatrical unions in Detroit, back in 1938, knew how tough he could be, along with the film distributors. Shortly after he had been placed in charge of the vast Paramount Theatre Division, when he had successfully reorganized some 260 Paramount theatres in New England, Leonard Goldenson had turned his attention to the United Detroit Theatre Corporation which was still in a financial mess. The operator of that chain, George Trendle, had "given away the store" by accepting onerous contracts from theatrical unions, and paying exorbitant fees to distributors for pictures. When Goldenson came to Detroit he ordered all payments stopped, which was tantamount to declaring war. A long and bitter strike ensued. But in the end Goldenson won. One year after he renegotiated all contracts with unions and distributors, the Detroit operation turned around from a $300,000 per year loss to a profit of $750,000.

When United Paramount Theatres was formed in 1950, Goldenson's determination to move UPT into television became almost fanatical. Some of his colleagues, however, were skeptical. What was the wisdom, they asked, in putting UPT's resources into the very medium that might mean the demise of theatres? Goldenson didn't see it that way. Each medium had its niche, he said. If theatrical exhibition declined in the long run, why shouldn't UPT have its stake in the new medium?

Hence, from the beginning, television had become Goldenson's secret game plan; as far back as 1948, a year before UPT had been formed; all through 1948 as details of the Consent Decree had been hammered out with the Department of Justice; on up to March 3, 1949 when the decree had been signed.

That had been a momentous date for the motion picture industry. The date when the industry had "thrown in the sponge," some said. Others congratulated Paramount for once more assuming the leadership of a frightened industry. No one, even diehards in the industry, questioned the propriety of the decision, or the fact that the picture industry was guilty of monopolistic practices. Yet it had been a long, drawn-out legal battle. Many lawyers put their kids through college just on fees from this case. When the Supreme Court said yes, the industry had been guilty of gross and flagrant monopoly practices, Paramount became the first to enter into a Consent Decree with the Justice Department. Paramount agreed to separate its production of pictures from its exhibition system. It agreed to cease its stranglehold on theaters in the U.S. and open up exhibition channels to competition.

Paramount, being the largest company, got most of the blame for the fix in which Hollywood found itself. It was the largest company of its kind in the world: a colossus with 1,500 theatres in the U.S., plus 350 in Canada; 14 in England; 2 in France; and several in South America. Many accused Paramount of having started this game of monopoly which led to the Justice Department invoking the Sherman Anti-Trust Act. But the trend had been started, ironically enough, by a theatre company called National Theatres back in the 'twenties. National, with some 500 theatres of its own, decided to "invade" Hollywood and set up its own production studio. Adolph Zukor, then head of Paramount, and considered even then the wisest sage of the industry, pleaded against this trend.

"It will be ruinous to the industry," he pleaded. And he turned out to be right.

So, in 1948, when the Paramount Board decided that wisdom was the better part of valor, and the company should be first to settle its problems with a meddlesome government, Leonard Goldenson had the forlorn pleasure of participating in the division of Paramount's assets. But the good news was that he would head up the new company to be called United Paramount Theatres which would be given all of Paramount's U.S. theatre assets, plus one of two television stations it owned.

Barney Balaban, Goldenson's cost conscious, no-nonsense boss, chose to remain as head of Paramount studios. In dividing the assets Balaban unquestionably gave himself the better of the bargain. He retained the production studios, the 18-story Paramount Building in New York, 369 theatres in Canada, England, France, and South America not affected by the consent decree, and the second of the company's two television stations. Balaban kept KTLA in Los Angeles and gave the new company WBKB in Chicago. Balaban did something else only a boss could do—he took out a $35 million loan on the entire company, gave United Paramount half the money, kept the other half for Paramount Pictures, and gave the new company, UPT, the obligation to *repay* the entire loan!

Balaban did something else that worried Goldenson. He retained 25% interest in Allen B. DuMont Laboratories, a company that not only made television sets but owned three VHF television stations in New York City, Pittsburgh, and Washington D.C., not to mention a television license application for the city of Boston. In addition, DuMont operated a fledgling television network which preceded ABC's television network by two years.

Therefore, Paramount was in a perfect posture to become the dominant force in U.S. television, exceeding even NBC or CBS. Yet in a stunning, and baffling example of missed opportunities, Paramount Pictures did not move forward. All through 1948 as the consent decree was being worked out, until it was signed March 3, 1949, Goldenson lived in trepidation thinking that Paramount, and Barney Balaban, would wake up and realize it was missing the opportunity of the century.

And that was odd, for Paramount had always been the most resourceful and far-sighted company in Hollywood—although it had owned half of CBS in the late 'twenties; needing cash, Paramount sold its interest back to CBS for $4 million cash. In television it had spent as much as a million dollars a year researching the new medium. It had an investment in the patents of the Scophony large screen theatre television process. It was talking about a new-fangled pay television system called International Telemeter. Later, through DuMont, it would develop the Lawrence chromatic color television tube. If one included the three DuMont stations, and the two fully owned Paramount stations, it already had the maximum number of stations a company could own. When one added to that Paramount's production capability and its backlog of pictures, it was clear that no company in America was better situated to become the dominant force in the new medium. So Goldenson waited and held his breath, hoping that Paramount would not move forward as he intended to do under the aegis of his new company, United Paramount Theatres.

The problem was not that Paramount was disinterested in television. Barney Balaban simply did not want to invest the kind of money it would take to succeed in the new medium. DuMont's struggling network got little support from Balaban or his television mentor, a brilliant mathematician named Paul Raibourn. They continually harassed Dr. Allen DuMont about costs. Rancor developed. DuMont wondered why he had ever gotten involved with Paramount. For Goldenson it was a sad experience to see all this happen—the opportunity of the century waiting to be grasped . . . while at the same time, the largest and most successful film company in the world was voluntarily dismantling itself.

Perhaps Paramount's lapse was symptomatic of a larger malaise, a kind of myopia that affected the entire picture industry during that period of shock, fear and paranoia, as television began to emerge.

Robert O'Brien, who served as assistant to Barney Balaban, remembers the time, at O'Brien's urging and Balaban's invitation, that Paul Porter, then Chairman of the FCC came to speak to the leaders of the industry in 1949. The subject, of course, was television, and why the picture moguls should not let television slip through their grasp.

"Paul Porter pleaded with them to climb aboard," recalls O'Brien. "Get in early, he told them. Become television pioneers. But whether it was from fear, or apathy, many of them left the dinner that night before Porter had finished his speech."

Perhaps Barney Balaban's very strength—his cost awareness—had become his greatest liability. That had been the reason that Balaban had been brought into Paramount back in 1933 when the company had been forced into bankruptcy by the less than brilliant fiscal policies of the great showman, Adolph Zukor.

Zukor, a fine old gentleman, had been the original architect of the grandiose Paramount scheme. If National Theatres, and others, were going to expand into both ends of the picture business, Paramount would do the same. Only Paramount would become the biggest. Zukor's nephew, Ralph Kohn, had gone around the country buying up theatre circuits by the dozen; buying them with Paramount stock. His enticement was irresistible: A stock guarantee! If Paramount's stock did not reach a figure of approximately $80, those who sold their theatres could get the difference from Paramount in cash! That scheme worked fine, as long as Paramount continued to pyramid its assets, put out a steady flow of profitable pictures, and as long as the boom of the 'twenties continued. But when the market collapsed in 1929, and Paramount's stock went down to $3, the owners of some 1,500 U.S. theatres asked for their money in cash. Hence, in 1933, Paramount filed voluntary bankruptcy.[3] The Federal Court appointed three trustees and they selected the most knowledgeable, the most cost-conscious theatre executive they could find in the United States—that person being Barney Balaban, President of one of Paramount's most successful theatre circuits, the profitable and aggressive Balaban & Katz circuit of some 100 theatres in Chicago.

One of eight brothers, Barney Balaban had come up the hard way, from the Maxwell Street area of Chicago. The glamor of making pictures scarcely existed for him. A motion picture was like any other product: you made it, packaged it, and sold it for a reasonable profit. When he went to Hollywood to run Paramount he put a ceiling of $1½ million on all Paramount Pictures. This did not endear him to producers or talent, but it helped put Paramount on the road back to fiscal health in a remarkably short time.

While Balaban was trimming costs at the studio, the court-appointed trustees were selecting law firms to oversee the enor-

---

[3] It was actually the Paramount Publix Corporation that filed for bankruptcy in 1933 in Federal District Court of the Southern District of New York. In June, 1935, the Company was reorganized under Section 77B of the Bankruptcy Act under the new name of Paramount Pictures, Inc.

mous task of reorganizing Paramount's theatres. One of these firms, Root, Clark, Buckner and Ballantine, hired a young lawyer in 1933 to help reorganize Paramount's New England theatres, including one group owned by Boston's Joseph Kennedy.

For a bright young lawyer only three years out of Harvard Law School, it was precisely the kind of job Leonard Goldenson dreamed of. As a boy in the small town of Scottdale, Pennsylvania, his father, a retail merchant, was also a partner in two of Scottdale's theatres. Young Leonard got bitten by the theatre bug at an early age. He helped out nights and weekends by selling tickets, ushering, and keeping the popcorn well buttered. Later, during his years at Harvard he had the feeling that, while a law degree would be fine, it would only be worth it if he could use it in the glamorous world of motion pictures.

The reorganization job turned out to be every bit as difficult as he expected it would be. First he had to learn the business; that took a year. He bounced from one circuit to another—from New England Theatres, Inc., to Olympia Theatres; to Western Massachusetts Theatres, to the Maine and New Hampshire circuit which Joseph Kennedy owned with an old friend.

He found the practical, confident, conservative New Englanders a pleasure to deal with. Their confidence in young Goldenson, and in Balaban's management, was justified, for in four years, 1933 to 1937, the time it took Goldenson to complete the job, all of their losses had been recouped. In fact, by that time, *all* Paramount theatre circuits in the U.S. were thriving again.

Goldenson's career was now assured. He was moved to New York theatre headquarters to become assistant to Y. Frank Freeman, head of the Paramount Theatre Division. But in 1938 Buddy DeSylva, Paramount's production chief in Hollywood, died of cancer. Balaban moved Freeman to that job and appointed Goldenson, at the young age of 33, to run Paramount's entire Theatre Division.

From that point on, Goldenson and Balaban made an extraordinarily good team. Though opposite types, they complemented each other. Their chemistry was great. Under their leadership the wounded colossus became well again. When television

began to emerge, Paramount showed the same kind of foresight
that caused it, in 1949, to become the first to enter into a Consent
Decree. Television, however, was really Leonard Goldenson's pet
enthusiasm.

"When I first saw television demonstrated at the New York
World's Fair, I was intrigued. I knew then that it would become
the greatest means of communication known to man."

When Barney Balaban's brother, John, President of the Balaban & Katz theatres in Chicago, called Goldenson in 1939 to say
that he had a chance to get an experimental television license for
Chicago, Leonard told him to go ahead. In 1940, Channel 4, the
third such experimental station in the country, under call letters
W9XBK, went on the air. In 1943, Paramount added a second
station in Los Angeles. Before the war ended, both stations filed
for, and were granted, commercial licenses under the call letters
of WBKB, Chicago; and KTLA, Los Angeles.

Leonard Goldenson.

Edward Noble.

Two more dissimilar types would be hard to imagine. But,
despite their differences, they were equally matched; equally formidable competitors. Now they would meet for the time in the
corporate arena.

◇   ◇   ◇

"What are the latest rumors about ABC?" Godenson asked
his top aide, Bob O'Brien, a few weeks after the first meeting
with Ed Noble. As usual, O'Brien had plenty of rumors. The financial grapevine was filled with them lately.

"Warner Brothers is said to be talking to them."

Could be, but Goldenson doubted if it was true. He was well
wired into Hollywood because UPT was the best customer the
picture industry had.

"I still say the price is too high."

Bob O'Brien didn't agree. They were going to have to pay
whatever price it took to get into television. The FCC freeze was
on and there was no telling how long it would last; there were no

other opportunities lurking anywhere. From the beginning of their association a year previously O'Brien had been an enthusiastic supporter of the idea of getting UPT into television. He sought advice from one of the company's largest stockholders, John J. Raskob, who voted the shares of the DuPont and General Motors interests. Raskob was bluntly in favor of the idea to merge with ABC:

"UPT needs more assets. Television is the coming giant. I say, move ahead."

"Tell that to Leonard," said Bob O'Brien.

"I will," said Raskob. And he did.

But then Goldenson and O'Brien got some shocking news. CBS was talking to ABC! More than that, serious negotiations were going on.

CBS, they thought. Incredible! Preposterous! What could CBS do with a second network? The answer soon came: CBS wanted ABC's five big city television stations. Not all five, because CBS owned its own station in New York. But CBS sure could use the other four—Chicago, Los Angeles, Detroit, and San Francisco. CBS had also been caught in the license freeze. In addition it was spending vast sums in programming its television network, and it was also locked into a bitter struggle with RCA on the standard that was to be used for color television. The FCC, a year before, had approved the CBS color disc system, but RCA claimed it had a better system, a compatible system that would not render some 20 million black-and-white sets obsolete. RCA had obtained a restraining order against promulgation of the CBS system; that vital issue would not be resolved until 1953 when the FCC would reverse itself and finally adopt RCA's compatible system. This was not one of the most clear-thinking periods in CBS' history. CBS owner William Paley also was reaching that year one of the most expensive, and ill-fated decisions CBS was ever to make: the decision to enter the television set manufacturing business. Before the year was out CBS would buy the Hytron Corporation, and before this misadventure was over, CBS would lose $50 million.

But, thought Goldenson, this idea of CBS wanting to buy

ABC had to be one of the more cockeyed ideas of the decade. If the deal were made it would mean that CBS would have to: 1) sell off ABC's five radio stations; 2) disband the ABC Radio Network; 3) sell off ABC's New York City television channel, since CBS already owned a station there; 4) disband the ABC Television Network.

Leonard decided it was time to end the cooling off period with Noble. He placed a call and put it to Noble bluntly:

"Ed, the FCC will never let you get away with such a deal. They won't permit you to collapse a television and radio network."

Ed Noble said, "Thanks for the advice. I know you mean well, but we think it's quite possible to put such a deal across." To him the conversation was a clear-cut signal that UPT was still interested. *Very* interested. And that was fine with him. His television costs were mounting. Expenses were rising faster than the projections that had been given him. Frankly, he was growing impatient with the enormous financial drain. He was getting exasperated with the whole situation, particularly by the ill timing of the advent of television. A decade later would have been so much better. By now he had built up an irrational, emotional grudge against the video tube. Every time his set went on the blink in his sumptious Waldorf Towers suite he would call Frank Marx, his vice president of engineering, and berate him:

"Frank, my damned set went out again. The picture is lousy even when the set works. I tell you this whole contraption is ahead of its time. It hasn't been perfected yet."

Frank Marx was one of the "culprits" who had helped get him into this mess. In fact, he had fired Marx a couple of years ago, but everyone said Marx was indispensable, so he had relented and permitted Marx to be rehired. Frank, along with Noble's trusted crony and fellow CAA Commissioner, Bob Hinckley, had been responsible for rushing all five ABC television stations on the air in the incredible short span of 12 months, between 1948 and 1949. *It's ridiculous*, he told himself. *We've got no money and we set a world's record for putting five stations on the air!*

All they were really doing was pulling RCA's chestnuts out of the fire; helping Sarnoff sell more television sets. Hell, even Bill Paley had more sense than that thought Noble. Paley was advising long-time CBS radio affiliates to go slow in getting into the new medium. Sometimes he wondered if his eager-beaver television fanatics at ABC had gone beserk. Their impulsive move had forced him to part with 35% of his stock in the form of 500,000 shares of common stock at $9 per share. The issue had sold out at once, but the funds were a mere pittance to what it would take to make television profitable. And now, with these five stations, his boys were rushing pell mell into developing a network! They claimed they already had three or four affiliates and were bragging that they now had a television network advertising rate card. What nonsense! A rate card with no stations.

Still, Ed Noble had this mystical feeling that, somehow, he would come out on top. It had happened that way when he had purchased Life Savers in 1913 for $1,900, and sold it in 1928 for $22 million.

It had happened that way when he picked his protege, Justin Dart of the Walgreen Drug Company, to reorganize the foundering drug holding company to which he had sold Life Savers. It had happened that way when he had bought radio station WMCA in New York City for $750,000 and sold it a year later to the Strauss family for $1,225,000. And it had happened that way when he bought the NBC Blue Network for $8 million, which seemed a high price to pay, even in 1943, for a company that owned only two full-time radio stations and one in Chicago that operated half time. What he inherited had definitely been a third rate company.

But that was what General Sarnoff had always wanted the Blue Network to be. In its first incarnation it got the name "Blue" as far back as 1926 when RCA Chief Engineer, Alfred N. Goldsmith, was riding the Congressional Limited from New York to the nation's capital. Engineer Goldsmith was plotting ways to implement Sarnoff's dreams of empire for RCA. On the way to Washington to get government permission to link multiple cities by use of telephone wire, Goldsmith was showing Elam Miller,

AT&T operations engineer, how they could interconnect certain cities. He drew the outline of one network with a red pencil; then, with a blue pencil, he drew a second network. Later, when the two networks were put into operation, their wiring at headquarters transmission points was done with red and blue wire to avoid confusion.

But the NBC Blue Network, which started January 1, 1927, about two months after the Red Network began, always seemed to get the programming leftovers that the Red did not want: Sustaining programs, talks, and public service programs that would please a government that was taking an increasing interest in monopoly aspects of the growing radio phenomenon.

There were those who said that Sarnoff enjoyed using the Blue Network as a dumping ground because it also served another more important purpose: It helped stave off competition from a fledgling network called CBS, led by William Paley.

But, as often happens, those good things which smack of monopoly must sooner or later come to an end. The Federal Communications Commission began an investigation. The results came in 1941 when the FCC ordered NBC to divest itself of one of its two broadcast chains.

NBC appealed to the Supreme Court and stalled for as much time as it could, though Sarnoff knew the results were inevitable. He instructed Mark Woods, then head of the Blue, to show as much profit as possible in operating the Blue as an independent company, though still owned by RCA. In one year Woods did exactly that. He showed a profit of $1½ million. This whetted the appetite of prospective purchasers, so much so that some 42 companies came knocking on Sarnoff's door.

In October, 1943, Ed Noble won the bidding contest with his bid of $8 million cash. Since then, despite everyone's efforts, ABC had remained a third network. Noble had inherited Mark Woods, who continued as president of the network, and his executive team of Edgar Kobak and Phillips Carlin. They were good men. They worked hard. But ABC simply did not have the programs, the stars, or the money to become fully competitive. It lacked powerful affiliates which could cover the country as well as the other networks. When ABC bragged about its larger number of affiliates, the competition could smugly respond that, obviously that was true, because it took *more* stations for ABC to do a comparable coverage job. And this was true. ABC had no mother lode to fall back on as NBC had with its owner, RCA. Nor did ABC have the long experience and success of CBS, or an owner with the entrepreneurial brilliance of a William Paley.

So, as ABC slowly developed, it had earned the reputation of being a network of commentators. News analysts came cheap in those days. ABC had dozens of them, including Walter Winchell and Drew Pearson. With dogged determination the company did make progress. After WW II ratings improved. So did sales. Bing Crosby became the showcase star because he wanted to do his weekly program on a new-fangled invention called tape, and NBC had refused Crosby permission to do his show on any basis except "live." In 1946 the network had the pleasant surprise of learning that its Joe Louis-Billy Conn fight, in June of that year, had been heard on 195 stations (vs. the usual 160), and had achieved the highest Hooper rating in broadcast history—67.8.

Profits continued to remain modest, however; never more than $1½ million per year; the network slogged along in third place; but at least it was comfortably ahead of Mutual Broadcasting System.

Then Noble met Robert E. Kintner during WW II, in which Kintner served as Lt. Colonel in Army Intelligence. Prior to the war Noble had admired the syndicated Washington political newspaper column Kintner had co-authored with Joseph Alsop. When the two met, Noble was impressed. He liked Kintner's no-nonsense style and decided that finally, he had found the man who would eventually work miracles for the company. Noble persuaded Kintner to cast his fortunes with ABC in 1944. Starting in public relations, Bob Kintner was pushed steadily up the ladder, with, or without, the approval of Mark Woods, so that Woods began to get the idea that his days with Ed Noble were numbered.

Bob Kintner was a brusque, sometimes truculent fellow who had an incisive mind and managed to get things done. He was the kind of fellow whom Noble saw as being in his image. In 1949, when Noble told Mark Woods that Bob Kintner would make an excellent vice president, Woods had no choice but to agree. And as Ed Noble saw the potential television debacle he was facing, he had at least one consolation—it gave him the chance of blaming the whole television problem on Mark Woods. He kicked Woods upstairs to the nebulous job of vice chairman of the Board and made Bob Kintner President in 1950 with a seven-year contract at $75,000 per year.

And so, when Leonard Goldenson called with his interest to buy ABC, Ed Noble was pleased to get the call. Considering all other candidates, United Paramount Theatres was a promising marriage partner. With all that cash flow coming from their theatres, plus their total lack of experience in broadcasting, and all those theatres to divest, which would keep Goldenson busy for years, Noble began to warm to the idea. Also, UPT stock was widely held. No individual stockholder, not even Goldenson, had a significant position in the stock. Noble, on the other hand, owned almost 58% of ABC's stock. In a tax free exchange of stock he would be the largest individual owner of shares in a new company. Yes, he could be the dominant force in a new company. Even—if it came to a test of power—the controlling force.

He picked up the phone a day later and called Goldenson:

"Leonard, I've been thinking over what you told me. While Bill Paley has no trouble with my price, I think you may be right. A CBS deal might be a little hard to get past the FCC."

"Good," replied Goldenson. "What are you doing for lunch?"

◇   ◇   ◇

Negotiations resumed. As they did, Goldenson reconfirmed what he already knew: There was no way that Ed Noble could be wooed to a lower price than $25 million. So, the dilemma was: how to justify that kind of a price for a company that, only a year ago, had shown a net loss of more than half a million dollars, and had run up $8 million of television losses in three years? How do you place a price on a dream? And even if he believed as strongly as he did in the future of television, how could he justify such a price to his Board of Directors? Even if he made a deal for $25 million, could he *sell* it to his Board? Bob O'Brien's enthusiasm was reassuring, but after all, Bob had only one vote on the Board.

Delaying further also had its risks, Goldenson knew. With each passing day the chance grew stronger that another company would pay the price; especially now that CBS had entered the bidding. If CBS was willing to pay that kind of money for, really, only four television stations, and was willing to sell off other ABC assets for whatever they would bring, this certainly put a new stamp of validity on Ed Noble's asking price.

The first stumbling block in negotiations was the matter of how Noble would take his stock. He liked the voting rights aspect of common stock, but he also liked the security of preferred. Could Mr. Noble have preferred stock with voting rights, asked Earl Anderson of Bob O'Brien at one of the dozen meetings that followed. "No way," said O'Brien. "We can't get into any Mickey Mouse deals that will later come back to haunt us."

Several meetings later, Anderson said, "I think Mr. Noble might like a fifty-fifty deal; fifty percent in preferred, and fifty percent in common."

"I see no problem in that," said O'Brien. "Let's put a pencil to it."

The pencil worked out to the following: UPT would issue $36/_{100}$ths of a share of 5% $20 par value preferred stock, and $15/_{38}$ths of a share of $1 par value common stock for each of the 1,689,017 outstanding shares of $1 par value common stock of ABC, Inc. This would require the issuance of 608,047 shares of 5% preferred stock, and 666,717 shares of common stock. ABC stockholders would receive for each share they owned, $7.50 in common stock of UPT measured at $19 per share, and $7.20 of preferred stock measured at par value. Noble himself would become the largest single shareholder with almost 9% of the stock of the new company.

The question of Noble's large percentage of stock gave Leonard Goldenson qualms. The size of the Board also became a problem, but that was resolved by agreeing that UPT would increase its Board representation from 7 to 13, while ABC, with its present 5-man Board, would be absorbed into the new Board which would have a total of 18 members.

Then came the matter of the structure of the new company, and here negotiations became protracted and troublesome. For Noble the key issue was one of autonomy for the broadcast division. His man, Bob Kintner, must be allowed to continue to run radio and television without the slightest interference from anyone. Goldenson assured that this would be the case. He went a step further.

"I'll give my word that I will give Bob Kintner a free hand in the broadcast division for a reasonable period."

"How do we define 'reasonable period'?" asked Noble.

"I define it as a minimum of three years."

That was acceptable to Noble. He felt even better when it was decided that, as the largest stockholder, he would head the company's most important committee, the Finance Committee.

Goldenson also asked for, and got, some concessions. There were three men he wanted inducted into the ABC management structure. One was his brilliant aide and Secretary-Treasurer, Bob O'Brien, who must be given the job of Executive Vice President of ABC. Another was veteran showman Robert Weitman, whose experience would add strength to ABC's program department. The third was Earl Hudson, who had done a fine job in UPT's Detroit theatre circuit. Earl had previous experience in Hollywood, so it seemed logical to position him as general management *factotum* in Hollywood.

Noble said: "Well, that's up to Bob Kintner. What do you think, Bob?"

"I don't really need any of them, but as long as they report to me, I have no objection," said Kintner.

All of the UPT contingent began to feel a decided chill in the air. And from there, things got worse. A major obstacle was the problem of what to do with one of the two stations owned by each company in Chicago. One would have to be sold to satisfy FCC regulations. UPT got a collective shock when it learned that Ed Noble had already solved that problem. In his negotiations with

William Paley, and in arriving at a price for individual ABC assets, Noble had set a valuation of $6 million for ABC's Chicago television Channel 7. In effect, said Noble, I have made a commitment to Paley that, if I should make a deal with UPT, I would sell one of the two stations to CBS.

The low price seemed bad enough until Goldenson learned that the station ABC now wanted to sell was not Channel 7, but UPT's Channel 4.

"We want to keep all of our channels on 7, so we think the UPT station should be sold to Bill Paley for $6 million," said Noble with a straight face.

"This guy's got some nerve," one of Goldenson's men whispered. "First of all he sells *our* station, not his. Then he sets a price that is about half of what WBKB is worth." This was true. ABC's Channel 7 was losing money, but WBKB was on its way to a profit, that year, of almost $2 million!

"This is very unfair," spoke Goldenson.

"I can't help it," Noble replied. "I gave my word to Bill Paley. That's the way it's got to be."

The impasse grew so serious that it threatened to scuttle the entire deal. Finally Goldenson resolved it by getting Noble to accept half a million dollars less in his preferred stock.

Now that Ed Noble knew that UPT was going to capitulate on the $25 million price he grew even more assertive and demanding. The atmosphere grew more chilly. "We must be left alone," Noble said, almost in anger. "Remember, you are not buying us. This is a merger. A true merger. You people run your theatre business. We'll run the broadcast business. We don't even need your three men, but we'll put up with them if we have to." By now Ed Noble was irritated over the fact that he had not asked for $30 million!

"We'll get back to you tomorrow," said a decidedly unhappy Leonard Goldenson.

"No later than tomorrow," snapped the wily Life Saver king. "We must have a decision."

It seemed a strange way to come to tentative agreement on terms for a merger. Both sides seemed unhappy. Especially Ed

Noble, despite the fact that he had come out ahead on practically everything he had wanted. Control was the big key, he told himself. In three years ABC revenues would exceed those of the declining UPT theatres. By then, his man, Kintner, would be so firmly entrenched that no one could unseat him. Even at the board level, Noble saw himself as winning. And that was the big thing, to have the power, the control. Yes, he decided, on balance the merger with UPT was a good deal. He only wished he were ten years younger, because the next ten years seemed sure to bring more excitement and adventure than the past nine years in radio.

◇   ◇   ◇

A rather grim UPT President, and his Board of Directors, adjourned in a pouring rain to the Carlyle hotel to discuss the deal they had tentatively agreed upon. All of them were tired. It was late at night. The meeting had gone on all afternoon, through the evening, and now that a general agreement had been reached, it was a dissatisfying, frustrating feeling. The vibrations were all wrong. It was almost as if ABC had the money and was taking over UPT—a company with $44 million in cash, assets of $68 million, and a profit in its first year of more than $12 million!

"Their attitude baffles me," said General Counsel, Walter Gross. "I didn't like what I heard. And I still say the price is too high."

Bob O'Brien was not pleased either with the way the last meeting had gone; and he had always been the most enthusiastic advocate of a merger, besides Leonard Goldenson himself.

Even Goldenson had his doubts. There were so many imponderables to consider. Perhaps this was too big a burden to place on a young company like UPT? And Ed Noble would have 9% of the stock. Was that a gamble worth taking? What they all needed, he said, was some solid advice from a neutral corner.

"Let's call Harry," suggested O'Brien.

"Harry" would be Harry Haggerty, Vice Chairman of the Board of Metropolitan Life Insurance Co., one of the most astute financiers in the country. Haggerty served on the Board of RCA, and his company also had loaned money to CBS, so he was particularly qualified to advise them in this matter.

"Good idea," said Goldenson. John A. Coleman, who was a tower of strength on UPT's Board, agreed with Goldenson that the matter was important enough to bother Haggerty at such a late hour. Since he was a close friend of Haggerty he was delegated to make the call to ask if the Board could impose on Haggerty at this late hour. He made the call. "It's all arranged," he said. "Harry is dressing. We'll go over to my apartment, which is only a block from Harry's apartment."

Goldenson and his Board found a cab in the rain and went directly to the East Side, mid-Manhattan apartment of John Coleman. A few minutes later, Harry Haggerty joined them. The discussion began anew with Leonard Goldenson setting down the pros and cons of the situation. They had a deal, but the question now was: should they proceed, or withdraw? Coleman, former Chairman of the Board of Governors of the New York Stock Exchange, and now a partner of his own investment firm, listened carefully.

There were many risks involved, Goldenson explained. It was true that ABC had only a skeleton of a network, some eight basic affiliates besides its five owned television stations. But it did own those five stations. Neither NBC or CBS could make that claim. These stations were located in five of the six largest cities in the U.S.

ABC's Radio Network was making some money, but admittedly, not enough to justify the $25 million price. Nevertheless, now seemed the time to move, to eke out this invaluable franchise of becoming a third major network. The economics of television at this stage justified only two, or maybe two-and-a-half, networks—but this was only 1951. "We must look ahead," said Goldenson. Five years, ten years (at that time, television sets covered only about 35% of the nation's homes) but look ahead to the time when television would be in 98% of the homes.

The others expressed their feelings. John Coleman asked some tough questions and seemed to be on the fence. Walter

Gross was dubious. Finally, when Harry Haggerty had heard all sides, he said:

"I think Leonard is right. In our lifetime I don't think there are going to be more than three networks. It may take five, six, or even seven years to get ABC on its feet. But ultimately it will be a vital force if it's properly managed. I've got faith in the future of television, and I've got faith in this deal. In fact, I've got so much faith in it that I'll be willing to back it with funds if that becomes necessary."

With that statement, Leonard Goldenson had sold his deal. Or, better, Harry Haggerty had sold it for him. One of the brightest minds in finance had given his blessing to the merger recommendation of Leonard Goldenson.

But still there were lingering doubts, as expressed by Walter Gross:

"Noble will own 9 or 10% of the stock. He can be in a position to control the company."

Haggerty had an answer for that. "If you fellows are foolish enough to let Noble control the company with only 9 or 10% of the stock, then you do not deserve to run the company."

That did it. There were no more questions. Harry Haggerty, an outsider, had answered the two thorny questions that had plagued the UPT Executive Committee. They agreed then and there to proceed with the merger.

Much later that night, Leonard Goldenson climbed into bed. It had been a long, arduous day. The next day, May 23, 1951, he would meet again with the remaining members of the UPT Board, then he would call Ed Noble and tell him that, yes, his Board had approved the merger.

He slept fitfully that night. After a year of difficult negotiations, that was understandable. What else could you expect when you had made the most important decision of your life—one that affected not only your personal career, but the lives and welfare of some 19,000 employees of United Paramount Theatres, and 27,000 stockholders.

2

Adjourn?
We Never Adjourn!

TWO COMPANIES SPRUNG from the loins of the Government (Justice Department and FCC) now returned to the womb to be reborn again. And while it did eventually happen, it was destined to go down as one of the most controversial corporate rebirths in the history of American capitalism.

To the surprise of both sides, the nation's trade, financial and consumer press generally approved the merger. Yes, the public would benefit, said the press. The country already had a third network in DuMont's network, but it would be well to have an even stronger network which ABC could become with its infusion of United Paramount's capital. There was sympathy, too, for "poor little ABC" as it tried to fight the goliaths, NBC and CBS.

In their joint euphoria, both ABC and UPT felt they could expect a quick settlement from the FCC despite the legal niceties that would have to be observed. Both Boards of Directors had to approve, which they did on May 28, 1951 for ABC; and June 6 for UPT. The two companies held special stockholders meetings on the same day, July 27, 1951, and each overwhelmingly approved the merger proposal.

There were, however, some probing questions from stockholders at the United Paramount meeting:

"How will the proposed merger affect the present two dollar dividend rate?" asked one.

Leonard Goldenson said he did not know. "I wish I could give a definite answer. But leaving the merger aside, I cannot predict the earnings or dividends of our theatre business."

Another shareholder pointed out that the tangible net worth of ABC amounted to a little over three dollars per share, but under terms of the merger, ABC stock was listed at $14.70 per share. Almost five times tangible book value.

Goldenson admitted that, based on book valuation, the merger did not appear warranted. But based on future prospects of the television industry it certainly could be justified. "When we decided to go into television we had two routes to go. One was to acquire licenses and build stations; the other was by means of this merger with ABC. We decided it would be far less expensive and time-consuming to go this way."

Another asked when ABC's earnings would improve. Goldenson said he had no crystal ball. ABC had earned only $84,000 in 1950; but for the first quarter of 1951 it appeared it would earn $220,000. Much depended on the FCC's approval of the merger.

Then came the question: "Will the government sometime in the future contend that broadcasting and theatres should not live together in the same company?"

Goldenson pondered this one, then said that their counsel had given the company the okay to proceed. "We think theatres and broadcasting enterprises can be operated in harmony with the antitrust laws."

A sympathetic murmur rippled through the room. After the hellfire and brimstone of the Justice Department's antitrust decree no one had any desire to go through a similar experience.

"When will the FCC approve the merger?" a stockholder asked—that surely was the key question. Goldenson, ever sanguine about the future, said cheerfully: "It's impossible to predict an exact date, but we think it can be approved in October or November of this year."

A chuckle came from a far corner of the room. Along with the words: "I'll believe it when I see it."

◇   ◇   ◇

By the end of July all necessary papers were placed on file at the FCC. On August 27, 1951 the matter was designated for a hearing before Hearing Examiner Leo A. Resnick. This time, said the experts, the papers would not get lost in the files. This was the most important, most highly visible case the FCC had ever had to adjudicate; the FCC would not muff its golden opportunity to move speedily so that millions of television fans could enjoy more and better programs.

But of course the FCC did nothing like that. The Broadcast Bureau of the Commission said it needed much more time to prepare its case. All government regulatory agencies run on slower clocks than the rest of the world. Summer passed; then fall. The stock of both ABC and UPT began to decline.

Soon word began to leak out that there would not be merely a hearing about the issues involving ABC and UPT. This was going to be a much larger "package." This would be a consolidated hearing involving many other issues such as: was Paramount Pictures entitled to own television stations in light of its antitrust violations? Was the new company, United Paramount Theatres, Inc., entitled to own television licenses? Should a picture producing company like Paramount, or a theatre company like UPT, be permitted *any* activity in broadcasting?

That wasn't all: Paramount admittedly owned 25% of the stock of Allen B. DuMont Laboratories, which in turn owned three VHF stations, and operated a television network. Did this percent of ownership constitute "control" of DuMont? If so, what effect should this have on DuMont stations in New York City, Pittsburgh, and Washington, D.C.? Should DuMont's licenses be suspended, and no grant made to DuMont's applications for Cleveland and Cincinnati? How about Paramount's license application for San Francisco? What about the status of Paramount's KTLA in Los Angeles, UPT's WBKB in Chicago, and UPT's tele-

vision applications in Boston, Detroit, Des Moines and Tampa?
How about CBS' intended purchase of WBKB, Chicago?

"Every issue has been thrown into this case except the price
of turnips in Russia," grumped Paul Porter, attorney for Paramount Pictures. Altogether the issues numbered 21!

And if that wasn't bad enough, one FCC Commissioner,
Robert Jones, objected strenuously to the package deal. Paramount Pictures still had pending at the FCC its transfer of license
of WBKB to UPT as a part of the division of assets at the time of
the Paramount consent decree. "We should solve that matter
before we ever take up the ABC-UPT merger," said Jones.

By late fall of 1951 there still was no word as to when the
hearing would begin. *Variety*, a trade paper with an excellent
record of accuracy, predicted that the hearing would end in
March of 1952, with a final decision to be rendered in the fall.
But *Variety* admitted that it had no idea when the hearing would
start. Petitions began being flung like confetti into the Commission by all parties, Paramount, United Paramount, DuMont,
ABC, and CBS. Several others, including Fanchon & Marco
Theatres, and Gordon Brown, owner of WSAY, Rochester, were
trying to join the case as intervenors. The Department of Justice
remained on the fence, but said it would be observing the case
"very closely."

At last the news came. Examiner Resnick announced the
hearing would begin in January of 1952—eight months from the
time the two companies had agreed to merge. Now, at last, the
Roman circus of 21 issues, far beyond the simple one of ABC and
UPT desiring to merge, would be heard.

◇   ◇   ◇

At 10 A.M. on January 15, 1952, in room 2230 of the ancient
post office building in Washington (which then housed the FCC),
Leo Resnick called the ABC-UPT hearing into official session.

Resnick was a rookie in the business of hearing cases. Being
thrust into the limelight of this unprecedented case was a heady
experience and he intended to make the most of it.

As far as counsel for ABC and UPT were concerned, they could have been on vacation. During many sessions of the hearing their services were virtually unneeded. The first issue concerned Paramount Pictures, Allen B. DuMont Laboratories, and whether Paramont indeed controlled DuMont; if so, what effect did that have on the licenses of DuMont's three stations? The bad blood between the two companies quickly became apparent. For a mere $164,000, back in 1938, Paramount had acquired stock in DuMont. Since then, according to testimony of Dr. Allen Du-Mont, the distinguished and outspoken inventor, Paramount had taken a kind of sadistic pleasure in stymieing DuMont's growth. Not so, replied Paramount. Oh yes, retorted DuMont. A querulous letter he had written only three months ago to Barney Bala-ban was placed on the record:

"What is Paramount going to do to remove any cloud over DuMont as the result of the Paramount antitrust decree, and what plans, if any, has Paramount for carrying out its intention, as stated to the FCC, of disposing of its stock interest in DuMont?"

Barney Balaban, after waiting three days to reply, answered that DuMont's letter was full of "misstatements and insinuations." And: "I don't intend to be drawn into a debating and letter-writing contest, since no useful purpose would be served."

Paul Raibourn, Paramount's enigmatic television expert, a fellow with a fixed, somewhat sinister smile, drew chuckles from the packed audience when he said that, as far as he knew, relations with DuMont had always been "fine." Paramount, he said, was not averse to selling its stock back to the good Dr. DuMont; the only problem was that DuMont did not have the money. Paramount now valued its stock in DuMont at 20 million dollars!

Hearing Examiner Resnick asked the Doctor: "Why did you accept Paramount's money in the first place?"

"Because we needed money to get our first three stations on the air. And we thought Paramount's program experience would be of help."

"Has it been?"

"No."

"Did you ever ask for Paramount's help with programs?"

"No."

The two companies agreed on only one thing: Paramount did *not* control DuMont. After two weeks of rancorous testimony, Resnick moved to a more substantive phase, the fulcrum, in fact, upon which would turn the fate of the merger: Could a mighty company like Paramount, an admitted antitrust violator, be qualified to hold broadcast licenses? Its own KTLA in Los Angeles had already been placed on temporary license status as a result of the consent decree—as had WBKB, Chicago, which had not yet been transferred officially from Paramount to UPT.

Barney Balaban thus returned to center stage again. An oddly colorless fellow, stoutish, his suit rumpled, Balaban did not seem much impressed with what went on. Resnick wanted to know if Paramount realized it was indulging in blatant monopolistic activities when it gobbled up so many theatres and restricted independent competition.

Paramount merely went along because of competitive reasons, answered Balaban. "The whole thing just grew like Topsy. We thought these practices were legal because everyone else was doing it. But once we knew what the law was, we decided to put our house in order, and accordingly we negotiated with the Department of Justice for the first consent decree."

"Yes, the very first," Paul Porter, counsel, emphasized. "And Paramount did it in less than ten months, setting a pattern for the entire industry. I think it is interesting to note that another great company, Loew's, has only now entered into a consent decree—2½ years later."[1]

"How are relations today with the new company that was created?" Resnick asked Balaban.

"You mean United Paramount Theatres? We are as far apart as the poles." There was more to the statement than anyone realized. The warm, boss-protégé relationship that once existed between Barney Balaban and Leonard Goldenson had ended. A rupture had occurred when UPT reduced its annual dividend

---

[1] RKO Pictures actually entered into a consent decree slightly ahead of Paramount, but that company was significantly smaller; thus Paramount's consent decree was considered to be the pacesetter for the industry.

from two dollars to one dollar per share. Balaban owned a large block of stock in UPT and that stock was held in trust because of the consent decree; he was miffed because Goldenson had not told him in advance that he was going to cut the dividend in half. Goldenson was legally and morally committed *not* to tell Balaban or anyone of his intention. The breach would grow larger as the years went by, although near the end of Balaban's life (he died in 1971) the two men had a reconciliation.

As for relationships now between the two companies, Balaban seemed pleased to point out that UPT's Paramount Theatre in New York had not shown a single Paramount film in six months.

"Why is that?" Resnick asked.

"We just have not been able to get together."

How was Paramount doing now under the consent decree? Balaban reacted as if he had tasted vinegar. "It's a different way of life," he said dryly. Paramount now was being forced to enter into some 350,000 separate film contracts each year! "The filing of private antitrust suits against major companies has become quite a business since the Supreme Court upheld the Justice Department antitrust action." Yes, there had been lots of law suits. "But out of 54 suits since the decree we've won 40 and lost 14. Not a bad record."

Frederick Ford, the handsome, urbane counsel for the FCC, drew a remark from the unflappable film mogul that brought down the house. "You say, Mr. Balaban, your daughter is pursuing television as a career? How is she doing?"

"Not too well. Last year she made only $600—just enough to keep me from claiming an exemption on my income tax."

All FCC hearings have their own flavor and style with moments of high drama and low comedy. This hearing, with 12 interested parties and some 32 lawyers vying to make points with their clients as well as with Resnick, was a gala show. Bob Kintner, representing ABC, underwent gruelling questioning on what ABC's policies would be if the merger was approved. His performance was brilliant for the most part, but occasionally he had lapses in judgment as when he prophesied that feature films would *never* work on television. "Too long," he said. "Sponsors would not want to pay for them. And stations would not clear the time for them." Programs had to be built for sponsors in blocks of 5, 10, 15, or 30 minutes of time, hence feature films would be useless.

Kintner was given a rough time by DuMont attorney Morton Galane, who interrupted Kintner during the latter's frequent pauses.

"Mr. Galane, I have not finished," Kintner would protest. "Will you kindly let me finish what I was going to say?"

"Mr. Kintner, I can't really tell when you're pausing, or when you're finished."

"Just then I was pausing."

A low bow from Galane. "Sorry, sir. I am too impetuous. I will pay more attention to your pauses from now on. Please pick up where your pause left off . . ."

Barney Balaban said that Adolph Zukor was a wonderful old gentleman who had started block booking back in 1916 when his company required theatres to take a mixed bag of pictures just to get Mary Pickford's pictures.

Yet, despite the fact that, from 1920 to 1951, Paramount had been hit with the astonishing number of 521 antitrust actions, the company had done well.

"Until 1947," said Balaban.

"What happened in 1947?" asked FCC counsel Ford.

"The whole industry got into a mess starting in 1947 due to blocked currencies, evaluations and restrictions placed on importing U.S. pictures into many countries. In one quarter of that year the industry was thrown from a profit to a substantial loss."

Leonard Goldenson acquitted himself well, but grew impatient when counsel inferred that a merged company would have unfair advantages in buying film, or talent. "And," asked FCC counsel Ford, "are you sufficiently aware of the history of mergers to know that one merger in a line of business usually is followed by competing companies making similar acquisitions in order to maintain their competitive ranking?'

Goldenson gazed around the packed room and heaved a sigh.

"Mr. Ford, this is the first merger I have ever had any experience with and I hope it will be the last!"

Leonard Goldenson did not know it, but this was to be a mere warmup for much more bitter and frustrating hearings to come.

◇   ◇   ◇

By now two months had passed. Several of the witnesses of the two principal companies, ABC and UPT, had not even yet been called. One newspaper columnist called the hearing a "new version of Alice in Wonderland."

While Examiner Resnick continued his education in how Paramount, the largest entertainment company in the world, ran its business, how it sold films, how it dealt with competitors, how it became the colossus of the business, ABC continued its painful education in how to subsist below the poverty level. By now ABC knew it had but one year to live. Its borrowing power had been extended to the limit. Its debt had jumped from 7 to 11 million dollars. Edward Noble had personally signed a note for 4 million. Paydays were met at the last minute. If the merger was denied, ABC clearly was facing bankruptcy. Its network would have to close along with some of its five invaluable television franchises. DuMont then would become the viable third network because certainly there was not room for four networks.[2]

Cutbacks in personnel continued at ABC that spring of 1952. Ad rates were slashed; outrageous bonuses were given advertisers to keep them on the air. At the same time compensation rates to network affiliates were cut, causing some stations to seek an affiliation with DuMont.

Yet none of this sense of urgency permeated steamy hot Room 2230 in the post office building in Washington. Leo Resnick was a methodical fellow. He was determined to make the record "complete". After all, this was the showcase hearing of all

---

[2] In one of the more mystifying aspects of the long hearing, DuMont did not *oppose* the merger. Had it done so, the chances are strong that the merger never would have been approved.

time for the FCC. This was a time to show the world how tough, how uncompromising the Commission could be—a new facade for a Commission that was beginning to have serious image problems. The Commission knew it was under scrutiny from diverse quarters. To begin with, it had underestimated the demand for television channels after World War II. It had not prepared a comprehensive allocation plan for the new industry. Its first plan had hardly been a plan at all; thus it had been forced to invoke a freeze on new channels on September 30, 1948. At that time there had been only 36 stations on the air, and 70 more were under construction. The problem of co-channel interference had begun to make itself felt. To continue without a comprehensive plan would bring chaos to the new medium.

In addition, the FCC was sensitive about accusations of low level politics in its hallowed halls. There was some truth to this, so the Commission knew that something had to be done. It needed the high visibility of the ABC-UPT merger to show the world that it was *not* a captive of an industry it presumed to regulate.

In March Resnick conceded that, yes, the hearings were considerably behind schedule. November looked to be the earliest date that a decision could be reached. Then he went blithely back to his educational course in how Paramount operated. He seemed fascinated to learn at the knees of Barney Balaban, Paul Raibourn, and Stanton Griffis, head of Paramount's Executive Committee.

Resnick: How do you sell your pictures, Mr. Balaban?

Balaban: By separate contract.

Resnick: How will you deal with television's need for films?

Balaban: I believe producers will make separate films for each medium.

Resnick: What are the reissue values of your films?

Balaban: $125,000 to $750,000.

Resnick: How do you get an honest count from exhibitors?

Balaban: Often we don't. We use checkers.

Resnick: What?

Balaban: Checkers. Some 20 million per year is lost in film rentals. This is money stolen at the box office. But we recover hundreds of thousands by use of checkers—they count admissions at the box office.

Back in his suite at Waldorf Towers, Edward Noble went into a funk over the long delay. He became so disgusted he pretended to have no interest in the hearing proceedings.

"We moved things a lot faster when I was Chairman of the CAA," he complained to his crony, Bob Hinckley. "Bob, most of those people are Democrats like you. Why can't you go over there and do something about it?"

Hinckley avowed he could do nothing. If Noble would keep his patience everything would eventually work out.

In his frustration Noble called Bob Kintner and asked him to figure out a way to make another personnel cut.

As the weeks passed the press began to take more than a cursory interest in the progress of the hearing. What was the Government's game, it asked. Was this process of "procedural strangulation" a calculated plan to kill the development of ABC?

"Something very nearly like panic reigns at ABC," wrote John Crosby in the *New York Herald Tribune*. "A great many key personnel have departed for other networks. Others have been let go. Directors have been made Assistant Directors, a loss of rank comparable to the unfrocking of an archduke. The network has very few sponsored shows, having just lost the sponsor of its excellent Herb Shriner program."

But while the FCC "fiddled", Crosby did not entirely blame the FCC for entertaining a "healthy and not unjustified" skepticism of UPT. In the words of one FCC Commissioner, UPT showed a "proclivity for predatory practises"—a wonderful phrase, Crosby called it, because "almost no corporation has had more antitrust suits filed against it, UPT collecting them like some of Paramount's lady stars collect husbands. Paramount, left unchecked, would like to own everything."

Then Crosby quoted Bob Kintner, whom he called "an extraordinarily able President": "CBS and NBC are up to their ears in manufacturing, and subsidiary interests."

Crosby agreed: "It's doubtful whether any television network can survive without a subsidiary bankroll of some sort. The merger will give ABC some 75 million of working capital to play with."

Crosby concluded that the FCC was simply perpetuating the preeminence of CBS and NBC, both of which were "fairly monopolistic empires. The suspicion exists that you have to be fairly monopolistic to keep a television network afloat."

◇　◇　◇

Welcome news came from another corner in late April. The FCC announced that, after four years, its freeze of television licensing was over. A group owner could now own two ultra high frequency (UHF) channels along with five very high frequency (VHF) stations. A mad scramble for channels began. More than 4,000 application forms were requested of the Commission. One law firm alone asked for 400! Some 1,200 applications were expected to be filed by July 1. The television "gold rush" had begun with a vengeance.

This was welcome news at ABC-UPT, provided the merger ever got approved; but that prospect still seemed a long way off.

The month of May found Leo Resnick still rummaging around in the Paramount closet for more skeletons to rattle. In June ABC and UPT lost all patience and filed a petition requesting a decision by summer so that ABC could be in a better competitive position to meet fall program commitments. The "hook" on which the petition hung fooled no one, least of all Resnick or FCC counsel, Fred Ford. Network program commitments are made much earlier than June for a fall start, but at least it gave ABC-UPT counsels a chance to explain more important matters, namely that ABC had been forced to use 2½ million dollars of its borrowed capital since November of 1951. Additional borrowed capital would be needed for the fall and winter operations. After that there be no more borrowed capital left.

Also, the petition pointed out, 75% of the testimony so far had been devoted to a history of old antitrust proceedings. 11,200 pages of oral testimony, and 7,000 exhibits had already been accumulated!

The petition plaintively concluded: "Testimony to come on the Paramount-DuMont issues will make available no facts or information that is essential to the ABC-UPT case. "Therefore, could the merger question, and the transfer of WBKB to CBS, be "severed for the purpose of an initial and final decision?"

CBS joined forces two days later with its own petition in support of ABC-UPT.

Resnick's answer was typical of most regulatory hearings. When pinned down by an unexpected action—take a recess. He recessed the hearing till June 19th.

◇　◇　◇

When the hearing resumed, Resnick received a vigorous dissent from DuMont television. "All the issues are interwoven, and the urgency of a swift decision is uniform to all applicants."

DuMont's position was growing desperate. If the merger were approved, DuMont's days were numbered as a television network. Its relations with Paramount had deteriorated so badly that there was little hope that it could ever get together again with Paramount and fill the golden vacuum that had existed for the past three years. Dr. Allen DuMont confided to his friends that he rued the day he had ever taken money from Paramount.

By now a ground swell of press reaction had begun to set in. Jack Gould, in the *New York Times*, described how a million dollar enterprise "can be practically paralyzed by bureaucratic delay and red tape."

"There is a vital matter of public interest at stake," he wrote, "when the FCC takes so much time to perform its operation that the survival of the patient is jeopardized."

The FCC might as well take apart the whole video network industry if "bigness alone" was the guiding criteria, said Gould. RCA was in manufacturing, recording, research, patents, and communications. CBS was getting into manufacturing; and in the record business it rivaled RCA. DuMont was manufacturing television sets and electronic equipment. Even Mutual Broadcasting System was, in effect, a subsidiary of General Tire and Radio. The very length of the delay was a "form of judgment that can have substantial and serious consequences".

The *Wall St. Journal*, on June 24, called the delay "needlessly punitive", and "just plain bad government".

Gene Smith, in the *New York Herald Tribune*, said the delay represented a gradual strangulation of investors' money—1,944 ABC stockholders; 26,995 UPT stockholders. ABC's indebtedness had risen to 11 million, he pointed out, and the company was helpless in getting more credit. Since May 24, 1951, the day the two companies had agreed to merge, ABC's stock had declined from 13⅜ to 9⅛. UPT stock had declined from 18⅞ to 13⅞ in addition to its having cut its dividend in half.

By contrast, wrote Smith, CBS class A and B stock had risen about 25%; and RCA had risen about 50% since May 24, 1951.

The hearing droned on, the written record and exhibits piling as high as all of the telephone books of the nation. The attorneys were getting as tired as Resnick who mentioned one afternoon that final adjournment seemed to be in sight. Duke Patrick, counsel for UPT, threw up his hands and cried out in mock horror: "Adjourn? Never! That is something we never do!" Patrick was sure they would be there till Christmas. But by August 20 there was simply nothing more to put into the record, so without further word Resnick brought the famous hearing to a close. Even the insatiably curious Resnick could think of no more questions to ask. He had learned all he wanted to know about Paramount, and how the motion picture business operated. Ironically, in all of the massive record there was relatively little in it about ABC or UPT. Testimony from Leonard Goldenson, Robert O'Brien, Edward Noble, and Robert Kintner did not occupy more than 15% of the record because their case was basic: ABC needed UPT's capital to expand and bring the country a strong third network. UPT wanted to invest its funds in the coming field of television and was prepared to do so with ABC as its partner. It was as simple as that.

There was something symbolic about the timing of the ending: Washington, dozing in the stifling heat and humidity of midsummer was a rather moribund city from which all the power-wielders had fled for more reasonable climes. Counsel for the major parties, James McKenna for ABC, Duke Patrick for UPT, Paul Porter for Paramount, William Roberts for DuMont, and their many assistants, packed their bags and went home.

"I can't believe it's over," said Jim McKenna. "But of course it isn't. We're only getting started. Ahead there are briefs to be written, then a recommended decision by Resnick, then more briefs, then an oral argument before the seven Commissioners, and finally a decision. More than a year so far! God, how much longer will this take?"

◇   ◇   ◇

Less than two months later, on October 3, ABC and UPT, plus Paramount and DuMont, were struck by a bombshell. The FCC's Broadcast Bureau which serves as an interested party at all broadcast hearings and has not only the right, but the duty, to make recommendations, came out with a resounding recommendation *against* the merger!

Curtis B. Plummer, Chief of the Bureau, minced no words in his stinging rebuke. Approving the merger, he said, would be the first step toward lumping the motion picture industry with the broadcast industry—a fate worse than death by Broadcast Bureau standards. Plummer said he was impressed by the some 180 antitrust actions involving Paramount in its long, colorful history.

The shock waves induced by this unexpected action caused sober reappraisals in the inner sanctums of all participants. For the first time ABC and UPT began to assess the dimensions of the disaster of a merger denial. If denied on antitrust grounds and if the Commission ruled that Paramount indeed controlled DuMont, the results would be catastrophic for DuMont because it would be declared unfit to own television stations in New York City, Pittsburgh, and Washington. Likewise, Paramount would be unfit to operate KTLA in Los Angeles. UPT would also be unable to operate WBKB in Chicago. CBS would not be able to acquire its own station in Chicago. And ABC, without funds, and with a deficit of $659,000 in the first nine months of that year, would be on the knife edge of bankruptcy.

Expected next was Leo Resnick's decision. If this, too, was negative there was every likelihood that the merger would be turned down by a majority of the seven person FCC Commission, two members of which were already on record as being against it.

But on November 13 hearing examiner Resnick sent hopes

soaring. He ruled *in favor* of the merger! In his decision he said
he saw no reason why ABC and UPT could not operate synergis-
tically in broadcasting and theatre exhibition. There was nothing
inherently monopolistic in this. And regardless of what clouds
remained over Paramount (and UPT as well) on the antitrust matter, the advantages accruing to ABC, with UPT's capital, sufficiently offset any negative aspects because the American public
would be the main benefactors.

Jubilation reigned within ABC and UPT, but only briefly,
because a surprise attack came from an unexpected quarter—
Congress!

The attack came from, not one, but two committees of Congress. The coincidence of both coming at the same time struck
many as odd: was this an orchestrated attack from powerful interests who had much to gain from a weak and impotent third network?

The first blow came from Paris where Senator Charles
Tobey, Republican of New Hampshire, was on a junket. Tobey
was Chairman of the powerful Senate Interstate and Foreign
Commerce Committee in the upcoming new Congress. He wired
Resnick:

"I am disturbed and shocked by the decision."

A day later Senator William Langer of North Dakota, and
Chairman of the Senate Judiciary Committee, wrote a letter to
FCC Chairman Paul A. Walker warning the FCC not to uphold
the Resnick decision:

"I sincerely hope that no action taken by your Commission
will require those of us charged with the supervision of antitrust
laws to inquire whether federal agencies are tearing down those
laws rather than seeking to further them."

Pointedly, Langer sent a copy to Attorney General James P.
McGranery for the purpose, he said, of having the Justice Department's antitrust division "make a thorough study of the matter and make recommendations to you and to the Senate Judiciary
Committee."

In conclusion, Langer called Resnick naive, while he hailed
the Broadcast Bureau's action for having strongly called attention

to the antitrust record of motion picture producers and exhibitors.

Predictably, DuMont, and the FCC Broadcast Bureau, filed an exception to Resnick's decision, scoring Resnick's "blind faith" that the new company would not try to suppress competition. "There is nothing in the record, or in the initial decision, to bind future officers and directors to their promises," said the petition.

By now it was Christmas time. All activity ceased for the holidays. But on January 5 all parties were summoned to participate in a one-day oral argument before the seven man Commission. Actually there were only six men. The seventh was a woman, the first to ever serve on this august body. She was Frieda Hennock, a testy, unequivocal person who never left doubt as to where she stood on any issue. On the ABC-UPT merger she was strongly opposed.

Respective counsel were given an hour each to present their views, including among them, the FCC's own counsel, Fred Ford, a distinguished, tall, articulate, gray haired man who might easily have been taken for a famous actor on loan from one of the Hollywood studios. Ford turned in one of his finest performances that day in terms of persuasive rhetoric, propounding once more his familiar argument that a merger between ABC and UPT would serve as a serious monopoly threat to the motion picture and television industries. Pounding the rostrum for emphasis, shooting phrases with the impact of bullets, Ford insisted that all major related issues should be resolved before the Commission ever acted on the merger issues such as Pay Television, and Theatre Television.

When Rosel Hyde, vice chairman of the Commission interjected: "Competition does not seem to have suffered from the joining of larger companies such as General Tire which now has control of Mutual Broadcasting."

Ford replied: "General Tire, sir, does not compete with Mutual for an audience; therefore that case is not a parallel one."

The one day oral hearing concluded on a note of gloom for ABC-UPT. Fred Ford very possibly could have carried the day.

A week later Senator Tobey, who had appeared at the oral hearing, surfaced once again. In a curt wire to Chairman Paul

Walker he said that his Interstate Commerce Committee would meet in two weeks "to determine if it would be helpful to prepare and pass legislation to prevent mergers of this kind in the future."

Attorney General McGranery followed with a letter to the Commission making it clear that, while the Justice Department had no official standing in the case, he wished to point out "certain factors of antitrust significance." With that he recited a list of points that should be noted by the Commission, such as trade restraint devices in buying or bidding for motion pictures; and other competitive advantages that should be "of concern to the Commission." Chairman Walker, in a letter filled with polite but cool legal rhetoric, replied that the Justice Department had not sought to participate when it had been given such an opportunity; nor had it, since the hearing began, ever sought to intervene.

There was nothing to do now but wait for the decision. Odds for a favorable decision grew slimmer as the days dragged on. ABC's finances were growing ever more critical. Alternative plans for its operation were being drawn up. Its television network service would be drastically cut back. One or more of its television stations would be put on the market. Meanwhile the press continued its general tone of concern: why this bureaucratic morass? Why the seemingly orchestrated attack by Senators Tobey and Langer? Who desired to see ABC forced into a helpless position? Was not the FCC's role to observe, and serve, the "public interest, convenience and necessity?" Was not a strong third network a service that met that criterion?

Then, quite suddenly, before anyone expected it to happen, the news came on a cloudy, blustery Monday, February 9, 1953. A simple announcement that came at the end of the working day, after the New York stock exchange had closed. The full Commission had met, deliberated, and voted to approve the merger!

The vote was 5–2 in favor of the merger. Chairman Walker, and Commissioners Rosel H. Hyde, Robert T. Bartley, George F. Sterling, and Eugene H. Merrill voted in favor of the merger.

Commissioners Frieda Hennock and Fred Webster were opposed. Frieda Hennock's 98-page dissent was more than a third as long as Resnick's 264-page decision and was one of the most acrimonious dissents ever filed by an FCC Commissioner. The merger, she said, was *not* in the public interest. It would establish "monopolistic multimedia economic power." It would not improve network competition. It would lead to "the amalgamation of the motion picture and television industries." It violated the Clayton Antitrust Act (to preserve competition). And finally, Paramount and UPT were not even qualified to hold broadcast licenses.

"The merger makes quite probable the early entrance of other motion picture interests into television which must eventually result in the substantial amalgamation of the two competitive media." Frieda Hennock, as the first woman Commissioner on the FCC, was a fierce and zealous advocate of her views on how communications should develop in America. Her FCC career was distinguished by a number of courageous actions; but in this case, history has proven Hennock to be wrong. None of the dire things she predicted came true. Far from creating a monopoly, the merged company still faced 20 years of uphill struggle to reach parity with RCA-controlled NBC; and CBS.

In any event the long process was over. After 93 days of hearings and 19 months of waiting a new corporate entity had been born.[3]

---

[3] Paramount was declared to be in control of DuMont; but by a narrow margin, 4–3, the licenses of DuMont's three stations were renewed. In 1955 the Du-Mont Network ceased to operate and its stations were sold. The Washington and New York stations were sold to Metropolitan Broadcasting Company, which later changed its name to Metromedia Corporation. The Pittsburgh station was sold to Westinghouse Broadcasting. Dr. Allen B. DuMont died in 1965.

CBS began operating in Chicago the next day on WBKB's Channel 4 under call letters WBBM-TV. (Later switched to Channel 2.)

ABC's Chicago Channel 7 dropped its call letters, WENR-TV, the next day and began using the older, more familiar call letters of WBKB.

At the time of the merger ABC had 355 radio affiliates and 14 primary television affiliates; assets of some 29 million; 2,085 stockholders; 1,689,017 shares outstanding; 1,991 employees; and a loss of $141,725 for the year 1952.

UPT had assets of 141 million; 26,214 stockholders; about 4 million shares outstanding; some 708 theatres in 215 communities in 37 states; some 20,000 employees; and a profit of $5,614,000 for 1952.

There were 159 commercial television stations on the air. CBS had 74 affiliates; NBC had 71; and ABC 14.

3

Shootout at 66th Corral

BEFORE THE MERGER Ed Noble liked to taunt his "eager beavers" for having prematurely thrust ABC into ownership of five television stations. "We've got a tent, but no circus," he would say.

So now the new company, American Broadcasting—Paramount Theatres Inc., (AB-PT) had its tent and the money to supply the circus. But what *kind* of a circus would it be?

Leonard Goldenson, Bob Weitman, and Bob Kintner pondered this question from the day the new company was born. They knew that no single network had the money, studios, or creative production talent to do the job alone. Sarnoff and Paley were in agreement that television was unlike any other medium; certainly it was unlike motion pictures. It was a live medium, indigenous unto itself.

When it came to talent, NBC and CBS already owned all the stars of the day; CBS had the cream of the crop as a result of William Paley's spectacular talent raids a few years before.

As for Hollywood, General Sarnoff loftily dismissed it as a source of programing. So did Paley, but to a lesser extent. Motion pictures were made for theatres, they said; feature films would play only a minor role in television's future.

Hollywood, of course, was openly hostile to television. Its stars were ordered not to appear on television in any form, not even to promote their pictures. Executives bragged that they had not yet purchased sets because the programs were so bad, and they did not want to ruin their eyes "squinting at that tiny tube." This kind of myopia was not new. In the late twenties Hollywood had issued similar edicts against radio, and stars had not been allowed to appear on network programs.

Thus the battle line between the two industries was drawn. Goldenson, however, was convinced that Sarnoff and Paley were both wrong. Television, he believed, absolutely needed the production genius of Hollywood. Without it the medium would never grow to its full potential. Viewers would tire of the sameness of all those quiz shows that cluttered up the air. Variety and comedy shows headed by major stars were interesting, but there could be too many of them. Live, original dramas like *Studio One* were commendable, but how many could a network turn out each week? There were some 28 hours of prime time to be filled. It was sheer folly, or blind egotism, to think that television could thrive without help from Hollywood.

But having reached that decision, the real question was: how to enlist Hollywood's cooperation? Goldenson was in a unique position to talk to leaders of the film industry because AB-PT still possessed some 650 theatres; therefore he was treated with tact by those who held power. He was not prepared, therefore, for the onslaught that came from his good friend, Nick Schenck, who invited him to lunch soon after the merger. Schenck, Chairman of Loew's Theatres, which had recently undergone its own consent decree separating its theatres from MGM Pictures, was considered one of the deans of the industry. Usually he was friendly and diplomatic. Today he was blunt and cryptic:

"Leonard, you are a traitor to the motion picture business!"

A shocked Goldenson asked, "Why do you say that?"

"You are one of the dominant forces in the business. Now you have acquired ABC."

The words upset Goldenson. They were typical of the thinking of film moguls. "Nick," he said, "let's assume someone came
to you and said they could put a trailer of every one of your pictures into the homes of every person in the United States?"

Schenck pondered this for a moment. "I would pay a lot of
money."

"I rest my case," said Goldenson. Schenck nodded, getting
the point. Nevertheless, MGM did not cooperate—at least not
then. Nor did any of the other studios.

Goldenson pursued his other friends. Spyros Skouras, President of Twentieth Century Fox, told him: "Leonard, I'd like to
help you. I'll talk to Darryl Zanuck about it."

But Zanuck was no more interested than was Y. Frank Freeman, or others. Freeman, as head of Paramount Production, was
a close friend. But Paramount gave him the shortest shrift of all
and was the last studio to cooperate with television in any form.

Moreover, Hollywood's prejudice was understandable. Television was making deeper inroads each day into the film industry's profits. AB-PT's own chain of theatres barely managed to
stay even with profits of the preceding year. The industry was
crying havoc, especially in those cities where new television stations opened. In addition the film industry was engaged in its
own expensive siege of technical change. Panoramic wide screen
processes like Cinemascope and Cinerama, with multiple track
sound systems, plus three dimensional processes, were hyping interest somewhat, but the technical installations were costly.

Goldenson continued to knock on Hollywood doors. Then, in
the summer of 1953, he achieved the breakthrough he had been
seeking. It came as a result of a long, marathon dinner he had
with his old friend, Jack Warner, who was known as being quick
of tongue, profane, and very anti-television. Goldenson recalls
that evening:

"Jack said, 'Leonard, I know you want to talk about television, but I don't want to waste valuable time talking about that
lousy subject. I'll talk about anything else—pictures, women,
horses, money . . . you name it'. So I named it. Television, I said,
was what I wanted to talk about. If we were not such good friends

I think he would have walked out. I told him I wanted Warners' to make some pictures for us. Jack stopped me and said, 'Hold it! I've been making those quickies for 40 years. I don't want to go back to them now.' 'No, I said, I don't want to go back to them. I want you to set up an independent management; a separate television production subsidiary. You've got story properties on the shelf that you'll never use for theatrical pictures. Put them on television. We'll pay you well for them . . .' Well, the upshot was I finally talked Jack Warner into it. It took me four hours to convince him that this would be worth doing."

That dinner was the opening wedge in the eventual breaking down of the Hollywood barrier, although it took five more years for the barrier to disappear entirely. And the results of that dinner did not appear on the video tubes of the country until the fall of 1955 when viewers, for the first time, saw the title: "Warner Brothers Presents". Three shows rotated weekly on Tuesday nights: *Cheyenne, Kings Row,* and *Casablanca. Cheyenne* clicked and that began the action-western-adventure trend that, in a few years, found shows like *Maverick, Lawman, Sugarfoot, Colt 45, Wyatt Earp, The Rebel, Rifleman, Zorro,* and others on ABC. Their success, in a few years, would put ABC in a virtual tie with the other two networks in those markets where the three had equal market coverage.

In the spring of 1954 Goldenson put another dent in the Hollywood barrier. A call came from an old friend:

"Leonard, this is Walt Disney. My brother, Roy, and I want to come to New York to see you."

"Come ahead," said Leonard. He knew what the Disney brothers wanted to talk about. They had a dream of building a super amusement park. There was industry skepticism about the idea. It would be a monument to Walt Disney's monumental ego; a project that "would never make a dime." Sarnoff and Paley had, according to reports, already turned it down. The Disney studio stock was selling at $7 per share and they were unable to borrow money for the project.

The Disneys appeared before the AB-PT Board to make their presentation. The amusement park would occupy 160 acres in

Anaheim, California. "It will be," said Walt Disney, "a combination of world's fair, playground, community center, museum of living facts, and a showcase of beauty and magic. It will be called Disneyland."

AB-PT could buy 35% of the stock for $500,000. In addition, AB-PT would be required to assist with additional financing to meet construction costs estimated at 4 million dollars. In return for this, Disney Studios would provide what ABC so badly needed—programing. An hour weekly show would be made, called *Disneyland*.

When the two brothers stepped out of the meeting so the proposal could be discussed, reactions were negative. Ed Noble and Bob Kintner liked the program possibilities, but not if the park were to be a liability. Nearly everyone thought the park would be a losing proposition.

"You know how Walt Disney is. That park is his dream. He'll never finish it."

"What do you mean?"

"Oh, he'll finish it, but as soon as he's got it finished, he'll begin expanding it, adding new things. He'll never declare any dividends."

John Coleman, the toughest Board member when it came to financial decisions, was also skeptical; but for another reason:

"The television program sounds fine, but I'm worried about the cost of financing the amusement park. That park will cost more like 8 million before it's finished."

Goldenson insisted that the deal would be worthwhile if he could tie the Disneys into a long term television program commitment.

"It's a big gamble, Leonard."

"Of course it is, but it's one I think we should take."

After much discussion the Board finally voted to go ahead provided Goldenson could work out a satisfactory program deal. He did. A $40 million deal for seven years at 5 million per year, plus an option for an eighth year—which eventually was exercised. But, true to John Coleman's prediction, the total cost of constructing Disneyland came to, not 4 million, not 8 million, but a staggering $15 million! And, while it was true Disneyland never paid any dividends, the park was successful beyond all expectations. The weekly Disney program became an instant hit and was followed a year later, in 1955, with an even more successful five-day-per-week series called *The Mickey Mouse Club*. And several years later, in 1960, when AB-PT sold its 35% interest in the amusement park, its profits came to 7½ million dollars, causing one of Goldenson's associates to remark:

"Leonard Goldenson has the manner of a Baptist minister, and the instincts of a river boat gambler. I guess that's what this business takes."

Even these prestigious breakthroughs, however, were not enough. The Warners' television series did not take the air until 1955, although the Disney program debuted October 27, 1954. By mid-summer of that year Goldenson realized that much more had to be done. A research study made by Columbia University's noted research expert, Paul Lazarsfeld, came up with results that Goldenson considered unassailable: it would not be enough to have only a few key shows each night. The entire schedule must be of such uniform strength that viewers would stay with ABC throughout the entire evening. Thus the cost of program commitments would have to be much higher than anticipated. Programing was the *only* key to success.

That fact impinged on another problem: who owned the programs? Some of the best shows on the air were owned, or controlled, by advertisers or their agencies. They could move their own programs around to the schedule detriment of any single network. Companies like U.S. Steel, Motorola, DuPont, Firestone, Pepsi-Cola, and others fell into this category. Goldenson took this problem to the Board in unequivocal terms:

"Gentlemen, we're all pleased because this year (1954) Bob Kinter got the U.S. Steel Hour for ABC. But next year, if CBS or NBC want the program, U.S. Steel's agency can take it away from us. If we're going to stay in business we've got to control our programs. If we don't have the judgment or the ability to make proper judgments you'd better get yourselves new managers. We cannot compete with CBS or NBC unless we control *every* program we have on the air!"

They were strong, but prophetic words for a struggling third network in 1954. It also meant that ABC had a long way to go.

◇   ◇   ◇

Set against this background of innovative program philosophy AB-PT was having serious internal problems of another kind. At first there had been the usual euphoria connected with the merger. Exuberant press conferences, optimistic press releases, full-page ads declaring: "WE MERGE!", and closed circuit intracompany conferences that were bursting with good faith, good will, and good intentions.

But at the human level, in the highest ranks of the new company there remained a deep and abiding distrust and suspicion that stemmed from the final negotiations between both companies.

It has been said that mergers work for all kinds of logical business reasons, but that they seldom, if ever, work at the human level. ABC's merger with UPT was to be no exception.

ABC's coup in obtaining the rights to the NCAA football schedule for 1954 was heading, that fall, toward a program triumph and a financial disaster. The protagonists were Bob Kintner and Bob O'Brien, each symbolizing the two separate camps that had divided the company from the day the two companies merged.

As always, in a human conflict, it is difficult to know where to begin to place the blame. And usually there is no single place to begin. Ed Noble's idea from the start was that this was to be a "true merger". His own lawyers had stressed this fact, that the FCC would not permit the merger to happen any other way. ABC was *not* being absorbed by UPT. It was to be run as a separate and autonomous division of the combined company. It must remain undisturbed, uninfluenced by UPT. Robert E. Kintner was to be its leader—in fact as well as in title—and he was to be left strictly alone.

Such assurances were given by UPT, but implicit in the understanding was that, since UPT had the money, it must, in the final sense, have ultimate control of the new company's destiny.

That condition, too, was accepted and understood by Noble. But he accepted it with the tacit understanding that Kintner would be left alone for at least three years. Kintner only grudgingly accepted the superimposition on his table of organization of two brilliant executives who, by no stretch of the imagination, could, or would, consider themselves to be supernumeraries, or "window dressing" in the ABC structure.

Bob Kintner, in all sincerity, felt he did not need either Bob O'Brien or Bob Weitman. With equal sincerity he felt that he was merely teaching both men the broadcast business. But, having accepted them, he had to go along and permit them to "do their thing" as long as they scrupulously observed the amenities of the corporate table of organization. Kintner certainly had to know that both O'Brien and Weitman were reporting their observations to Leonard Goldenson, just as Kintner was doing with Ed Noble whom he still considered to be his only boss. Undoubtedly Noble was soothing Kintner's occasional irritation about this problem, and assuring him to "go along" and play the game; if it eventually came to a showdown the old guard at ABC would prevail. Thus, with Noble's oft-repeated support, Kintner stubbornly held his line.

Further, Kintner was not pleased by the daily rumors that circulated. These rumors were both good and bad. The ones he liked were those that said the theatre mentality and the broadcast mentality were like oil and water. ABC, after all, had done a Horatio Alger job of lifting itself up by its bootstraps. It had gradually improved its radio network. Its brilliant stroke of grabbing off five television licenses in one swift move, without even so much as a hearing, then getting them on the air in one year, was conceded to be a stroke far more brilliant than Paley's talent raids; and equal to RCA's coup of blocking CBS' color disc system. Hence, the rumors went, ABC, with Kintner at the helm, had proven itself. It did not *need* any executive help from UPT. It needed only UPT's money.

The rumors Kintner did not like were those from the financial community to the effect that "money talks." UPT had the
money, hence it had the power. Neither did he like to hear that
Leonard Goldenson was not your run-of-the-mill executive, but a
brilliant strategist, a man with creative drive who would, sooner
or later, put his own imprint on ABC. Indeed, if Goldenson was
really inclined to leave ABC strictly alone, why would he have
put into ABC two such qualified executives as O'Brien and Weitman?

So Bob Kintner, who was not an outgoing person and had a
tendency to be moody, only became more tense, more watchful
and suspicious. Kintner was often called by his friends, a "loner."
He was a man who kept his own counsel, confided to very few,
and kept his executives on a short leash. He liked to keep them
off guard. His penchant for "chewing them out", usually in group
meetings in his office after working hours, was well known.

Robert H. O'Brien was the opposite. He was an outgoing,
gregarious fellow who liked to philosophize. He was much more
of an intellectual than financial men usually are. Though a mathematician, he preferred debating the merits of Plato. He made
friends easily and expressed himself with great flourish and persuasion. Kintner could be equally articulate, but because of his
newspaper training, preferred to sum up his thoughts in a few
words.

Robert Weitman, on the other hand, epitomized the theatrical showman stereotype. He spoke in a "showbiz" jargon, had his
name frequently in Ed Sullivan's column, and was buddy-buddy
with most of the top entertainers of the day. He had been responsible for furthering the careers of such stars as Frank Sinatra,
Danny Kaye, Red Skelton, Perry Como, the Andrews Sisters,
Betty Hutton, Tony Martin and Frankie Laine. His management
of the Paramount Theatre in New York gave him stature.

Kintner had a certain disdain for the brash, extroverted style
of Weitman. O'Brien, on the other hand, was anathema to him.
O'Brien was the one he knew he must watch, because Bob
O'Brien wasted no time in making his presence felt as executive
vice president of the new company. A few weeks after the

merger, ABC's Treasurer, Nick Priaulx, resigned. Simon B. Siegel was sent over from the theatre division to fill that job. Then, at O'Brien's instigation, Kintner approved a drastic change in the management structure of ABC's Chicago operation. This author, in fact, was given the job as General Manager. The repercussions of this move were greeted with consternation by Kintner's loyalists, adding more grist to the rumor mill. *Maybe Bob Kintner's days were numbered,* the rumors went. And with Bob Weitman making waves in the program department, Kintner grew more watchful.

Credit for the NCAA football coup belonged to O'Brien who had made staunch friends of NCAA officials and coaches during the preceding years when UPT experimented successfully with college football games on theatre television.

"Bob always understood our problem," said Tug Wilson, then head of the Big Ten Conference. "He had a knack for making us see the positive side of television—not just the negative side, which was that nationally televised games would hurt the attendance of smaller college games."

As a result, to the industry's surprise, and to the astonishment of NBC which had carried the games, ABC, in the summer of 1954 won the rights to the NCAA fall grid schedule for a rights payment of 2½ million dollars. The O'Brien concept included rights for an extensive list of other NCAA events that would unfold during spring and summer, and was prophetically similar to ABC's later concept of "Wide World of Sports." It was considered a major acquisition, in the same league with Leonard Goldenson's bold moves in the Hollywood arena. The press was generous in its praise for the "new ABC."

Sale of the games was taken for granted. But now, in late summer, with the schedule to start soon, advertisers seemed cool to the package. General Motors had been the sponsor the year before on NBC, but this year was not interested. Everyone was mystified. Audience estimates, upon which rates had been set, were said to be reasonable. Rumors began to fly. Was Bob Kintner dragging his heels because O'Brien had negotiated the deal?

In August, O'Brien personally led the sales effort. He travelled from city to city with sales head Slocum Chapin, and a young research whiz named Oliver Treyz. Rates were slashed, but still sponsors seemed to have little interest. For the first time Bob O'Brien began to think that someone was trying to set him up.

"Too many strange things happened," he recalls. "Everywhere we went, advertisers seemed to have made up their minds in advance. They knew our prices and seemed to have carefully rehearsed reasons why they should not buy the schedule. It was almost as if they had been coached in advance by someone."

Leonard Goldenson watched the development in growing consternation. He knew of the deep divisions within the company. Bob Weitman told him of his growing frustrations in trying to get new pilot programs ready. "If my name's on it, forget it," said Weitman. "These guys are experts at finding reasons why something won't work!"

Still, Goldenson exhorted his two friends—"Keep trying. Build a team. We've got to build a team."

"How can we build a team when the Captain doesn't want to use his players?" they asked.

The NCAA sales effort continued, but now with a kind of desperation. Goldenson called Kintner in the south of France where he was vacationing, and asked him to return and personally direct the sales effort. Kintner did so, but he, too, found sales resistance. He vehemently denied that he was "dragging his heels". Advertisers, for some reason, seemed intent on waiting for bargain basement discounts which they knew would be offered as September neared.

Finally some modest sales success was achieved. Kintner made a sale to a national appliance company; other "giveaway" regional sales were made. The final result was a fiasco.[1]

---

[1] The loss was estimated to be 1.8 million. Because of ABC's poor sales performance, the NCAA switched the games back to NBC for the next year, 1955, where they remained for the next five years. In 1960 ABC reacquired them for a payment of 6.2 million. CBS acquired them for 1962–63, and NBC for 1964–65. ABC got them back in 1966 for a payment of 15.5 million and has retained the rights since then.

Leonard Goldenson was a troubled man. It was one thing to have personal differences in his executive ranks, but when it affected the bottom line, the profits of the company, and the performance of AB-PT stock, it became a matter that he could no longer ignore.

In September of that year, as the NCAA games were starting, Goldenson called Bob O'Brien to his office in the Paramount Building. The conversation was painful.

"Bob, I think you'll agree that the situation at ABC has become untenable."

Bob O'Brien agreed that it had.

"I see no chance of it getting any better. I think, in the best interests of the company, you should come back to headquarters and help me here with various projects that need attending."

O'Brien said he understood, but that, in his opinion, Goldenson was backing the wrong man. Yet if Leonard wanted it that way he would move out of ABC at once.

The experience was a bitter one for O'Brien. He remained convinced that Goldenson was backing the wrong man.

Goldenson, if he had personal doubts, was still plagued by the promise he had given not to disturb Kintner for three years. So O'Brien was quietly removed from ABC's headquarters on West 66th Street. The studios were located in an old riding academy; on hot, humid days the place still remained redolent of the pungent odor of horse manure. Bob O'Brien had lost the battle of the 66th Street Corral.

The rumor mills now ground anew. The O'Brien pull-back was viewed as a "victory" by ABC forces over the entire theatre division. A smashing personal victory for Bob Kintner. Gossip abounded:

"I understand Kintner really laid it on the line to Goldenson. He put it this way: 'Either O'Brien goes, or I go.' "

"No, it was Noble who had the showdown with Goldenson. And Noble won."

The truth was that none of these rumors were true. Yet this did not stop them from circulating. Staff executives who had been sitting on the fence now plumped into one camp or the other. Oliver Treyz, the research expert who had "stuck his neck out" by trying to help Bob O'Brien sell the games, decided he was in Kintner's doghouse. So he quit and accepted a job as head of a newly established television media bureau called Television Bureau of Advertising (TVB).

In the hope that the differences could be ameliorated, Leonard Goldenson decided to put another of his trusted UPT aides into ABC. John Mitchell, who had come from Chicago where he had done an outstanding job managing UPT's Chicago station, and had recently been brought to New York to improve the status of ABC's New York flagship station, was given the assignment to make peace and "build a team." He was a tall, genial Hoosier whom everyone liked. On the surface at least, he seemed to have established a reasonable rapport with Kintner.

But this move helped not at all. The situation had deteriorated so badly that Mitchell was dubbed a "stooge" by Kintner supporters.

"All Mitchell does is give a daily report to Goldenson," said one detractor. Mitchell, who had performed well at every job he had been asked to perform, began complaining that Kintner gave him nothing to do.

"After five o'clock, that's the worst time," he told Goldenson. "That's when Bob has 'open house.' The scotch bottle is brought out and those who are in favor at the time are invited to drop by. As soon as Bob has a couple he starts telling people off. It gets embarrassing. The smart ones pop in and out before Bob gets belligerent."

After a few months of this, John Mitchell became ill.

Another of the UPT execs who "politely declined" those after hours scotch sessions was Simon B. Siegel, who functioned as Treasurer of the company. Siegel's relationship with Kintner was generally good and he chose not to jeopardize it by attending the 'happy hours.' Besides, he was too busy trying to unravel the complicated bookkeeping procedures of the many ABC divisions. A number of fiscal surprises had come to his attention since he had come over to ABC. Not that he thought Nick Priaulx and his capable staff were playing tricks with the books. They were simply deferring charges, doing their best to make every dollar do

the work of two. The ABC accountants did, however, have an annoying propensity for under-estimating costs, failing to meet de-
partmental projections, and failing to properly justify budget
needs.

Siegel's most ticklish task came when he was asked to dispos-
sess Ed Noble from his large corner office at ABC's corporate
headquarters. Noble used the office only occasionally. Most of his
duties as Chairman of Life Savers were performed at his Waldorf
Towers suite. Frequently he was out of town at his 250-acre St.
Catherine's Island estate off the coast of Georgia, where he raised
Black Angus cattle; or he would be at his Thousand Islands estate
tending his "third business", that of running the Edward John
Noble Foundation. In December of 1953 he had given the Foundation a check for $2 million and said he hoped to make equally
sizeable donations to the Foundation from then on. The Foundation supported three upstate New York hospitals. Noble's current
fascination was the idea that philanthropic organizations should
"make money." Also that industry could be more philanthropic.
"Industry now gives about ½ of 1% of its earnings to charity. If it
were more diligent it could boost that figure to 5%."

When Si Siegel realized that he was the one delegated to
take back Ed Noble's office, he approached Nobel with definite
trepidation.

"We really need that space," he began cautiously. "And since
you're hardly ever here, we'd like to get it back."

Noble took the news more gracefully than Siegel had expected. A mischevious glint came into his eyes:

"Well, let's see, Si, if I move, how much rent is the company
going to pay me?"

Si thought this over and replied, "Well, Ed, I thought we'd
pay you five times the amount of rent you're paying us—which is
nothing."

Ed Noble laughed heartily. He enjoyed getting back as much
as he gave. The damned office was a nuisance anyway, he said.
Besides, who wanted to work in an old riding stable. That ended
the matter.

By 1956 the dissension had not abated. John Mitchell was

ready to throw in the towel and wondered how he could get out of this miserable situation. He had fallen ill not once, but twice, and began to wish he had never left Chicago.

Bob O'Brien continued working on numerous projects at headquarters, not the least of which was a subsidiary that put AB-PT into the record business. O'Brien also handled the company's interests in various small electronic companies. Yet he was not a happy man. He continued to brood over the fact that Goldenson had backed the wrong man.

Early in 1956 Bob Weitman decided he had had enough. After agonizing over his decision for weeks he went to his boss and said:

"Leonard, I just can't take it anymore. This thing is getting me ill. I've got to resign or I'll end up in the hospital like John Mitchell."

Weitman was so distraught he could not be dissuaded. He said he had virtually no communications with Kintner and felt that his ideas were being sabotaged. Goldenson reluctantly accepted his old friend's resignation effective in February of 1956. Weitman promptly signed a contract with CBS.

The loss of Weitman affected Goldenson more than he cared to admit. First it had been O'Brien, then Mitchell, and now Bob Weitman. Three years had passed since the merger. It was time to come to grips with a decision he knew, sooner or later, he must make. On balance he could not say that the first three years of the company had been a disaster. Lacklustre, perhaps, but not a disaster. When one discounted the capital gains profit from the sale of WBKB Chicago, to CBS, net profits for 1953 were about the same as UPT had made the year before the merger. In 1954, profits had risen dramatically, almost double, to 8 million. Television gross had risen 53% with almost 21 hours of prime time sold, compared to 10¼ hours in 1953.

Warner Brothers programs were now on the air; Disney's programs were in their second year; the evening schedule attracted substantially more viewers; the network increased its coverage with new affiliates in several major cities.

But this was progress that was inevitable, Goldenson realized. The other networks were making progress, too. It was almost impossible *not* to make progress in these early years of the medium.

The real problem, as Goldenson saw it, was that AB-PT was a badly splintered company led by a "loner" who had his own peculiar style of operation; an executive whose ideas of "teamwork" did not mesh with his. Morale seemed low. Radio was going nowhere, but again he could not blame that on Kintner. Radio was simply suffering from the inroads of television just as theatres were suffering.

No, it was a general malaise within ABC. Everytime he talked to Bob Kintner, or to his aides, it seemed that he heard only reasons why things could *not* be done, instead of how they *could* be done.

Even the Board had become restive about the situation; several had mentioned that perhaps the time had come to make a change.

Ed Noble, however, would not think that such a time had come. Noble was *pleased* with Kintner's performance. Kintner was still very much his man and he made that abundantly clear to anyone who asked.

Thus if it came to a showdown, Goldenson realized, there probably would be one hell of a fight. Did this company need a showdown at the Board level this soon? Plus the threat of a proxy fight?

He wrestled with the problem through the summer and into autumn. One evening, unannounced, he dropped in at Kintner's office after 5 PM. Happy hour was in progress. Kintner was in a sour mood. Goldenson listened in embarrassment as Kintner berated one of his top aides. It was a bad scene. No question about it, he told himself, something had to be done.

Finally he came to grips with the inevitable. It happened at night in bed as he lay tossing and turning, thinking that maybe some of his well-meaning banker friends were right; maybe UPT had bitten off more than it could chew.

That morning at breakfast he told his wife, Isabelle, that he had come to a decision. "I've got to make a change at ABC."

Later that morning, he phoned all members of the Board except Ed Noble's contingent of five. Noble would have to be told in person. That evening he had his driver take him to Ed Noble's home in Greenwich. Ed was surprised to see him.

"I've come to tell you, Ed, that the time has come when I must make a change at the top."

"You mean Bob Kintner?"

"Yes."

Noble's face turned red. "I will see you in hell first!"

"I've got to do it, Ed."

"No sir! You fire Bob Kintner and I'll start a proxy fight!"

"That's your prerogative. I just want you to know I'm going to make a change."

Events gathered momentum swiftly after that. At a Board meeting the next day, Ed Noble and his coterie unleashed an astonishing string of charges against UPT and its executives. There were charges of ineptitude, meddling, ignorance, ineffectuality, and many more. The Board was told that ABC had already made sustantial progress *in spite* of UPT's interference. If only Leonard Goldenson and his henchmen would tend to their own knitting, keep the popcorn buttered at their damned theatres, ABC would prosper very nicely, thank you. As for Bob Kintner's management, it was fine, and it would be even better if Kintner did not have to spend so much time wet nursing UPT greenhorns, correcting UPT's mistakes (such as the NCAA fiasco), etc. Leave Kintner alone and things would be fine. As for Goldenson, said Noble, Leonard should spend more of his time trying to stem the fortunes of the theatres, because this year it looked inevitable that ABC would make more revenue than the declining theatre division.

After this diatribe John Coleman responded somberly:

"These are very serious charges. I suggest you put them in writing."

Noble said he would be glad to do that. A day later, Earl Anderson, Kintner, and others put their charges on paper. Copies were hand delivered to all members of the Board except Bob Hinckley, who was in Washington and could not be reached.

Now it was incumbent upon Leonard Goldenson and his team to respond. He, Si Siegel, Jerry Golden, and others, stayed up the entire night answering each charge, point by point. The document was delivered the next morning to all Board members, except Hinckley who still could not be located.

The Board reconvened the next day. This time, however, Ed Noble did not show up. None of his associates appeared either, except the unsuspecting Hinckley who walked in totally ignorant of the tense developments.

Ed Noble had learned by telephone earlier in the day how the Board intended to vote. He knew he did not have enough votes to win the battle. The Board voted overwhelmingly (except for ABC's five votes) for Bob Kintner's removal. Not only that, but there was an expression from some to the effect that perhaps the matter should have been resolved sooner.

Kintner was bitter, yet stoical, about the forced resignation. "I saw it coming at least a year before it happened," he said. "UPT had control of the Board, so there was nothing that could be done about it."

However, according to Kintner, despite the fact that the majority of the Board remained behind Goldenson, Ed Noble was prepared to wage a proxy fight if Kintner had not intervened.

"I was the one who stopped it," said Kintner. "I went to Ed Noble and told him that I did not want him to go through with a proxy fight, that it was best for all parties that I resign, and I was willing to resign as long as the rest of my contract was honored. By then I already had feelers from both CBS and NBC, and figured that I would have little trouble landing on my feet."

Thus Ed Noble did not pursue his threatened proxy fight and Kintner resigned on October 22, 1956. Edward Noble continued as Chairman of the Finance Committee and served on the Board until his death two years later. But relations between Noble and Goldenson remained more strained than ever until Noble died.

There are second guessers to this day who think that Leonard Goldenson should not have fired Kintner. Others say he should have acted sooner. Others believe that, when it came to the schism between Bob O'Brien and Bob Kintner, that Goldenson supported the wrong man. One of those is Noble's closest friend, Bob Hinckley, who said, "I always believed O'Brien was the better man of the two."

The crisis, ABC's first of many, seems to confirm again that on the human level mergers never work. Nevertheless all three "victims" of this first major intra-company dispute went on to distinguished careers elsewhere.

Bob Weitman, who left first, went on to become a successful program executive for CBS, then became head of production for MGM under the leadership of none other than Bob O'Brien. Today Weitman continues his career in Hollywood as an independent film producer.

Bob Kintner went to NBC. After a short time as an executive in charge of developing color for NBC, Kintner became President of the television network. He rose to Chairman of NBC and resigned in March, 1966.

Bob O'Brien stayed with AB-PT long enough to outlast his nemesis but resigned the next year in August, 1957 to join MGM as Treasurer. In 1963 he was made President and reigned there during the last six years of MGM's existence as a major film company. He retired as Chairman in 1969. O'Brien contributed much to Paramount Pictures, United Paramount Theatres, and ABC in his eleven-year career with these companies.

Nor can one fail to recognize that Bob Kintner, who joined Ed Noble in 1944, also contributed greatly to the early development of a struggling ABC.

Edward J. Noble remained the testy, unpredictable "character" that he enjoyed playing until his death in 1958 at age 76.

All of these men were, in one sense or another, unfortunate victims of that peculiarly American social phenomenon that is played on the battlefields of economics and business—the phenomenon known as *merger*.

4

High Jinks, Hardball, and Mavericks

HISTORY, in its infinite wisdom of hindsight may adjudge three men to have been the most influential programmers in the history of television—apart from William Paley and Leonard Goldenson, who as chief executives of their companies have always exercised a great deal of authority in program matters. First would be:

Sylvester "Pat" Weaver (NBC, 1950–1955), who contributed many of the formats that are still popular today; and who endeavored to create for the medium the kind of programs he thought the public *should* have.

Second: Oliver E. Treyz (ABC, 1956–1962), who gave the public what research, and his instincts, told him the public *wanted*.

Third is Fred Silverman (CBS, ABC, NBC), who also, with research and instinct, has "fine-tuned" the mass denominated program machine to its ultimate in terms of maximum audience.

As a study in character, Ollie Treyz is by far the most fascinating. His meteoric rise and fall in six short years exemplifies in dramatic and poignant terms the volatility of the medium, and why stories of what goes in executive suites of networks seem so unbelievably bizarre.

There are still today conflicting opinions about Treyz and what made him tick:

"Ollie Treyz was a kind of genius."

"Ollie was a jungle fighter who never learned to change with the times."

"ABC, when Treyz was there, was maverick land, and Ollie was the biggest maverick of them all."

The program, "Maverick" did not start until 1957, but within the company the era of mavericks began when Leonard Goldenson personally took command of ABC and picked Treyz to head ABC's television network. This was to begin a riotous, rambunctious go-go era, the likes of which the company would never see again: 1957–1962.

The personal command by Goldenson signalled a whole new direction representing Goldenson's style of the broadest kind of autonomy for his executives. He had watched Paramount Theatres operate under centralized and decentralized policies and found decentralization by far the best. His key words were: *Innovation. Broad autonomy. Rugged individualism.* Fear of failure should bother no one unless you failed too often, in which case you were handed your head as your body was pushed out the door. Imitation was scorned; conscious imitation was in itself considered a sign of failure.

No one had yet written the rulebook for television. Certainly CBS and NBC had not written it; they had merely adapted radio to television. After all, CBS and NBC were thirty years old, while ABC was a brash upstart of a mere 14 years—and only 4 years as a merged company. ABC was known as a "shirtsleeve company," whereas CBS—as Jack Schneider, former CBS President, put it in his earlier years—was a company you did not "join." You were "pledged" to CBS.

At ABC you were definitely "hired," but only if you liked the rough and tumble of a good fight; if you could dish out punishment, as well as take it.

Ollie Treyz suited Leonard Goldenson's style. Goldenson

was, and remains today, the kind of executive who likes to be "sold." He doesn't even mind if he is being *over* sold. He will even forgive being sold a wrong proposition. What he wants, essentially, is:

Enthusiasm! Raw, bubbling, irrepressible enthusiasm.

No one had more of that quality than Treyz. He fit perfectly the canard coined by some unknown author of one-liners: "Anything is possible; the impossible only takes a little longer." Ollie Treyz was one of the most glib, rapier-minded, research-oriented men ever to come upon the television scene. He could extract any results he wanted, or needed, from research "numbers."

He was aided in that department by another maverick in the person of Julie Barnathan, a rugged character whose appearance belied his virtuoso talents. Barnathan was a Phi Beta Kappa from Brooklyn College where he wrote his master's thesis on the possibilities of rolling dice. He did not merely walk into a room, he barrelled in with a rolling gait that reminded one of a sailor back from a long cruise. He had the appearance and mien of a teamster organizer. When Julie charged on stage to confront, not address, ABC affiliates with his bar charts, quintiles, and other research proof of stations' performances, he began without ceremony. No greetings. No friendly smiles. His opening barrage was:

"All right, you guys, you're all full of shit, and I've got the numbers here to prove it!"

A roar of laughter would flood the room as the affiliates stood and replied: "Yes, Julie, we know we're full of shit, but so are you!" On that note a head knocking session would begin.

The word "demographics" was becoming fashionable in the 'fifties; Treyz, and Barnathan as Director of Research, were two of its most ardent proponents. Together they articulated the formula that prescribed that ABC must go after younger families, a direction and technique that ABC has mastered today to an unparalleled degree.

In the winter of 1956, Treyz put his team together, a hardheaded group of research experts who "spoke his language." The goal: to question all past concepts and replace them, where necessary, with new ones. Sales, programing, promotion techniques

were to be mercilessly scrutinized. ABC had far less primary affiliates than NBC or CBS, but did that mean ABC could not be
competitive? *No!*

But how?

ABC had less than a third of the revenues of the other networks, but did that mean that ABC could not catch up? *No!*

But how?

ABC had fewer hit programs than NBC or CBS, but did that
mean they could not compete and catch up? *No!*

But how?

He spent his first month searching for answers to these questions. Pacing back and forth in a room filled with his cohorts, he
delighted in playing "intellectual tennis" with his men. He would
throw out outrageous ideas and defy his men to shoot them down.
They had very little time to put together ABC's new sales story
which would be travelled to hundreds of clients and agencies.

Several months after he took over, Treyz hired Jim Aubrey
away from CBS to serve as his program chief. The immediate conflict of wills between the two only added a further quality of pan-
demonium that kept many of the staff looking for a bomb shel-
ter. Aubrey insisted that Treyz keep his nose out of programing.
Treyz could no more do that than he could permit his new sales
chief, Tom Moore, to handle sales. Treyz had to do everything.
He was like a man possessed. Indeed he was possessed of such incredible drive and inexhaustible energy that he worked seven
days a week and slept only four hours per night, causing one of
his aides to remark:

"Ollie can't be on pills. There are no pills that can keep a
man so constantly high!"

But the disagreements between Treyz and Aubrey grew
worse. Aubrey came from the CBS mold and had a disdain, if not
outright scorn, for Treyz and the entire ABC organization. It was
clear that Jim Aubrey was trying to use ABC as a stepping stone
for a higher position back at CBS. This became even clearer when
he began brazenly telling his associates that there was only one
way ABC could succeed, and that would be for both Goldenson

and Siegel to go back to the theatre business; put Ollie in Washington to handle government affairs; fire all the ABC station managers except Jimmy Riddell; and let Aubrey run the broadcast division without interference from anyone. If that were done he would have ABC in the number one position in a very short time.

Aubrey, understandably, remained at ABC only 14 months. When he left no one had any regrets.

But even without Aubrey all the combustible elements were in place for the inevitable explosion that had to happen. Treyz ran roughshod over those who disagreed with him and branded them as "obstructionists." He began a whirlwind pace of "deal-making," criss-crossed the country almost continuously, often in company with Goldenson, and made ABC's aggressive presence known in every major advertising agency, and to every potential client, in the country. He made it clear that he was not going to be thwarted by any "bookkeepers," a reference intended to sting the chief bookkeeper of them all—none other than the Treasurer and Financial Vice President of the company, Simon B. Siegel.

Siegel was considered the closest man to Goldenson, not only an alter ego, but the Executive Vice President without portfolio.

Siegel did not qualify as one of Goldenson's "enthusiasts." He was low key, sometimes droll, with an inscrutable expression that reminded some of the Sphinx. He could chill and wither with a glance and was a moderating influence on Goldenson's susceptibility to pepper-pots. If Siegel thought his boss was making a mistake he would bide his time, then approach and say, "Leonard there may be some risks here that we should take a second look at." Goldenson's faith in his old friend dated back to the days when Si Siegel helped unravel incredibly complex theatre reorganization problems.

In addition to Siegel's loyalty and dependability, Leonard Goldenson appreciated Siegel's succinct solutions to problems. Si Siegel never wrote a long memo in his life; his views were summed up in one or two paragraphs.

But while the Goldenson-Siegel relationship was akin to

Damon and Pythias, the relationship of Goldenson to Treyz was more like a father to a son—the son he never had. For Goldenson developed a genuine affection for the buoyant Treyz. Leonard found it easy to excuse both Ollie's excesses of enthusiasm and the rapidity with which he made decisions. If Treyz made a mistake, Leonard would say, "One thing about Ollie, he never takes 'no' for an answer. He's always in there trying."

In addition, Ollie made Goldenson laugh, and laughter was something he needed, because the past seven years had been somber and tragic years in the Goldenson family.

In 1945, at breakfast one morning, Isabelle Goldenson said to her husband, "Leonard, I'm convinced there is something wrong with Genise. She isn't even trying to walk or talk." Their daughter was then two years old.

Leonard replied, "Darling, calm down. This is our first baby and you're just an overwrought, nervous mother."

Nothing more was said, even though the subject of Genise's passive behavior had been bothering them for months. Then he happened to read a copy of *Time Magazine* containing an article about a German measles epidemic in the South Pacific, where a number of GI wives had contracted German measles in the early months of their pregnancies. The result, said the article, was a surprising number of cases of cerebral palsy. Suddenly, the Goldensons knew that their daughter was afflicted with cerebral palsy because Isabelle Goldenson had contracted German measles in the early months of her pregnancy.

They took their child to the best medical experts in the east and learned that there was little that could be done to alleviate, or eliminate, the affliction. The Goldensons were able to afford the best attention and care for their daughter, and this bothered Isabelle for another reason:

"What about all the people who cannot afford this expensive care?" she asked. Thus was born, within a year, the United Cerebral Palsy Foundation, which is today the sixth largest public health agency in the United States. The Goldensons contributed to, and raised the necessary seed money, and ever since have devoted vast amounts of their time, energies, and funds to this cause.[1]

So Ollie Treyz, with his boyish laugh, quizzical grin, and penchant for doing the unpredictable, added new zest and excitement to Goldenson's life. NBC and CBS were the enemy and the battle was on.

Treyz built the new ABC schedule carefully, building one night at a time. Wednesday was already strong, so he built Tuesday. Then Sunday. Then Friday. Spinoff programs were created for the first time, long before Fred Silverman, Paul Klein, and others carried on the idea. *Sugarfoot* was born of *Cheyenne*. *Sunset Strip* begat *Surfside Six* and *Hawaiian Eye*. And so on. All of them hard-hitting action-adventure programs. ABC had little faith in comedies, because they took too long to build an audience. The new ABC had to have results fast!

Traditional patterns of selling programs gave way to single minutes, ideal for those advertisers who had only single products to sell. ABC locked up the tobacco, soap, and food companies. In one year the company made tremendous improvement.

Then he made another daring move. To lock out his competitors, he made commitments with major film studios for *all* the television programs they could deliver.

Daytime had been a problem for ABC. In fact the company scarcely existed in daytime, with the main program being Dick Clark's American Bandstand program from 3:30 to 5 PM. ABC could not find advertisers willing to support any programs that ABC suggested. And if they did, ABC could not have broken even, because its station compensation rates were too high. In a

---

[1] Genise Goldenson died January 4, 1973, at the age of thirty. (The Goldenson's have two other daughters, Loreen and Maxine.) The Goldensons are justifiably proud of the work that United Cerebral Palsy has done in the early detection, correction, and relief of birth defects. UCP was largely responsible for isolating the rubella virus as a major cause of congenital brain damage and also for reducing the incidence of German measles among pregnant women. With space age technology, Goldenson believes, mankind will see the day when youngsters born with physical and mental disabilities will be able to lead nearly normal lives.

bitter fight, Treyz persuaded affiliates to accept less compensation. Then, in a brilliant coup, worked out with Young & Rubicam Agency, ABC, in one fell swoop, introduced 21 half-hour programs per week, beginning at 11:00 in the morning. And with it came such prized Y&R clients as Bristol-Myers and General Foods, plus American Home Products from the Bates Agency. The co-architect of this maneuver was Everett H. Erlick, who, a few years later, would join ABC as General Counsel.

The daytime schedule did not achieve the ratings that Treyz wanted, and he was baffled. Perhaps, he told his staff, they had too many game and variety shows. Maybe they needed soap operas. He called his friend Tom McDermott at Benton & Bowles Agency, which, through its client, Procter & Gamble, owned many of the successful soap operas on the air.

"Tom," he asked, "how long does it take a soap opera to succeed?"

McDermott, with a straight face, replied, "Well, Ollie, after one is on the air about a year and a half you begin to get some kind of idea. After about three years you can pretty well make up your mind."

Ollie groaned. No soap operas for him. At least not yet. Nevertheless the new daytime schedule gradually began to succeed. He turned his attention back to prime time. Wheeling and dealing. Gillette placed virtually its entire budget on ABC in a broad, diversified sports schedule. Kaiser Company was sold *Maverick,* and in doing so, Ollie considered giving away ABC's affiliation contract to a station owned by Kaiser in Honolulu. But wiser heads back at headquarters prevailed.

Inside the company, Ollie's deal-making continued to create friction. Many of his deals actually cost the company money. Others barely covered the cost of station compensation and the cost of the program. *What's the difference,* said Ollie. *We're building a network. We have the overhead anyhow, so why not eat it?* And in terms of upward movement, Treyz was right, at least for that time in the company's development. Ratings grew. Revenues grew. And as the ratings grew the profits increased. But at the same time rumors began circulating that Ollie was being high-handed with agencies; that he was alienating some of the button-down minds of agencies and clients. It was said that his handshake on a deal could not be trusted: "If you're dealing with Ollie, get it in writing."

"Not true," Ollie would reply. "I just found their contract unacceptable." Which, translated, meant that if a deal came in on Monday and paid more money than the deal he had accepted on Friday, the higher deal would be accepted. Agency executives were all mercenary whores anyhow, he maintained. Why shouldn't he do what was best for his company?

Inside the company, relations between Siegel and Treyz grew more strained. Treyz, by now, was completely ignoring the chief financial officer of the company. To settle things down, Leonard Goldenson installed James Riddell, popular manager of the station's successful Detroit station, as Executive Vice President of the company, a notch above Treyz.

This disturbed Treyz, but did not cause him to change his ways. He ignored Riddell as much as he did Siegel. "I report only to Leonard Goldenson, as I have in the past," he boasted. After one year of this Riddell became so disgusted he asked to be transferred as far away from headquarters as possible, which happened to be Los Angeles.

While all this was going on ABC was moving in other areas. Telstar was coming. The world was shrinking. ABC decided it would go international. In 1959 it began to buy into television stations in foreign countries. That success led to expansion into some 14 countries in Central and South America, the Mid-East, and Far East. The Disneyland amusement park was such an enormous success (although, as predicted, it never paid dividends) that the company purchased a swimming mermaid amusement attraction in Florida called Weekee Wachee Spring. ABC's record division, under Sam Clark, continued to expand and exceed profit projections. A solid, medium-sized publishing company in Chicago, called Prairie Farmer Publishing Company, was acquired, along with its half ownership of WLS radio station. Radio networking continued to be anathema as it was to the other networks, but the ABC-owned radio stations were doing well. And the five ABC-owned television stations were doing even better. The rights to the NCAA football games, which had been such a sales fiasco in 1954, were reacquired for the 1960–61 seasons at a rights fee of 6.2 million dollars—and the producer for those games turned out to be an eager, young redheaded director named Roone Arledge. A year later, in 1961, the same young Arledge became producer of ABC's *Wide World of Sports*, television's longest running, and most successful sports series. In news, Leonard Goldenson persuaded James Hagerty to leave President Eisenhower and direct the news and public affairs destiny of the company.

Despite all of Ollie Treyz' mounting problems, by 1961 it had to be said that he had "arrived." ABC's "perpetual motion machine," as some called him, or that "wild bull from the pampas of mavericks" as others called him, had truly arrived. Primary affiliates had grown to 100. Treyz was able to announce, with figures to back him, that the era of the 2½ network economy was over. More importantly, in those markets where ABC was equally competitive with NBC and CBS, the third network had achieved audience leadership! More important than anything else, ABC's television revenues had risen from 83 million in 1957, to 190 million in 1961!

But problems that had been relegated to the background now came to the foreground. The tides of the fortunes of men change as mysteriously as do those of nations, and now Ollie Treyz, at the peak of his career began to reap the harvest of his own destruction, the seeds of which he had sown for some time. Treyz was the last one to know that things were happening that would inevitably lead to his downfall.

His selling methods, and the integrity of his "solemn word," began to be questioned in half the agencies that dealt in television advertising. His refusal to honor verbal commitments led to a cocktail cliche throughout the advertising fraternity:

"Yes, but Ollie you said . . ."

One of the largest agencies in America, Leo Burnett Company, refused to have anything to do with ABC because of some alleged misrepresentations by Treyz. One of their large clients, Philip Morris tobacco, was moved out of its expected schedule because Treyz got better deals elsewhere. Another of Burnett's clients, Kellogg's cereals, was paying full rate card when other advertisers were getting fantastic rate-cutting deals. The very agency that handled ABC's own advertising account, Batten, Barton, Durstine, Osborne (BBD&O), turned the account back because it could no longer tolerate Treyz' "unreasonable and cruel treatment."

The impasse grew so great at Leo Burnett Company that one of Treyz' Chicago salesmen, John Beebe, sent a desperate, but whimsical wire to the great Leo Burnett himself, to the effect that ABC had top level problems with Burnett's company, and therefore a meeting would be in order; a personal meeting with the legendary Leo Burnett would be the "equivalent of meeting with the Pope."

A day later Beebe received a phone call. A burred, guttural voice said:

"Mr. Beebe, this is Pope Leo calling."

Thus a meeting was set up at the highest level, which Ollie Treyz attended. He flew into Chicago and was met by Jim Beach, John Beebe, and the Chicago ABC network sales contingent. As they drove from Midway Airport down Cicero Avenue, Treyz ordered the hired limousine to stop at a rundown diner. He wanted coffee. Jim Beach, his Chicago sales chief, looked at his watch and protested. "Ollie, we'll be late for the big meeting."

It turned out that this was exactly Ollie's intention. He would not let the limousine proceed until he was sure they would be at least 45 minutes late for the critical Burnett meeting.

Obviously the Burnett meeting did not turn out well, but that did not bother Treyz. He had more important things to do than to "baby" sensitive advertising agencies. He much preferred getting over to the Ambassador East hotel where a minimum of six phones had to be installed; there he delighted in demonstrating how he could keep three phone conversations going at once.

His reputation for "veracity," or for "remembering what happened," spread as far as Minneapolis, where Art Lund, executive of Campbell-Mithun Agency, had gathered top executives of Pillsbury for a personal presentation by the great Treyz himself. After welcoming Treyz, and expressing gratitude for the honor of the personal presentation, Art Lund said, with a straight face:

"There's only one thing, Ollie. If you don't mind, we'd like to tape this meeting."

Ollie's face fell. There, sitting on Lund's desk was a Wollensak tape recorder with microphone facing the room. The meaning was clear: none of them *trusted* what Treyz had to say. Ollie proceeded somewhat hesitantly, and gave one of the few presentations that were less than superb.

The time had come for Treyz to change his opportunistic sales practices; to mend his fences and build solid alliances in the way that NBC and CBS had done. Julie Barnathan pleaded with him to change, but Ollie would have none of it. "Why should I change? I'm doing it for the good of the company," he insisted.

"But Ollie, this will bring you down," Barnathan said. "It's a new ball game. The rules have changed. We don't need to play by those old rules."

"Bullshit. They're all whores. Julie, if I didn't know you better, I'd begin thinking you've become an obstructionist."

Then Barnathan heard some news that upset him deeply. It concerned Terry Clyne, television major domo for the McCann-Erickson agency which handled the Liggett and Myers tobacco account. Ollie had performed radical surgery on the client's advertising schedule.

"I don't know how to say this," Clyne said, "but what Ollie has just done to our schedule has cost me my job."

Shortly after that the McCann-Erickson agency lost the Liggett and Myers account, worth some ten million dollars in billing!

Within the company, Treyz by now had totally alienated Si Siegel and the powerful TV station managers, all of whom qualified as mavericks themselves. Treyz refused to raise the stations' network rate, even though they deserved the increase. In addition, he appropriated their local time periods with less than 48 hours warning. Periodic company meetings between the two divisions—network and stations—were held out of the country, it was said, so that if real mayhem erupted, the U.S. press would not

THE ORIGINAL WHEELER DEALERS: Edward J. Noble, far right, who bought ABC the Blue Network from NBC and named it American Broadcasting Company. Next to him, Mark Woods who presided over ABC until Robert Kintner replaced him. Earl Mullen, ABC executive, carries bags, and Robert Hinckley, longtime Noble crony, leads the group to a meeting.

HINCKLEY, NOBLE, AND WOODS arrive in Atlantic City for the 25th meeting of the National Association of Broadcasters in 1947.

ED NOBLE'S CHOICE: Robert E. Kintner, who replaced Mark Woods shortly after Noble purchased the Blue Network and named it ABC.

"HIGH HOPES AND TOTAL HARMONY": So read the press announcements after the ABC-UPT merger in February of 1953. Shown (seated) are Leonard H. Goldenson; Robert E. Kintner; Robert H. O'Brien; and (standing) Robert Weitman.

BREAKTHROUGH: Leonard Goldenson, shown with Jack Warner, President of Warner Pictures in 1961. It took all of Goldenson's persuasion to convince Warner that he should "join television".

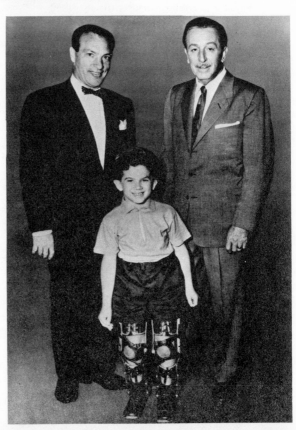

ABC BUYS INTO MICKEY MOUSE:
One of ABC's early coups was to convince Walt Disney, shown here with Goldenson in the early fifties, to join forces with ABC. Shown with them is Jackie Mortin, a victim of Cerebral Palsy, a disease to which Goldenson has devoted much of his life.

"THE INSCRUTABLE BUDDHA": Simon B. Siegel, Executive Vice President during ABC's early years when the going was difficult. Siegel's stern manner belied his extraordinary sensitivity. 1962

A FAMILY PORTRAIT: Taken in the late fifties, Leonard and Isabelle Goldenson sit with their two daughters, Maxine on the left, and Loreen on right.

IN THE DAYS BEFORE CAMELOT: Senator John F. Kennedy is flanked by Goldenson, Oliver Treyz, and John Daly. 1960.

ELEANOR ROOSEVELT conducts a press conference to herald an ABC series dealing with her husband. With her are Goldenson, James Hagerty, and Oliver Treyz. 1961.

DYNAMIC TRIO: Oliver Treyz, Julius Barnathan, and Thomas Moore prepare for an industry convention in 1961.

NEWS RESPECTABILITY: Elmer Lower, who moved from NBC to ABC in 1963, gave the third network a vigorous thrust toward parity in network news competition.

A VOICE FROM CHICAGO: Of the many mavericks who distinguished ABC from its more sedate competitors, none was more outspoken than Red Quinlan, the author of this book, who managed ABC's Chicago television station from 1953 to 1964. Photo: 1958

THE ELUSIVE HAROLD GENEEN AND ERSTWHILE FRIENDS: Two years of waiting for a merger to be approved with International Telephone and Telegraph enervated ABC badly. Here in the euphoric days when the merger seemed like a wonderful idea are shown Simon Siegal, Harold Geneen, Leonard Goldenson, and Hart Perry, an ITT executive.

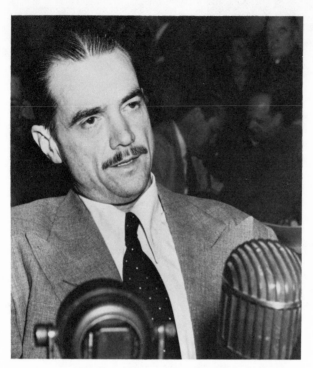

RALPH BEAUDIN: Whose nimble brain came up with ABC's four radio network concept.

YES, THERE WAS A HOWARD HUGHES: In the summer of 1968 he tried to take over ABC, and almost succeeded. Following the ITT disappointment, and the abortive Hughes takeover attempt, ABC's fortunes slowly began to rise.

SAM CLARK: Bad luck in feature films ruined his chances to go higher in the company.

HAROLD L. NEAL, Jr.: After 35 years with ABC he resigned suddenly in 1979 as President of ABC Radio. His leadership and contributions were exceptional.

BEN HOBERMAN was moved up from manager of KABC-AM, Los Angeles, to replace Neal as head of all ABC radio activities. Hoberman has 29 years with ABC. KABC-AM is considered to be the nation's leading talk station.

THEODORE SHAKER: There were few tears shed when he missed the brass ring.

hear about it. The stormy battles that went on were classics of adversary confrontation between intra-company divisions. "We make the dough that the network pisses away," the stations cried. "Ollie's programs are so bad that we can't give them away to the local educational station."

Treyz complained that the stations were not cooperating; not promoting the network sufficiently. He had heard rumors that the Chicago station was cutting its transmitting power in prime time just to undermine the network.

"Hell of an idea," said the Chicago manager. "I'll start doing it next week!"

Another cried out: "Ollie, you're so full of shit you should be sentenced to ten years at NBC!" This was a current gag within the company. NBC, with its many-tiered layers of management, and its rather stodgy style, was considered a dull place to work. CBS would be even worse, but for other reasons. At CBS the atmosphere would be so rarified that ABC alumni would suffocate from lack of oxygen.

Physical altercations were narrowly averted even in the august presence of President Leonard Goldenson. All he could do was look off into space, hoping that fists would not fly. After all, this was his definition of "teamwork"—not that namby-pamby concept that implied old-fashioned virtues like harmony and togetherness. No, gentlemen, this was hardball. Goldenson's kind of hardball. *Stomp on yourselves if you must, just remember, our common goal is to be first, and best, among the three networks, and we still have a long ways to go.*

The station divisions' mutiny grew so strong that individual station managers began to reduce their annual profit projections, not only to embarrass Treyz, but for the very real reason that they never quite knew what local time they could sell.

Still, Goldenson stubbornly supported his "perpetual motion machine." "You must remember," he told the stations managers, and Si Siegel, at one critical meeting, "that Ollie is a very busy guy. He can't be expected to remember everything. No one is perfect. I just want to say that I think Ollie is doing a hell of a job."

That ended that battle, and it was another victory for Treyz. Siegel himself began to feel that perhaps it was time to look for greener pastures. He had a close friend, Selig Seligman, write his resignation letter, but then decided not to submit it because it was becoming apparent to him that Treyz, sooner or later, would dig his own grave.

In the spring of 1961, as the new fall schedule was being sold, it soon became clear that Siegel's hunch was right. Something drastic began to happen. ABC's new programs failed. Not only that, but Treyz' former scheduling genius had gone by the boards. For the first time, Treyz had chosen not to "listen to the numbers," but to appease certain powerhouse advertisers like Procter and Gamble, and in doing so, he not only ruined his schedule, but alienated lesser clients who disliked being pushed around by the big boys.

This was compounded by another error that had taken a year to catch up with him. When Treyz had signed for exclusive product from the major studios, he had removed the competitive element from these suppliers. The result was that the new shows were weak. He also failed to recognize the signs that had been unmistakable a year before: action and adventure shows, and detective shows, were losing audience appeal. The public wanted more situation comedies and ABC did not have them.

Before 1961 ended, the industry knew that ABC's new fall schedule was a disaster.[2] Ollie knew it, too, but refused to admit it. He continued to treat Si Siegel like a lackey. One day he called Siegel and ordered him to visit an agency and solve some pressing financial problem. Siegel said he was too busy, but would send one of his staff.

"You don't understand, Si," said Ollie. "I'm telling *you* to handle it personally."

"Ollie, I'm too busy."

"We'll see about that."

Leonard Goldenson happened to be in Europe on a com-

---

[2] New shows like *The Islanders, Stagecoach West, Hong Kong, Guestward Ho,* and *Harrigan and Son* were repudiated by television audiences.

bined vacation and business trip. When he returned the matter was promptly laid on Goldenson's carpet.

"Ollie," said Leonard, "you read the note I sent around before I left. I made it clear that, in my absence, Si would be in charge."

Ollie was unimpressed. "Leonard, you don't understand. I'm the President of the Television Network. How would it look if the word got out that I was reporting to someone in the financial area?"

Goldenson pondered that remark only for a moment, then replied:

"Well, if that's your problem, I'll change Si's title to that of Executive Vice President. Then you'll have to report to him."

Still Ollie continued to ignore Siegel. Julie Barnathan began to think that Treyz had taken total leave of his senses. "Calm down," he urged. "Stop making waves. Give the owned stations their rate increase. Give Si Siegel the time of day."

"Screw him!" Treyz replied. "I'm not reporting to any goddam bookkeeper!" The following Monday the news came out: Treyz now reported to Siegal.

Then Barnathan received another call from an advertising agency friend, a fellow who handled the Peter Paul Mounds candy account. Treyz had shuffled his client's schedule around, and the fellow sounded like he was in a daze.

"Julie, do you know what happened? You promised me that Sunday schedule. You said I would not be moved. You said Ollie guaranteed there would be no change. Now I don't have that schedule. And do you know what else? I no longer have my job."

Barnathan decided he could take no more. At a Christmas party Barnathan got an offer to run a station in Buffalo. He went there over New Year's, with his wife, and decided to accept the job. The following Monday he saw Si Siegel. Before he could get the words out, tears began rolling down his face. "Life's too short," he said. "I can't take it anymore. I can't work for Ollie any longer, but I don't want to hurt him either because he gave me my chance. I'll never do anything to hurt Ollie, but I just can't work for him anymore."

Siegel talked Barnathan out of resigning. One man could not be permitted to ruin a whole company, said Siegel. *Hang on. Be patient, and calm down.* Siegel put Barnathan in charge of the recalcitrant station group, figuring that this would keep him occupied for a while. Before that happened, however, Treyz' two top lieutenants, Tom Moore in programing, and Ed Scherick in sales, tried to enlist Barnathan in a conspiracy to go to Siegel and force Treyz out of his job. Barnathan refused. He wanted nothing more to do with the ABC television network.

Then there came a blow from another quarter—from the U.S. Senate Juvenile Delinquency Subcommittee, a vote of censure against ABC for having carried an episode of excessive violence in a series called *Bus Stop.*

But that did not really matter. For Ollie Treyz, the die had been cast. In the winter of 1962 Leonard Goldenson knew that he had to make a change. Treyz had to go. It was not an easy decision to make, because he still had a strong affection for his firebrand; but, considering all the complaints he had received from so many quarters, for so many months, Goldenson knew also that he had probably waited longer than he should have waited. At a weekend meeting in Goldenson's Mamaroneck home it was decided that Tom Moore would replace Treyz as head of the television network; Dan Melnick would move into programing; Scherick would continue in sales; and the disenchanted Julie Barnathan would move back to the network as General Manager of the network. Julie viewed the prospect with dim misgivings, because, while he admired and liked Ollie Treyz with all of his shortcomings, he had very little respect for Tom Moore's ability.

Treyz was given his walking papers the following Monday. He was in Chicago, on a sales call at Alberto Culver company, trying to make amends with Leonard Lavin who also had been pushed around in his television schedule. Ollie was told to return to New York at once and come straight to the President's office. There, he was told that the ballgame was over. He would receive severance of one year's salary. Plus one unexpected feature: Goldenson had arranged for Warner Brothers to hire Treyz at once, if Treyz wanted to take the job.

Oliver E. Treyz, on March 19th, finished his career at ABC. To say that he was stunned when he heard the news is an understatement. Weeks passed by and he still could not believe what happened; or *why* it happened. Some say he is not able to believe it today, many years later.

"Whatever I did, I did for the good of the company," Ollie Treyz says to this day.

They still talk about what happened to Treyz. The key word is "integrity," some say—or, in Ollie's case, the *lack* of it. Others say that in some strange way, Ollie was divorced from reality. "He never really believed that he lied to anyone. He had a genius for rationalizing whatever he did, so that purple came out green. As Julie Barnathan put it: "I heard Ollie explain a problem one way to me, and then when I heard him explain it to Goldenson, it came out totally different. And in both instances, Ollie believed he was saying the same thing."

The irony of it all is the fact that his closest friend, Julie Barnathan, unwittingly, probably did more to end Ollie Treyz's career than anyone else: it was Barnathan's heroic gesture of wanting to resign rather than oppose, or expose, Treyz' methods, which made the deepest impression on Leonard Goldenson and caused him to reach a decision. But then the decision would have been made sooner or later because that seemed to be the way fate destined it. Ollie could not change. How can you change if you think you have done nothing wrong?

Nevertheless his contributions to ABC were enormous. By 1962 the company had a respectable 25% of all network revenues. Profits had risen, during his tenure, from 4 to 10 million dollars. The near-monopoly dynasty of NBC and CBS had been broken, but it had taken a lot out of many ABC people; the high energy six years of Ollie Treyz—of high jincks, hardball, and mavericks—left everyone somewhat depleted.[3]

◊   ◊   ◊

[3] Treyz later set up a television spot sales company. In the mid-sixties he tried to establish a fourth television network which failed. Then he set up a consulting firm which continued until a few years ago. His present activities are unknown.

Part Two

Crisis Time

5

Minefields and ITT

BY THE END of its first decade ABC had managed to traverse the usual minefields endemic to a merger. The new company had shaken down to a single management philosophy and point of view. It had begun to establish itself as something of an unorthodox but healthy third player in the game. It had entered international television on a much larger scale than either NBC or CBS, and acted as though it were willing to join anyone's high stakes poker game.

Externally, as the turbulent sixties loomed, new minefields lurked ahead. RCA had won its battle of color standards; its satellite company, NBC, now had the key role of getting America to buy color television sets. NBC's role was to push color harder and faster than either CBS or ABC. And it was doing a good job, ironically, under the supervision of Robert Kintner who worked closely with General Sarnoff in this area. CBS, always adjustable and not accustomed to be a follower, refused to concede leadership in any area, so it began its own campaign to introduce color programing faster than NBC. CBS "colorized" its production plant every bit as rapidly as NBC.

ABC, as regards color, was reluctant to proceed, for economic reasons. It was just beginning to catch up with the other two networks in black and white programing; a switch to color was the last thing it wanted. Yet, being attuned to the marketplace, ABC knew that sooner, rather than later, it must colorize.

Advertisers at first were asked to pay a premium for color programs. They balked at this, so NBC gave in. CBS had to capitulate, too. ABC did not really care; it had no color to offer as the sixties began. With less than 5% of sets in color by the start of the sixties, advertisers began giving that slight edge to color as a factor in buying programs. The reasons were obvious: color enhanced a product so incredibly that clients became much more enthused about spending more advertising dollars in the medium. Research be damned; if the client wanted color, give it to him, especially when there was no cost premium to pay.

Thus, by the early sixties, certainly by 1962, the chicken-vs-egg syndrome regarding color was broken. Color was on its way, 1) because the public wanted it; and 2) because products looked and sold so much better in color.

Facing these realities, ABC had the serious problem of lack of sufficient capital to introduce color programs into its schedule. It was not an NBC sheltered by mighty RCA; it was not CBS with its established leadership in programing, nor did it have anything like CBS' financial viability. In 1962 CBS profits were $29 million compared to ABC's $10.7 million. A year later, when CBS abandoned its abortive television set manufacturing subsidiary, its profits leaped to 41 million. So, while NBC was the "advance man" for RCA in the expansion into color, CBS could handle its capital needs very nicely. ABC could not.

A second minefield appeared in the matter of ABC's need for theatrical films for its prime time entertainment schedule. Movies, that ubiquitous product that doughty General Sarnoff and dapper William Paley said was not suitable for the new medium, had now become a necessary program staple to a successful evening schedule. And the imperious Hollywood studios, needing money, were now delighted to sell to the highest bidder. Prices had quadrupled in three years' time, and ABC had to stake out its own franchise in this new program sweepstakes. The cost was millions that ABC did not have.

Combined, these two needs—colorization of its studios, production, and transmission plants; and theatrical movies—came to a colossal capital need of some *$134 million!*

A third minefield existed in the form of that always fashionable game played in the corporate jungle: make-it-big-but-if-you-show-any-signs-of-weakness-we'll-take-you-over.

In other words, corporate raiders.

The rules of the game were basic, not complex at all, if your company was publicly held; if the stock was widely dispersed, and the principals, members of the board, and key employees did not hold, or control, large blocks of stock, the game could be played with relative ease.

ABC was this kind of company. Large blocks of stock were held by financial institutions—trusts, holding companies, insurance companies among them. While their confidence in ABC management was strong, it was not so strong that it could not be swayed by articulate dissidents. There were some two million shares floating out there among the approximate 4.7 million ABC shares outstanding at the time. This "floating" increment provided a real temptation to corporate raiders, and for a very good reason: ABC was in the vanguard of a new technology. It was the third player in a game of only three, in the most promising profit-oriented arena since WW II. ABC was, in other words, *vulnerable.*

For years, at annual meetings of the company, held in the spring of the year, persistent questioners asked the same question: why did Board members hold virtually no shares of ABC stock?[1] Leonard Goldenson defended his practice by saying that, as far as outside directors were concerned, these gentlemen were distinguished in other fields; they brought the company distinction and expertise; as for Board members from within the com-

---

[1] The official name of the company at that time was still American Broadcasting-Paramount Theatres, Inc. (AB-PT) The name was not changed to American Broadcasting Companies, Inc. (ABC) until 1965. But to simplify matters for the reader, the company will be called from this point on: ABC.

pany, these men had the incentive of generous stock options; there was every reason to expect they would exercise those options when option dates came due.

This of itself may have provided an additional incentive for two large corporations who began, in the early sixties, to buy heavily into ABC stock.

Rumors first circulated around McCall Corporation, a large publishing company. In 1964 McCall was said to have bought some 332,000 shares of ABC for something like 16.5 million dollars—about 3.2% of the company.

While this was quietly (but not so secretly) going on, a noted California industrialist named Norton Simon was also said to be buying ABC stock. Simon was known as a "collector of art and companies," and before he was through he owned 9% of ABC! He presided over the vast holdings of Hunt Food and Industries. Also, by coincidence, Hunt Foods also owned 29% of McCall Corporation.

One did not have to be very bright to add up the implications of these moves. Clearly, Norton Simon was trying to take over ABC.

In the winter of 1964 Norton Simon made his first contact with Goldenson and asked for a meeting. With him were Gus Levy and Simon's President of McCall Publishing Company, Herb Mayes. Goldenson brought with him his staunch Board member and financial expert, John Coleman.

Simon said that, despite the substantial stock position of the two companies he controlled—adding up to more stock than was being held by the Edward J. Noble Foundation—and despite the fact that he was entitled to, and intended to seek, a position on ABC's Board, he was not coming as an adversary, but as a friend. The synergism of McCall's publishing interests with its vast library of literary properties, augured well for ABC. He was thinking, he said, only of the overall advantages that would accrue to ABC by his presence in the company. The friendly overtures did not stay friendly very long. In fact Mr. Mayes offended John Coleman at the outset by a remark he made concerning Coleman's penchant for contributing to Jewish charities despite Coleman's well known philanthropies to his own faith, the Catholic Church.

In March of 1964, two months before ABC's spring stock-holders meeting, Goldenson and Simon Siegel had another meeting with Norton Simon at the Hotel Pierre in New York. It was also an unpleasant encounter. Simon was obviously looking for weak spots in ABC's method of operation; things he could criticize; similar tactics to those used in past takeover activities.

"Let me ask," he began. "Do you use accelerated depreciation at ABC?" He was referring to a procedure favored by some companies which saved taxes now, but was considered detrimental to profits later on.

"Absolutely not," said Siegel. "We have depreciation we have already taken, but which is still available for taxes. We could increase our profits if we wanted to."

Norton Simon seemed disappointed by such conservative accounting methods. He probed some more but without success. He had already advised Goldenson of the name of the individual he wanted on the Board. Under the present corporate structure, there was no way that Simon could be denied a seat on the Board. And once that happened, the scenario would be a familiar one: the dissident board member would attempt to divide the Board; sew seeds of unrest and dissension; he would object to every move management tried to make. That would be followed by an attempt to gain enough support to take over without even a tender offer or a proxy fight. If this Trojan horse technique failed, a tender offer and proxy fight would follow, usually at great expense to stockholders who ended up paying the bills for the proxy fight. With approximately 45% of its stock held by financial institutions, ABC was in a particularly vulnerable position for a well executed corporate raid, and Norton Simon was a formidable raider. His sales pitch regarding the ABC situation was a persuasive one: McCall was already in communications; its strength could be synergistic to ABC, especially in the area of story material for its television programs.

After the meeting at the Pierre, Goldenson decided that the Norton Simon threat had to be eliminated quickly and finally. He did precisely that at the annual meeting in May, when despite vigorous protests from McCall-Simon forces, he eliminated the cumulative voting rule whereby each share was entitled to one vote. The meeting was a stormy one. Opposition representatives shouted, "Unfair! Unfair!" but they were outvoted by a count of 3,204,039 to 517,382—which gave ABC an idea of how much stock was held by the opposition.

The battle was not over, however. Indeed, it had hardly begun. ABC knew that the time had come when it must entertain the idea of getting under the protection of some large corporate umbrella; but a company of *its* choosing, not one that would force itself upon ABC.

So Goldenson called his friend, Larry Tisch, who was a close friend of Harold Geneen. "Larry, remember the conversation we had about ITT?"

"I do."

"I think it's time I get acquainted with Mr. Geneen."

"I understand. I'll arrange it."

Si Siegel accompanied Goldenson on that first visit with Harold Geneen a few days later. It was a cautiously exploratory meeting, congenial and in low key. Geneen spoke softly. He did not fit the mold of the formidable taskmaster that he had been pictured to be. He spoke modestly about the dimensions of the vast conglomerate he had built. Goldenson and Siegel knew those dimensions—sales of 1.78 billion in 1965; profits of 76.1 million; 60% of its revenue came from overseas, and 6½% of its 22 million shares were owned by foreign interests. This might present a problem at the FCC, in the event of a merger. They knew that ITT was engaged in international communications, defense, and space contracts; auto rentals through Avis, insurance, and publishing. They also knew that ITT had been formed in 1920 by Sosthenes Behn and his brother, Hernand, and started as a holding company to operate telephone and telegraph companies in Puerto Rico and Cuba. In 1925 it had purchased the Western Electric Company's international telecommunications manufacturing operation.

International Telephone and Telegraph had lost some of its foreign assets during WW II. After the war, in trying to increase its domestic holdings, it had disastrous consumer product experiences with the Coolerator Corporation and Capehard-Farnsworth Corporation. Its fortunes had begun to turn around in 1959 when Harold S. Geneen moved from Raytheon Corporation, where he had been Executive Vice President, to become President of ITT.

Geneen's leadership had been effective from the start. He was determined to increase the company's domestic holdings to counterbalance the vagaries of international politics and set as his goal for the 1965-69 period an annual volume of 3 billion dollars. His criteria for corporate acquisitions was crystal clear: any company that was growing faster than ITT, and had room to grow in an industry that, itself, was growing, was a prospective acquisition candidate for ITT.

ABC met these criteria perfectly. But still there was a missing element in their discussion that first meeting. Just *why* did Harold Geneen want ABC? The idea sounded good; it "listened" good; but there must be something else, thought Goldenson; some other reason Geneen had not yet explained.

"Yes, there is," Geneen admitted. He leaned forward in his chair and spoke with great earnestness:

"If you walk down the street today and ask someone, what is ITT, they'll answer, 'Oh, it's some foreign corporation'. Eight out of ten won't know *anything* about ITT. Well, I want to get our company's name known in the U.S. Here we are, one of the largest companies in the country and our multiple on earnings is only about 7-1. If we were as well known as other companies who are much smaller than we are, we could raise that multiple to 15-1. I could double the price of my stock if we were well known. And whatever I paid for ABC stock I would more than get back in the value of my stock. ABC could do that for me."

Goldenson and Siegel left the meeting impressed. No one could refute Geneen's logic. Also there appeared to be no antitrust problem in a merger. ITT had taken a brief fling in cable television, but had never entered broadcasting (although there had been rumors that it would like to do so, and might even be a prime candidate to start a fourth network).

Philosophically the merger made sense, as much so as the

merger with ABC had made sense in 1953. Also, now that ABC had entered the international television field (recklessly, some said), ITT, with its 195,000 employees scattered throughout 52 countries, could add real strength and muscle to ABC's International Division.

But then, at least for Leonard Goldenson, the question came: how would he personally get along with Harold Geneen? Indeed, *could* he get along with Geneen? He had heard about Geneen's committee style of management, exactly the opposite of his own almost totally autonomous style. Could he sit around the world's longest conference table with executives from all over the world and make monthly written, as well as oral, reports? Goldenson was no good at giving written reports. In his business no one had time to write reports.

That would be no problem, said Geneen. Leonard would be removed from all that. Si Siegel could give the reports. When Si heard that, he began to have serious misgivings of his own. He, too, was poor at making reports. In his entire life he couldn't remember writing a report longer than three pages. And most of that was simply columns of figures.

Geneen's style was said to be: divide, rule, and never mind questions of loyalty. His management cadre totalled some 1,100 men and the top corporate heads had to fly in once a month to report personally to Geneen and their peers in marathon sessions that lasted far into the night. They were said to be excruciating experiences for those executives who did not have the right answers. Executive turnover at ITT was high. The more Siegel checked around the more doubtful he became.

"Those meetings are more exhausting than the job of running the company you're responsible for," said one of Geneen's men. "They can take on the character of an inquisition. When Geneen gets unhappy with the answers he is getting from some poor bastard, you can just see his guts dripping on the floor!"

On the other hand, Harold Geneen was known throughout the world as a brilliant innovator in international management. His executives, though given overlapping responsibilities in an intricate web of checks and balances, were among the highest paid in the world. But in terms of personal styles, Goldenson and Geneen, no two executives could have been more antithetical. Still, by some alchemy the two men began to develop a good rapport. They sized each other up over numerous luncheons and found that they could talk about, and enjoy, other subjects besides business. Geneen was far from the ogre he had been pictured to be. Of medium height, he spoke in a clear, soft, but rapid voice. Autonomy, Geneen reiterated, would not be a problem.

"I don't think we are unreasonable in the way we operate," he said. "My job, basically, is to monitor all of our activities on a regular basis. If things are going well, we never interfere. If things go wrong we try to make suggestions to improve the situation."

Goldenson liked the sound of that. He also liked, as negotiations proceeded, the idea that "Hal" Geneen believed in paying his executives every dollar they deserved. Geneen said he believed Goldenson should be paid a salary more commensurate with what William Paley was getting at CBS, and what Robert Sarnoff was getting at NBC. Therefore, eighty thousand dollars more per year, suggested Geneen, would be quite justified. As for Si Siegel, ABC's Executive Vice President, his salary should be more in line with what Frank Stanton was getting at CBS, and what Bob Kintner was getting at NBC: $46,500 more per year would remedy that problem. Both men would receive five-year contracts.

Contracts were fine, but how long, Goldenson wanted to know, would he be guaranteed "complete autonomy" in his management of ABC?

Geneen's reply had a quality of *deja vu.* "Three years," he said. *Shades of the past!* An echo of the words Goldenson had given 14 years ago to Ed Noble regarding Bob Kintner!

In addition both men would go on ITT's Board, plus two other ABC representatives. Two ITT directors would go on ABC's Board.

The rapport between the two became so good that finally it came down only to the matter of the price ITT would pay ABC for its stock on a share for share, tax free basis.

Si Siegel became the trench fighter for that sensitive part of the deal. Siegel was not known as the "sly fox" for nothing. Despite his company's pressing need for cash, and the ominous threat of Norton Simon still actively buying stock, Siegel played a cool, almost indifferent hand, deliberately giving the impression that there were other suitors desiring to talk to ABC. And there were.

Negotiations of mergers have a life of their own. They must be made relatively soon or they break down beyond recapture. In late 1965 the negotiations broke down. But in mid-November ITT came back and agreed to Siegel's "forceful" bargaining demands which drove the price up from an equivalent of $70 per share on pro forma, to $100 per share, bringing the total price to be paid for ABC to approximately 350 million dollars.

Finally the details were worked out: ITT would issue 0.5719 of a share of regular common stock, and 0.5719 of a new convertible preferred stock ($10 stated value) for each new outstanding share of ABC common on a record date to be determined in the future.

Preference stock would be convertible on a share for share basis into ITT common and would carry a dividend which was cumulative, equal to twice the dividend on its ITT common stock, but not less than $2.40 per share. New convertible preferred could not be called for 10 years, and in the 11th year the initial redemption price would be $150 per share and would decrease thereafter at a rate of $5 per year to a minimum of $100. Also, certain "anti-dilution provisions" would protect stockholders. ITT would issue about 2,677,750 new shares of common stock and an identical number of new convertible preferred shares at the closing.

The news was released on December 7, 1965. "Largest Merger In History of Communications!" the headlines blared.

Wall Street called it a "natural."

A financial reporter, unable to get a comment from Norton

Simon in Fullerton, California, wrote, "Well, at least ABC is no longer in danger of being *simonized!*"

Another analyst wrote: "If I were Leonard Goldenson, I'd be looking for another job."

Now ABC would go back to the well for the third time, back to the loins of the Government that begat it—to be reborn again.

6

Autonomy Has Been Overemphasized— Harold Geneen

ON DECEMBER 7TH, 1965, trading in ABC stock was brisk, closing at a year's high of 74. ITT closed at 67½, below its 1965 high of 75.

On February 15, 1966, both companies' boards approved the merger. On April 27, stockholders of both companies approved the merger by overwhelming margins. Harold Geneen pointed out that the merger would give the two companies revenues in excess of 2½ billion dollars, and move ITT from 31st in ranking of the world's largest corporations to a position "within the top twenty." On the sensitive question of "autonomy," Geneen told his shareholders something that must have given pause, if not panic, to ABC's President. The subject of autonomy, said Geneen, had been "overemphasized" to the point where the FCC had informed ITT that it must accept authority for its newest acquisition. Word in financial circles was that, despite ITT's assurance of ABC's continued autonomy, ITT "would take a very active hand in management."

At ABC's annual meeting in the spring of 1965, Goldenson

was plagued again with protests by McCall and Norton Simon representatives about the abolishment of cumulative voting. In fact John Henry Campbell and Wilma Soss proposed a joint resolution to establish cumulative voting but were voted down. "This is unfair!" they shouted. "It is undemocratic to deny Norton Simon a seat on the Board." Goldenson replied that Simon had not personally asked for a seat on the Board, and in any event, the company had no way of knowing precisely how many shares Simon held.

On August 18, the first of many surprises to occur over the next two years came in the form of an announcement by the FCC that it would take cognizance of the ABC-ITT merger not in its usual manner, but instead would consider the case in a single day of Oral Hearing before the seven-person Commission.

One day. On September 19, the largest and most important case in broadcast history was to be disposed of in a single day! Industry leaders were incredulous. Even the pro-industry trade press was astonished. What magic had been performed to bring about this miracle of expeditious determination?

Nicholas Johnson, the fresh new firebrand Commissioner, and Kenneth Cox, teamed together to ask that question. They were joined by a third democrat, Robert T. Bartley, who called for a full hearing to explore all phases of the complex case. "The 13 percent broadcasting tail must not be permitted to wag the 87 percent nonbroadcasting dog," said Bartley, who a month before had issued a list of some 18 points and issues that, he said, were crucial to reaching a decision.

Commissioners Johnson and Cox, however, surprised many by agreeing to the single day's procedure as long as both parties were responsive to Bartley's list of 18 points, most of which centered around possible monopolistic implications of a merger, and on the extent of ABC's independence under an ITT corporate umbrella.

The hearing day was long and arduous for all participants. Goldenson himself was subjected to four hours of gruelling questions. Tempers flared. It was almost as if everyone was in tacit agreement that this was an incredible, and perhaps impossible task—trying to do in one day what a full hearing might accomplish in several months.

At the end of the day there was still testimony to be presented and questions to be asked, so Chairman Rosel Hyde recessed the hearing until 9:30 the next morning.

Again the relentless questioning continued:

—How would the public interest be served?

—What specific technological advances could ABC expect from ITT?

—Would not such a merger also force CBS to merge with a giant conglomerate?

—Did ITT plan any other expansion into mass media?

—How would ABC policy be affected by a merger with ITT? Especially in the news area? Might not ABC documentaries be subtly slanted to promote ITT interests in foreign countries?

Geneen, Goldenson, and their staffs did their best to answer all questions. As the second day ended, press reaction seemed generally favorable. ITT and ABC had presented a "persuasive case." Besides, said the experts, the rare two-day oral hearing was merely "window dressing." The majority of the seven-man Commission were said to be in favor of the merger. And the decision would not take long. Certainly it would be handed down before the end of 1966.

But strong negative reactions came before the fall leaves turned. Senator Gaylord Nelson, Democrat, Wisconsin, launched the first attack on October 24:

"The merger should be delayed until there is a full study by the Department of Justice."

On October 28, Senator Wayne Morse, Democrat, Oregon, joined in: "There is not the slightest evidence that the public interest requires a quick decision," said Morse. "More than half of ITT's income comes from foreign countries. Its control of ABC could conflict with FCC aims to insulate domestic mass media from foreign influence."

An orchestrated attack seemed to have been launched. On November 1 the Chairman of the Senate antitrust and monopoly subcommittee, Philip A. Hart, Democrat, Michigan, called for a "full customary hearing," and agreed with others who questioned the two day oral hearing.

Three days later, Commissioners Cox and Johnson demanded more information from ITT concerning its foreign interests. Again that nagging suspicion: ITT, with interests in 52 countries, and more than 60% of its income abroad, could be tempted to "tailor its news commentary and reporting so as to minimize any conflict with local governments."

Not true, replied ITT, and it would be most willing to provide the voluminous documents demanded by Cox and Johnson. As for the possibility of "news interference," both Leonard Goldenson and Harold Geneen personally pledged that there would be none of that.

A day later, November 5, a blast came from a more serious source: Department of Justice's Donald F. Turner said that a preliminary investigation of the Justice Antitrust Division, which he headed, revealed possible antitrust violations. There was, wrote Turner in a letter to FCC Chairman Hyde, "a sufficient possibility of significant anticompetitive effects to indicate that substantial antitrust questions are presented."

This should have raised a red flag of warning to both ITT and ABC. Perhaps it did, but both companies were too well committed to back out. The history of American business is replete with examples to prove that corporations do not successfully lock horns with the Department of Justice. It is a broad, uniquely powerful arm of government and has many cards to play, including that subtle and most damaging of all cards—time.

Following Turner's statement, the three Democratic members of the Commission—Cox, Johnson, and Bartley—announced with dramatic effect that they were emphatically against the merger.

This left four Republican members: Chairman Rosel Hyde, Robert E. Lee, James J. Wadsworth, and Lee Loevinger. The favorable votes of Hyde and Lee were considered assured. The voting patterns of Wadsworth and Loevinger were considered more unpredictable.

However, on December 21, all four came through as hoped.

The Commission voted 4–3 to approve the largest broadcast transaction ever to come before it, and in the shortest hearing on record. The licenses of 17 ABC AM, FM, TV stations would be transferred whenever the two companies wished to officially begin their merged identity. Of course there would be the usual legal delay for opposition filings by interested parties, but this was considered unlikely. The Department of Justice had only protested, not acted. Opposition from other quarters seemed to be more in the nature of polemics from those who had political grist to grind. Senator Morse once again said he was shocked at the hasty action. Silvio Conte, Republican, Massachusetts, agreed. So did Senator Nelson of Wisconsin.

Commissioner Nick Johnson wrote an angry dissent warning that the public interest was being "significantly harmed":

"It (the merger) will place one of the three largest purveyors of news and opinion in America under the control of one of the largest conglomerates in the world; a company that derives 60% of its earnings from foreign sources, and 40% of its domestic income from defense and space contracts. These reasons alone should leave little doubt in anyone's mind that the merger should not receive the blithe imprimatur of this Commission."

But the voice that ABC-ITT feared most remained noticeably silent and unthreatening. Donald F. Turner said, "For the present, the Justice Department is not contemplating bringing suit against the merger."

For the present? What does that mean, asked an ABC news reporter. Turner gave no answer. Later an ABC lawyer explained what Turner had meant. " 'For the present' means: don't relax for 28 more days because Justice has that much time to file an appeal."

7

That Phantom
Department
Called Justice

IMPLEMENTATION DAY of the merger was to be January 21. On January 19 the Department of Justice filed two separate petitions, both bristling with criticism and asking for a stay on the merger until the questions it raised could be answered. Its questions were substantive, said Justice, and ran the gamut of objections:

—The FCC violated its own rules by jamming all issues into a two day oral hearing.

—The hearing was incomplete. ABC's need for cash was not a significant factor; the reverse appeared to be true. ITT expected a large cash flow from ABC for use in investments outside the broadcast industry.

—The record should be "truly informative on all known aspects of the public interest."

—ITT's attempted move into the cable industry in New York City was evidence of the company's intention to get into broadcasting; but, the petition noted, in two different cases the Supreme Court had upheld the principle that elimination of a potential new competitor could be grounds for holding a merger invalid. If the merger were prohibited there were other ways ITT could get into the field.

"We do not wish to drag out the proceedings beyond the end of the year," said Justice. "We know that is when the agreement between ITT and ABC terminates. We are certain the matter can be disposed of before the year ends."

This move shocked both companies. Counsel burned the midnight oil as strategies and tactics were determined. The next day, January 20, ITT pulled a maneuver that was designed to take the pressure off the FCC. It "volunteered" a two-week delay to give all parties time to straighten matters out. Justice Department questions were "immaterial and inconsequential," said ITT, but it was willing to wait until 5 PM, February 2 for the FCC to render its decision in answer to Justice.

The FCC accepted ITT's voluntary postponement, and Donald F. Turner won the first of many skirmishes that were to follow.

Stock trading was heavy that day, particularly in the stock of ABC. ITT traded from 80½ to a close of 82. ABC did not fare as well. It closed at 79, down 14⅝ points, reflecting the activity of arbitrageurs who hoped to capitalize on price spreads between stocks by trading one issue against the other.

"If the merger does not go through," one broker explained, "the arbitrageurs are killed—that is, they are left holding the bag, holding ABC, the stock that has most to lose if the merger does not go through, and short on ITT along with everybody else."

On January 27 ABC and ITT filed a joint petition, a strongly worded appeal to the FCC's integrity:

"This is an eleventh hour maneuver . . . a startling and unprecedented attack on the competence and administrative integrity of the Commission . . . if this device is permitted to succeed, the Justice Department will have a ready made weapon to hamstring *any* merger before a regulatory agency where the Department's case would not stand the test of a separate suit."

Three days later, Justice filed a stronger petition in support of its position. It now said it had information to prove that ITT did not expect to pour capital into ABC, but was planning to take capital *out*, and that the FCC's entire justification for the merger had been based on ABC's capital needs.

With only two days to go, the FCC found itself in a real dilemma. Its four member majority remained firm: Hyde, Lee, Wadsworth, and Loevinger were still convinced they had done the right thing in adjudicating the decision in a two day oral hearing. The other route meant long months of game-playing that would only decrease ABC's chances of remaining a viable third competitor in television. Despite all other carping they remained firm that the merger had no antitrust taint, and indeed if there were, Justice, by now, would have filed strong objections based on antitrust considerations.

But if they denied Justice' plea to reopen the case, would not Justice take its next option and appeal to the U.S. Court of Appeals? Indeed, that intention began to be leaked by Justice the day before a decision had to be made.

So, feeling it had no other recourse, on February 1, the day before the merger was to take effect, an angry FCC said, yes, it would agree to look at evidence Justice said it had, and which Justice said it had been preparing for a year.

Scathingly the Commission asked why Justice had been so slow in raising its objections? Thus two government agencies were now at loggerheads, a situation that did not augur well for the two companies. In conclusion, said the FCC's order of February 1, it had no alternative but to reopen the case because of the "unique status of the Department of Justice." The Commission voted 5–2. The two dissenters, oddly enough, were Bartley, who had previously voted against the merger; and Wadsworth who had voted for it. Cox and Johnson were delighted to join the majority this time; but there would be five separate opinions filed by Commissioners, both in concurrence and dissent.

All evidence, the order read, would be submitted by February 15. ITT and ABC would have until February 23 to submit evidence of their own, and Justice would have until March 6 to supply rebuttal information.

Now the die was cast. ABC was locked into a situation that it had desperately hoped to avoid—long months of legal delay, and capital attrition.

◇   ◇   ◇

The flurry of charges and counter charges reached blitz proportions in the next month. Justice filed an ITT company memo purporting to show that ITT truly looked upon ABC as a ripe harvest of "cash throwoff" which it intended to use elsewhere. The two day hearing had not permitted Justice enough time to voice all of its old objections, let alone new ones raised by its antitrust investigation. And if, after the brief reopening period, the FCC reapproved the merger, Justice intimated that it would likely seek a court order to reopen the case.

The *New York Times* voiced its concern in an editorial on February 18: "A full public hearing is required to answer the serious antitrust questions belatedly raised by the Department of Justice."

On that same day, ABC reinforced its claim that it needed cash when it announced it had been forced to borrow 25 million dollars from ITT to be paid out in five monthly installments starting at once and repaid a year later.

ABC's ratings for the 66–67 season had slipped. A "second season" of new shows had hastily been introduced in January. The ITT loan would be spent entirely on converting its schedule to color, and to pay for expensive feature films. Even this loan would be "substantially less than what is needed over the next several years," said Goldenson. As for Justice' charges, both ABC and ITT called them "flimsy . . . misguided . . . and glaringly insufficient."

Such protestations were not enough. On March 16 the ax fell. The Commission voted 4–0 to reopen the case! This time the customary rules would apply. A full dress hearing would be held with James D. Cunningham appointed as Hearing Examiner. This time it was Cox, Johnson, and Bartley who were in the majority, and they were joined by the Chairman himself, Rosel Hyde. The others abstained.

The hearing would start March 27, but was later delayed until April 10. The issues themselves were unclear. But the ubiquitous, pervasively powerful arm of Government known as the Justice Department had won again. As one lawyer put it: "Fighting Justice is like fighting a phantom."

◇   ◇   ◇

To everyone's relief, the hearing did not stretch out for months, but lasted only 17 days punctuated by wrangling, shouting, gavel pounding, and bursts of intemperate language. David R. Hunter, Justice attorney, caught ITT general counsel, Raymond Brittenham, passing notes in the corridor to future witnesses. Hearing examiner Cunningham reprimanded him. R. H. Kenmore, an ITT vice president bragged about the amount of cash ABC would generate. "An earnings growth of some 16% a year is expected from ABC in the five years from 1965–69," he said. "ABC has a higher return on its investment than ITT." ABC's expected earnings plus depreciation from 1964 through 1969 would "approach 100 million, almost all of which will be available for investment outside the television industry."

When asked if he knew about ABC's cash needs, Kenmore said, no, Leonard Goldenson had never told him about this. Goldenson said the 100 million dollar projection was "nonsense." If the merger were not approved, ABC would be in a precarious position. Expenses would have to be cut on the radio network and in the news area. "And," he added, "I don't think that's in the public interest." ABC's efforts to become the leading television network had resulted in network losses aggregating 27 million dollars in the past four years.

"But the overall company runs at a profit, does it not?" asked Cunningham.

"Oh yes. Those losses are balanced by revenues from our theatres, radio and television stations, and other properties," answered Goldenson.

FCC counsel observed, "That is like saying, see this pocket is empty; but it's all right, because the other pocket is full."

Harold Geneen stressed again the ABC would operate as an autonomous company under Goldenson and there would be no attempt by ITT to interfere with ABC's news judgment.

However, on April 19, three reporters testified on a charge raised by Justice to the effect that pressures had been exerted on them by ITT as a result of stories they had written about the merger. Lionel Kestenbaum, a Justice attorney, read into the record an article printed in the previous Monday's *Wall Street Journal:*

"ITT's news management efforts have backfired," the article stated. And: *"Veteran Washington newspapermen consider the extent and intensity of ITT's efforts to be extraordinary."*

Eileen Shanahan of the *New York Times* testified that she believed the article to be correct as far as it went. "But there was more," she said ominously. Under further questioning she admitted that an official of ITT had "questioned my integrity and that of the *Times.*"

Stephen M. Aug of Associated Press, and Jed Stout of United Press International, also testified and gave similar opinions.

These charges came like bombshells. The inference was drawn that if ITT had the audacity to try to influence the working press, what would deter it from trying to influence the news departments of ABC's television and radio networks?

"Not as long as I'm there," said James Hagerty, former press secretary to President Eisenhower, and now a top ABC executive in the area of news and corporate affairs. "If ITT tried to do that I would resign."

Elmer Lower, operating head of ABC news, went Hagerty one better:

"I'd be out the door ahead of Jim Hagerty!"

Thomas Moore, President of ABC's television network, and successor to Ollie Treyz, raised some eyebrows when he admitted that he had sent messages to ABC television affiliates suggesting that they discuss the matter with their senators and congressmen.

Even Wall Street put in an appearance. Wilbur Ross, partner in Faulkner, Dawkins and Sullivan, an investment banking firm, said that, not only would ABC suffer if the merger were denied, but the public would suffer as well. ABC's stock was then selling in the eighties, but could drop as low as fifty if the merger did not go through. And the public would suffer in another way. The sale of color sets in the nation had increased from 9% to 16% in one year, which meant that viewers were switching to color at a rapid rate. They wanted color programs on ABC, and ABC needed some 134 million dollars to completely colorize its production plant—all of which ITT could provide.

On April 27 the hearing ended. Another month went by before the usual one-day oral argument was held. During that period the FCC's Broadcast Bureau made it clear that if the grounds for approving the merger were "principally" ABC's need for capital, the merger should be denied; but on the criticial issue of possible news censorship by ITT the Bureau took a middle ground.

At the oral argument Nick Johnson asked Thomas B. Fitzpatrick, chief of the Commission's hearing division, the question:

"As the one Commission employee who has lived with this case since it reopened, give us your personal opinion about the desirability of the merger."

Fitzpatrick answered bluntly: "The public interest would *not* be served!"

ABC's counsel, Jim McKenna, took issue with this. Too much emphasis was being placed on this, he said. There were other benefits, such as the contribution ITT could make to broadcast technology, particularly in the development of UHF if it had the incentive ownership of a major network. In addition the public would benefit if ABC were in the hands of a diversified company so that "every adverse rating does not produce a disastrous drop in the price of the stock."

On the sensitive matter of ITT's influence on ABC's news policy, both companies pledged that they would notify the FCC in writing if ABC ever changed its news policy. Nick Johnson demurred with biting sarcasm. "How can we believe that ITT will follow higher principles with ABC than it did with reporters covering the merger with whom it had no business connection?"

Marcus Cohn, ITT counsel, found this one tough to answer.

Aware of how much damage the press harrassment incident had done, he replied cautiously: "ITT now has a greater sensitivity and a greater awareness of the need for freedom of the press."

Nick Johnson did not seem in the least convinced. Then Lionel Kestenbaum, counsel for Justice, put a chill on both companies when he said that his department had not yet addressed itself to the question of whether Justice might have an antitrust case against the merger under the Clayton Act. "However," he added, "I expect that we will soon be doing so."

Within ABC belts were being pulled tighter. Pencils were sharpened down to the stubs. The general economy was soft, and so were ABC's ratings. Color expansion was being done slowly, on a piecemeal basis because of lack of funds. Bills were being paid by the rule that all companies follow when faced with a cash crisis: pay only those creditors who scream the loudest. Si Siegel dreaded seeing the mail come in each morning. Nothing but bills! He would sort them out in piles, and those that began, "This is our *third* notice!" went into a special pile. He held off making any payments until he checked the amount of receipts for that day. One morning a call came from Twentieth Century Fox. ABC was delinquent in its film inventory payment.

"Mr. Siegel," said the voice, "we have come to the conclusion that we are now your banker."

"What do you mean?" asked Siegel.

"Well, you owe us $300,000. We haven't seen any money for so long, we figure that, since we're banking you, we should add on interest. So you now owe us, by our reckoning, $325,000."

Si almost choked. "You got to be kidding!"

"No, we're not kidding."

"I'm positive you're kidding. Anyhow, it's academic, cause a check went out to you this morning." Regardless of the day's receipts, *that* check definitely went out that day.

Good news, however, came on June 23. The FCC voted to approve the merger for the second time! The same four Commissioners voted in favor, and the same three dissenters, Bartley, Cox, and Johnson voted against it, and filed a 131 page dissent.

In essence, the decision noted that ABC, by reason of the

merger, would be in a better competitive position. The FCC would accept the "solemn assurances" of ITT that there would be no attempts at news censorship. In addition ITT must report for the next three years on what it was doing on behalf of UHF technology.

The Department of Justice again remained strangely silent. But two former antagonists did not. Congressmen Dingell and Conte at once called for a further delay by Justice which had thirty days to appeal the decision. A week later Conte went further and called for an investigation of the FCC itself because, he said, there is "legitimate public doubt and lack of confidence in the FCC."

Despite a great sense of relief at both ABC and ITT, there was no real jubilation because of the spectre of possible Justice action. Rumors began to circulate that Justice was determined to block the merger at all cost. Somewhere, perhaps at the White House itself, there had been a decision made that this merger must never be allowed to happen. With a sense of foreboding, the two companies moved forward with their implementation plan. On July 22 new incorporation papers would be filed by both companies and ABC would begin its new identity as a subsidiary of ITT.

However on July 20, two days before the legal filing period expired, Justice notified the world that, tomorrow, on July 21, it would take the case to the U.S. Court of Appeals!

Citing 17 points of error it thought the FCC had made, Justice said, "We believe the briefing of this appeal can be so scheduled as to permit presentation of argument in October of this year, enabling a decision before the end of the year, and we are willing to cooperate to that end."

The news, although not entirely unexpected, struck ABC particularly hard. Its stock tumbled 21 points in one day. The vagaries and delays of the original merger seemed mild compared to the buzz saw they now faced. A year and a half had passed. What if the Court of Appeals did not act before the end of the year? The agreement between both companies terminated the last day of 1967. Or what if Appeals denied the Justice petition?

Would Justice take the case all the way to the Supreme Court? That could take another year! ABC would have given anything to extricate itself from this hopeless mess, but there was no way out. The legal charade had to be played till the end. The next act of the drama would unfold the week of October 16 before a three judge panel of the District of Columbia Court of Appeals: Chief Judge David L. Bazelon, and Judges Spottswood W. Robinson III, and Edward A. Tamm. They were considered neither admirers of television, nor of big business. ABC postponed its annual spring meeting to August 3, at which Leonard Goldenson put on a brave show of continuing optimism.

"Personally, I feel we'll win," he said. "We've already won two times at the FCC."

But this was a new kind of hardball which ABC stockholders sensed. When Goldenson explained that the company was conserving its cash during the delay, one stockholder suggested that it might help if top executives cut, or deferred, their salaries during the crisis. Another asked, "How about our dividends? Will they be cut?"

"No," said Goldenson in answer to the latter question. As to the first suggestion he said he would take it under advisement.

Both companies kept a low profile during the waiting period, but Justice Department did not. In statements to the press it scoffed at the FCC's plan to "police" the network's news programs. "It is plainly absurd to think that the FCC will receive advance written notice before ITT tries to kill an ABC documentary, or before ABC officials on their own shelve subjects which would be embarrassing or detrimental to ITT."

As for approving the merger to help the cause of UHF television, that was simply "fallacious," said Justice.

Most damaging of all perhaps was the continuous reminder by Justice spokesmen to the world that the attempts of some ITT officials to improperly influence the press constituted "outrageous conduct" and related to the very matter of the department's concern over "ITT's assuming responsibility for ABC's news and public affairs activities." The same day, a new allegation came from another source. *New Republic Magazine* writer James Ridgeway charged that ITT was conducting an investigation of one of its staff writers because that person had written "a critical piece about the merger."

So the long fall season dragged on. ABC's stock remained sluggish, in the mid sixties, versus a high of 102 for the year. Morale at the company was not as low as it might have been; instead the mood was one of exasperation and frustration; helplessness, not hopelessness. ABC employees adopted an attitude of: things can't get much worse, so they've *got* to get better!

ITT on the other hand was scarcely affected at all. Its stock had performed exactly the reverse of ABC: from a low of 68 in 1966 to more than 100 as 1967 came to a close.

But at least it could be said that Harold Geneen had attained his primary objective: everyone in the United States now knew who, and what, ITT was. He had achieved that goal even without a merger.

8

Two Years
Down the Drain

ON NEW YEARS DAY, 1968, Si Siegel received a call early in the morning. The voice was familiar:

"Si? This is Hal Geneen calling." Siegel's heart fell. Here it comes, he thought. *Two years down the drain!* Much of the preceding week had been spent discussing this possibility with Leonard Goldenson and chief counsel, Everett Erlick.

"Happy New Year, Hal."

"Same to you. I wanted you to be the first to know that our Board met this morning and voted to cancel the merger."

Siegel thought: what an auspicious way to start the new year! And *so* early in the morning! Si wasn't hung over because he had spent a quiet News Year's Eve, but he was still sleepy, and sat there on the edge of the bed in his bathrobe staring at his toes. It seemed unlikely to him that the ITT Board had actually met. A simple resolution made before the holidays authorizing Geneen to cancel the merger on New Year's morning was all that was necessary. "Hal" Geneen, he thought, was probably home in his bathrobe, also.

"Have you talked to Leonard yet?" asked Siegel.

"No, I couldn't reach him."

Siegel doubted that, too. Goldenson was in Florida getting a few days rest. He would certainly still be in the hotel at this early hour of the morning. "I think, before you do anything else, you owe it to Leonard to call him personally and tell him this. Have you got his number?"

"Yes, his secretary gave it to my office before he left. I'll try it again." A radio was playing somewhere in the house. Si wished his wife, Rose, would turn it down.

"Si," Geneen was saying, "I wish you would call Ned . . ."

"Who?"

"Ned Gerrity. Our P.R. director. Our two companies should put out a press announcement."

Just then the radio program was interrupted by an announcer who said, "We interrupt this program to bring you a special news bulletin. The ITT merger with ABC has been canceled. ITT, in an unusual Board meeting held early this morning has voted to terminate its merger with ABC. The outcome of that merger has been pending before the U.S. Court of Appeals since last October . . ."

Siegel wondered if Geneen was listening to the same station. It seemed to him that Ned Gerrity had already handled the matter of a press release. But Si went along.

"I'll give Ned a call."

"Thanks. He's standing by."

Instead of calling Gerrity, Siegel put in an immediate call to Goldenson in Miami.

"Have you heard from Hal Geneen?"

Leonard said no.

"You should be getting a call as soon as I hang up. ITT has terminated the merger."

There was a moment's silence. "Okay. I'll wait for his call and call you back." There was no tone of surprise. The odds had been figured about even that ITT might terminate the very instant it could legally do so. Since the Court of Appeals had heard the case in October there had been an ominous silence, both from the court, and from ITT. Speculation was rife. Was the court purposely sitting on its decision? Everyone knew that the contract between both parties expired with the last day of 1967. Based on a valuation of the stock of both companies, ITT would now have to pay much more than it had planned to pay when the agreement had been made. In February of 1966 ITT would have paid about 366 million for ABC based on 1.14 shares of ITT stock for each ABC share. Now ITT's commitment would cost it about 620 million.

During the last few weeks there had been virtually no communication between the two companies. General Counsel Everett Erlick, Goldenson, and Siegel agreed that this probably was an ominous sign.

"No news is bad news in this instance," said Erlick.

"Maybe ITT knows something we don't know."

"What do you mean?"

Several scenarios presented themselves. One was that ITT, with its not inconsiderable influence in Washington, had decided that it preferred not to go ahead with the merger. Such a signal could have been sent to the court which might have decided that all it had to do was sit on the case and soon it would go away.

But it seemed needlessly dramatic to call the merger off on New Year's Day! An hour later, Goldenson called Siegel back. Geneen meanwhile, had reached him and had expressed his regrets.

"Did he give any explanation," asked Siegel.

"None. Nor did I ask for any."

The two talked briefly. They understood each other so well that words weren't necessary. Regret, relief, and disappointment were all mixed together. *Two years down the drain!* Two years in which the company had been stopped dead in its tracks. Two years in which NBC and CBS had been able to pull further ahead. There was regret that they had not been able to foresee the many entanglements that would arise between ITT and the government. But who could have foreseen that? The Justice Department was such a cunning octopus, with tentacles reaching in so many different directions. Justice had played its cards with consummate skill and subtlety.

And then there was a feeling of relief because now, at last, it was all over. Thank God for that. Now their fetters were removed. It was almost like having one say to them: here's your company back. Now you may run it again.

"When are you coming back?" Siegel asked.

"Right away," said Goldenson. "Call everyone together for a meeting tomorrow. Si, we've got losts of work to do."

◊   ◊   ◊

ABC, despite its vicissitudes over 25 years, has also had at times incredible luck. No company has had better support from the government, especially from the FCC. That can be said to be a combined function of excellent legal advocacy by its Washington counsel, McKenna, Wilkinson, Kittrick, plus the FCC's own policy of encouragment of diversification and competition in the broadcast industry. The only failure ABC ever had was at the hands of the U.S. Court of Appeals, but this, ironically, turned out to be the most *fortuitous piece of luck the company ever had!*

Under an ITT banner the American public would have been served by another NBC, a company that has labored mightily to forge its own path, but instead has had to chafe, languish, and even suffer at times under an RCA management that really does not understand the broadcast business. This is not to say that there has been no synergism between the two companies; there has been in the testing, and use, of new equipment. It is also true that, in spite of RCA, NBC has at times distinguished itself. But these periods have been accidents of timing and circumstances . . . individual human situations illustrated by the regime of Pat Weaver who, single-handed, led NBC to breathtaking heights; and by Bob Kintner who led NBC into news leadership for nearly a decade. Other than this, however, the record is clear: manufacturing and broadcasting do not go very well together. In fact no other business mixes very well with broadcasting. So the lesson should be clear: one conglomerate ownership (in which broadcasting is the lesser element) is enough. The country would not be well served by another. Two conglomerate ownerships would be one too many.

Under the Geneen management style it is not likely that Leonard Goldenson would have survived, or remained contented for very long. Just what kind of company ABC would have become under ITT is hard to predict. But one can conjure numerous depressing possibilities. One thing however is certain: it is hard to imagine that ABC would have been as *interesting* a company if it had merged with ITT. Adversity has a way of molding the character of corporations as well as people. ABC needed all the "character" it could get, because there were other surprises in the not too distant future.

Part Three

The Turning Point

9

That Crazy Radio Idea

LEONARD GOLDENSON had plenty to think about as he returned to New York. Broadcasting being the kind of business it was, risks had to be taken whether the timing was right or not; blockbuster films had to be purchased regardless of timing or cash problems. *Bridge On The River Kwai*, had proven that two years ago by racking up a record 60 million viewers. Still, that did not answer the question: how was ABC going to get the cash to continue to buy films it must have in order to remain competitive?

Likewise, color could not be stopped; that expansion had to continue, regardless of cost or timing. Some radical fiscal policies and innovations would have to be implemented.

Two years ago, the company had moved into a shiny new forty-story building in mid-Manhattan and that represented an additional cash drain. Expansion in the International Division was still going on, with no decision yet as to whether the gamble was going to pay off. ABC International Division via the new satellites could now link Asia, Europe and North America in a single broadcast. The prospects still seemed mind boggling, but the losses also were mounting. A growing spirit of nationalism in many countries boded ill for the venture, especially now without the influence of ITT's vast worldwide empire.

Another outdoor leisure attraction had been acquired a few years before in the form of Silver Springs, a 3,900 acre park near Ocala, Florida. Expansion funds were still required for that investment. But the biggest gamble of all, perhaps, was ABC's entry into motion picture production. Not pictures made primarily for television, but expensive theatrical pictures made for ABC's chain of theatres which still numbered 401. Product for theatres continued to be scarce and high priced, and since it was such a seller's market, ABC, a year before, almost out of a sense of desperation, had taken the plunge into the production or co-production of theatrical feature films. Some considered this another wild gamble for ABC. Goldenson frankly had to admit that it was. But it also might spur others to jump in, and that would be good because it was becoming extremely expensive trying to fill 401 theatres without good films, or to have to enter sky-high bidding contests for what product was available.

Another worry for the President was the changing nature of the record business, particularly in the distribution area. Discount retail chains were changing the nature of the business; to stay competitive in this changing business ABC had formed its own record and tape sales division, and now it looked as though the company would also have to enter the rack jobbing business to protect its flanks in a business that was becoming increasingly dominated by large retail chains.

Yes, there was much to think about as the plane flew north that day and ABC entered its 15th year. Then, almost as an afterthought, because he had completely forgotten, Leonard Goldenson remembered that today was the day that voices were being heard in homes throughout the country, introducing a new concept in radio network broadcasting. Four different announcers were saying each hour:

"This is the American Contemporary Network."
"This is the American Information Network."

"This is the American Entertainment Network."
"This is the American FM Network."

These four identifications represented the biggest gamble any company had ever taken in radio and was ironic in itself, for only a few years before ABC had come near to abandoning its radio operations and selling its stations to Westinghouse for some 50 million dollars. Now the company was embarked upon an idea that was considered exceedingly risky; even reckless; a further cash drain that could not have come at a worse time.

Already Goldenson was crestfallen over the advance criticism that had befallen the four network project. It seemed so grandiose in concept that one critic had written: "Only ABC would come up with an idea as wild as this."

Little did Goldenson know that at this unpropitious hour, this critical time in ABC's history, the off-the-wall scheme, beginning today, would begin a complete turnaround of ABC's radio network losses, and more importantly, would set in motion a chain of events that, rough though they turned out to be, represented a turning of the tide in ABC's fortunes.

The idea had had its genesis almost two years before, when one of ABC's eager young mavericks had walked into the office of Simon B. Siegel. . . .

◇   ◇   ◇

The man who walked into Siegel's office that day in 1966 was a tall, acerbic fellow named Ralph Beaudin. His outspoken manner often ruffled the feathers of his fellow executives. He cared little whether others agreed with him or not. One thing could be said about Beaudin: you always knew where you stood with him; and where he stood on any issue.

Ralph Beaudin had made his reputation running ABC's radio station in Pittsburgh. He had turned that station into a "rocker," which blared out high decibel rock and roll music all day long. Then he had been sent to Chicago where ABC owned a floundering radio station, WLS, which had a split image because of its former identity as being two stations: for decades half of its transmission time had been programmed to a farm audience; the other half went under the call letters of WENR which tried unsuccessfully to appeal to an urban audience. The result was a horrible mish mash. To gain control of the station ABC had bought the parent company, Prairie Farmer, which owned three successful midwestern farm magazines in Chicago, Des Moines, and Racine. That acquisition caused the company to "back in" to the publishing business. It was an uncommon stroke of good luck and a move that ABC never had cause to regret. In short order Beaudin turned the image of WLS-WENR completely around. Within a year, under the call letters of WLS, the station had achieved impressive ratings and profits. Again the format was hard rock presented by screaming announcers who turned off everyone but those who made up the target audience: the young, the very young, and the still younger.

After that, Beaudin had been brought to New York, where he was *not* given the responsibility for running ABC's New York station; that station, WABC, had made rapid strides under Harold L. Neal, Jr. who had earned his reputation in Detroit. Neal had then been promoted to the job of supervising all of ABC's owned AM and FM radio stations. Walter Schwartz had been made manager of WABC and he, too was doing a splendid job. So Beaudin was given the challenge of trying to rescue ABC's languishing Radio Network.

The most logical idea was to shut it down, for ABC's Radio Network, like those of NBC and CBS, was a financial disaster. Losses of two to four million dollars a year were being racked up with maddening consistency. Each year a loss of that magnitude was "plugged in" to annual operating projections and it was driving management up the wall. There were those who seriously believed the time had come to get out of radio networking, cut off this hemorrhage of cash. Yet, there was an institutional value in maintaining a radio network. The loss of face incurred by shutting it down would downgrade ABC as a competitive company, so the radio network doggedly continued to operate.

Not that new and novel formats had not been tried. Robert

Eastman, and later Robert Pauley, had made valiant attempts to put the network on a profitable basis. Their ideas had been innovative, their efforts commendable and persevering, but the result never changed the bottom line to any great extent. Radio networks had to face the reality that television had drastically changed the shape and pattern of modern listening habits. Radio was no longer a multiple service, but a personalized, individual medium. The average listener now was a single individual, or small groups of people who searched the dial for a sound that spoke to them and no one else. Small, inexpensive transistorized radio sets represented the medium. No single network could appeal to all of the diverse audiences that were developing across the land, Radio networks were an anomaly, a relic of the past, performing a service that few needed.

So, on this day, Beaudin approached his boss, Si Siegel, in a manner that was not typical of him—tentative and guarded.

"Si," he began, "I've got a crazy idea."

"That's what we need," Siegel responded sourly, "another crazy idea."

"But I mean, this idea is *really* crazy."

"Crackpot?"

"Totally crackpot!"

"We can't make our other crazy ideas work."

"That's why maybe we've got to try this one."

Siegel looked at Beaudin, his face an inscrutable mask. When he wore this expression, which was often, his callers usually felt a bit unnerved.

"Can I sit down?"

Siegel remained impassive. His silences often spoke more profoundly than his words. This was one of those times. Baudin thought better of sitting down. He began striding around Siegel's office and talked rapidly.

"Si, I mean, this idea is *really* far out. So far out that I won't mind if you throw me out of your office. If you do, I promise I'll never bring it up again."

As formidable as Si Siegel was, he indeed had a sense of humor. He liked those who laid it on the line. A flicker of a grin appeared. "Well, I promise I won't throw you out at least until I hear the idea. Sit down."

Ralph Beaudin sank his lanky frame into the softest chair and draped his leg over one arm. "We all know that radio networks are dead. Television has killed them. But radio itself is not dead. Technology has changed the nature of radio. The transistor set has changed listening habits. It's now a personal one-on-one medium. All kinds of new sounds are springing up. . . ."

Siegel gestured impatiently. "I know all that. You've been telling me that for months."

"This idea could be the salvation of network radio. At least for us. Why not create *four* radio networks?"

"*Four?*" Si Siegel almost choked. "What the hell are you talking about? We can't even make *one* work!"

"That's why I say *four* networks. Each one different. Each one with its own group of affiliated stations."

"You mean buy *four* sets of AT&T lines?"

"No."

"We're not even using the lines we've got."

"I know. That's why this idea might not be so crazy after all. Look, we now use only a portion—seven or eight minutes an hour—of the lines we've got. All the rest of the time goes to waste. If we do this right maybe we can fill up each hour, all day and night, with four different, non-competing services."

"That *is* crazy," said Siegel.

"I know it. As I said, if you want to throw me out . . . I'll leave now."

"Keep talking."

"Well, we haven't worked it all out yet. This is just the germ of the idea. It's such a radical concept I don't want to go further unless you think I should. I've talked it over with Hal Neal and Wally Schwartz and they, too, think it's worth developing. Right now, at this stage, we're thinking of one network being a personality network, a sort of middle of the road format of news, popular music, and feature stuff like *Don McNeill's Breakfast Club.* A second would be news and information aimed at "talk" stations. A third might be a contemporary network with special music and features that would appeal to all those AM stations that are trying to find their way. A fourth would be strictly for FM."

"Would you do this with one set of AT&T lines?"

"Yes. No extra line costs. We'd use to full capacity the lines we now have."

"I like that part of it."

"So do we. Now for the downside risks . . ."

Siegel pulled himself back to reality. There were always, of course, "downside risks" and they always required rather fantastic sums of additional money. He was not disappointed.

"This will cost a hell of a lot of money," said Beaudin. "Furthermore, it's a hell of a risk because what we've got to do, if we go into this, is shut down the entire radio network as we now have it. That means cancelling every advertiser . . ."

Siegel suffered a slight spasm of his facial muscles. "*Every advertiser?*"

"Yes. We'd have to notify them almost a year ahead that it's a new ball game. Same with our stations. We'd have to cancel every one of our present affiliate contracts."

"What you're saying is that we'd be going out of business?" Siegel asked in utter astonishment.

"That's right, Si. Close the old store. Open a brand new store. There's no other way we can do it. In addition there's a lot of FCC hurdles to get over. So many, in fact, that maybe Ev Erlick and his guys will tell us to forget it."

"What are your profit projections?"

"We haven't gone too far into that as yet. Probably the first year we'd lose four to six million bucks. But the next year we might make six million. Now, do you want to throw me out and forget the whole thing? Or shall I go ahead?"

Siegel pondered the situation. This was a hell of a time to be trying any new or fancy ideas, what with the ITT merger having just been announced. Who could tell how long that would take? And with the enormous amounts of capital needed to "colorize" the television network, it seemed insane to encourage Beaudin at this time. But losing two million or more per year in the radio network now and for the foreseeable future wasn't a very happy prospect either. But increasing the loss for one year to six million dollars in the hope of breaking even a year or two later . . . plus the risks inherent in throwing the present system up for grabs . . . it was all rather mind boggling. If the idea failed, it was tantamount to throwing out the baby with the bath water. Still . . .

"No, I'm not going to throw you out of the office," Siegel finally said. "I'll talk it over with Leonard. In the meanwhile I think you should go ahead with the others and develop the idea further."

◇   ◇   ◇

Beaudin's "crazy idea" was developed fully over the next few months of 1966. In its final stage, the "personality" network was re-identified as the "American Entertainment Radio Network." The others remained as originally envisioned: American Information Network; American Contemporary Network, and American FM Network. The four would be fed consecutively from 7 AM to 7 PM EST, with one of them providing news feeds to 11 PM EST. Each specialized network would affiliate with different local stations in markets and each would be programmed, "separately, consecutively, and non-simultaneously on one line;" each program service would also be "separately and distinctively designated, programed, and sold to advertisers." However, to abide by an FCC rule against dual network operations, none of the new ABC affiliates would program opposite each other.[1]

Before 1966 ended, ABC had given notice to all of its advertisers and affiliated stations to the effect that the year 1967 would be ABC's last year in business in its old single network format.

By mid-1967 the company began heavy promotion and selling efforts on its new idea. The response was not gratifying.

In fact it was scoffed at by many elements of the industry.

---

[1] A waiver was requested and obtained from the FCC to waive the rule in the specific case of one program, *Breakfast Club*, which then still retained high popularity and was accepted by affiliates of one or more of the four networks. The structure of the concept, despite a few refinements, remains basically the same to this day.

ABC had "gone off the deep end once again," said critics. This was a reckless, crackpot, hare-brained scheme, said certain advertisers and agencies. As for affiliates, they were confused, leery of signing with any of the four proposed services.

"How do we know what it's really going to be like?" protested one affiliate in New Orleans. "How long will ABC stay with the idea if it flops?"

Another said scornfully: "Now I know what the letters ABC stand for: Always Be Crazy!"

To add to the confusion, not to mention the tension, and in another classic example of the kind of brinkmanship ABC enjoyed playing, the company, for some reason, chose to wait until November 6, 1967—less than two months before the new plan was to start—before it filed its request to the FCC for an interpretative ruling on Section 73.137 of the Commission's Rules barring dual network operations.

The broadcast trade organization called Station Representatives Association (SRA) took a dim view of the whole idea. They feared it would be ruinously confusing and unfairly competitive to standard network formats.

SRA had a long list of objections: if ABC obtained a waiver on *Breakfast Club*, would it not soon be back asking for similar waivers on football games and vital news feeds? Would not the plan give ABC "significant common interest or control" of affiliates? And, pleaded SRA, "There is inherent in the ABC plan the possibility of illegal group sales and combinations (of sales)."

The FCC enjoys playing a kind of brinkmanship of its own. It was not until December 28, 1967—*three days before the new concept was to begin*—that the Commission adopted a favorable ruling on behalf of ABC. The proposal, said the Commission, merited "encouragement as a new and imaginative approach to networking in the radically changed field of radio broadcasting, and the public interest is served by our action herein." However, it added, the experiment would be watched carefully for "problems or abuses" that could develop. And the proposal would be implemented *only* for one year, after which further study and evaluation would be done. The Commission said it would keenly

scrutinize the operation from a standpoint of "selling of each network on an individual basis, the barring of group sales, combined
rates or inter-network discounts." In addition ABC must submit a
comprehensive report every six months on the progress of its new
concept.

No one in the company today talks about what would have
happened if the FCC had not acted in time to meet the January
1, 1968 deadline. As for the lateness of the hour in getting FCC
approval, that scarcely raises an eyebrow.

"All life is a gamble," said a very nervous Walter A.
Schwartz, who was appointed operating head of the four-network
scheme. Schwartz had done such an outstanding job as Manager
of ABC's New York radio station (WABC) that he was rewarded
by being given the dubious honor of making the idea work.

"There's a moral there somewhere," said Schwartz, "but I've
never quite been able to figure it out."[2]

◇   ◇   ◇

Historically, January 1, 1968 must go down as a watershed
date in ABC's history, because the day of the disappointing news
from ITT was also the day of the beginning of ABC's four-network
radio concept, and paradoxically, it marked the date that the company's fortunes began to turn upward.

Not that they turned much. Or soon. Indeed, the postscript
on the radio network idea is that it was *not* a turnaround overnight. Its projected losses for the first year of operation were $4-6
million. The actual losses came closer to $8 million! Nor did the
turnaround come in the second year as projected. Rumors were
well placed by competitors to the effect that ABC, by launching
this preposterous idea, was signalling its intention of going out of
radio networking; and that after giving it a noble try, would throw

---

[2] ABC began its new plan with approximately 500 affiliates and today has about
1,600. On October 30, 1968 Mutual Broadcasting System, Inc. petitioned the
FCC to rescind the ABC plan, claiming that it was ruining its business and that
it might be forced to go out of business. The FCC denied that petition on September 12, 1969. On April 26, 1972 Mutual was permitted by the FCC to begin
its *own* version of the ABC plan.

in the towel and say, "We did our best to succeed, so don't blame us for getting out of the network radio business." This in turn created confusion among potential affiliates and made them reluctant to sign with ABC. Eventually, however, it did catch on. Four years later the operation broke even. In the fifth year, 1972, ABC's Radio Network made 4 million dollars. Since then it has become known as the "biggest game in town" among the three major companies. Its latest profits exceeded 17 million dollars.

Along with the network, ABC put together the two most successful AM and FM broadcast operations in the industry. Under Hal Neal, President of all ABC radio operations, with Edward F. McLaughlin heading the four radio networks, Charles A. DeBare heading the ABC owned AM stations, and Allen B. Shaw, heading ABC's owned FM stations, ABC is considered today to be the undisputed leader in radio among the three networks.

Another irony to the postscript is the fact that Ralph Beaudin, who put together the four-in-one radio scheme with the help of Hal Neal and Wally Schwartz, is no longer with the company. Soon after the success of his idea became assured, Beaudin, true to his nature, grew bored with his job and resigned. He disliked living in New York City and decided to strike out on his own. It is hard to comprehend, but even a lively company like ABC grew too tame for a true maverick like Ralph Beaudin who now continues his career in the southwestern part of the country. He has not switched to western clothes, but he likes the living "just fine".[3]

---

[3] As of 1979 ABC's four networks broke down as follows:
   American Contemporary Radio Network—396 affiliates.
   American Information Network—488 affiliates.
   American Entertainment Network—476 affiliates.
   American FM Network—193 affiliates.

   Paul Harvey is virtually a network by himself. His daily news programs cut across *all* the four networks making him the most listened-to, and highest paid, radio news personality in history.

   In addition ABC provides service to 132 stations who have the right to delete ABC commercials. Another 164 small power college FM stations, noncommercial, receive ABC's programs without charge. Altogether ABC affiliates outnumber all of the other three networks combined. Mutual Broadcasting System is said to have about 750 affiliates; NBC has about 350 affiliates; and CBS has about 300 affiliates.

As the plane flew back to New York, Leonard Goldenson gave only a fleeting thought to the commencing of the four radio networks that day. Too many other problems demanded attention. ABC needed cash and needed it badly. One solution, he thought, would be to find another merger partner. There were others in the wings, but time was a factor. FCC delays were always a factor.

In addition, speaking of time, there was the matter of his age. And Si Siegel's age. Both of them would reach 65 in about three years. And while he had no intention of retiring, if the Board desired that he stay on, he assumed that Siegel would opt to retire at 65. That left him with the problem of who would succeed his trusted and competent Executive Vice President.

That raised another problem. Besides himself and Siegel, three other top executives had been "locked in" to the ITT merger with five year contracts. They were Sam Clark, Everett Erlick, and Thomas Moore. Now these contracts were inoperative. Therefore he was free to move ahead on a contingency plan he had formed some time ago. In fact he had concluded his conversation with Si Siegel earlier that day with the pointed remark:

"I think we now should go ahead with that executive change we've discussed."

Siegel agreed. That change involved one of the three men who would have benefitted by a long term ITT contract, and this would now become the top priority item when Goldenson returned from Miami.

Thus was set in motion a series of events that would lead to the most intense power struggle in the history of ABC's executive suite.

ABC's owned AM stations are: WABC, New York; WLS, Chicago; KABC, Los Angeles; WXYZ, Detroit; KGO, San Francisco; WMAL, Washington D.C.

ABC owned FM stations are: WPLJ, New York; WDAI, Chicago; KLOS, Los Angeles; KSFX, San Francisco; WRIF, Detroit; KAUM, Houston; WRQX, Washington D.C.

10

An Offer You Can't Refuse

THE POWER STRUGGLE began three days later on January 4, 1968 when Elton Rule in Hollywood got a surprise call from Tom Moore in New York. The struggle, however, was not between these two men, for the fate of one of them had already been sealed when that call was made. The struggle concerned another top ABC executive, Theodore Shaker, who was a close friend and ally of Moore's, but a decided adversary of Rule's.

Rule received the call in his car as he drove through Griffith Park to the ABC Television Center, where Elton Rule managed ABC's owned station, KABC-TV in Los Angeles. It was a Friday morning, and the last one he expected to hear from was Tom Moore, President of the ABC Television Network. He hadn't seen or talked to Moore in weeks. When the phone rang he was sure it was Ted Shaker, his boss, who seemed to take perverse delight in calling his station managers at any hour of the day or night.

"Elton, how you doing?"

Rule laughed. "I'm doing fine, Tom, considering that New

Year's is over, the smog is light and it's Friday. How you doing?"

"What are you doing tomorrow?"

"I'm going to my place in Malibu."

"How would you like to come to New York?"

Elton laughed again. "I'd rather be in California."

"I'm serious. Can you come to New York?"

"What's up?"

"I'm moving up to a higher level. I'd like to discuss with you the possibility of your becoming President of the network. All of this is highly confidential."

If so, thought Rule, broadcasting it on a shortwave telephone frequency hardly seemed the best way to keep it confidential, so he suggested that they continue the conversation when he reached his office. There, on a private line, Tom Moore outlined the situation. He was being promoted to a Group level and since the network would be one of the divisions that would report to him, it was incumbent upon him to select his successor at the network.

Rule said he was flattered to be considered for such an important job, so under the circumstances he would certainly fly at once to New York.

"You won't believe this," he said, "but my bags are already packed and in the trunk of my car."

Moore thought that odd. "Did you know about this?"

"Not a damned thing. But I planned to fly to San Francisco Monday morning with my sales manager, Jim Osborne. Since I'll be at Malibu I didn't want to have to stop at my house in Sherman Oaks to pick up a fresh change of clothes on Monday morning."

"Good, then you can fly in today. I'll reserve a room for you at the Hilton. We'll have a limousine meet you at the airport."

Again Moore urged strict secrecy because the decision probably would be made that weekend and they wanted to avoid any leaks to the press.

"Betty will be the only one to know," said Elton. But as it turned out, his wife was the last one to know. She was not home, but on the golf course. He called her again from the airport, but she had not returned so Betty Rule learned the news later that night when her husband called from New York.

On the plane Elton Rule had four hours to reflect on the opportunity that presumably awaited him. The ITT merger cancellation was only four days old. Things were moving fast. He also thought it odd that no rumors had leaked out within the company; not a hint of anything from Ted Shaker or Si Siegel. Maybe Shaker did not know. But Siegel certainly did. It also intrigued him that *he* was a candidate, and that Tom Moore apparently had done the selecting. Why? He and Moore had never been close. Yet Moore also had been careful not to say, or imply, that he was the *only* candidate. Who could the others be? And how should he play this overture?

The opportunity, he also knew, was fraught with career peril. Being the President of a television network was as deadly a spot as the eye of a hurricane. Few lasted in that job for very long. Tom Moore had held it for six years. Was Tom now being kicked upstairs? Or was Moore kicking *himself* upstairs?

There were many other reasons to give Elton Rule misgivings. He knew he had done a good job in Los Angeles. The company also knew it. He had survived Ted Shaker's quixotic management style, was in fact only one of two of ABC's "old guard" station managers to survive Shaker's regime. Rule had actually done such a good job in Los Angeles that he had been offered opportunities in the past to come to New York and accept headquarters management challenges. There had been several conversations with both Si Siegel and Leonard Goldenson. He remembered the last one with Goldenson, who had asked:

"Elton, what will it take to get you to come to New York?"

Rule had replied: "Leonard, I don't expect that it will happen, but if ever the time comes when I can be given the chance to run the television network, you won't have to ask me—just tell me and I'll come running."

So in a sense, if Tom Moore's offer was genuine, it was something like an offer he could not refuse. But all of that had been months ago. Now, after 16 years with the company, his big chance might be forthcoming. He wondered about the fact that

Tom Moore, not Goldenson or Siegel, was doing the inviting. What did that mean? And that raised still another question: could he and Tom Moore work as a team? Yes, he mused, there were many questions that had to be resolved. With it all, however, there was one bright spot: if he were specifically offered the job, and accepted it, he would no longer be reporting to Ted Shaker. That certainly was a consolation to consider . . .

He pushed his seat back and resolved to think no more about the situation. In a few hours all the answers would be on the table.

◇ ◇ ◇

What Elton Rule did not know was that Tom Moore was indeed being promoted upstairs. Yet it was not put to Moore in those blunt terms. The time-honored corporate custom of promoting one "up and out" was not being followed in this case. At least that's how it was put to him. Moore was told that he was definitely wanted, but that he should move up to a Group level status which would put him on a par with Sam Clark, who controlled the theatres and leisure entertainment division; Ralph Beaudin who now controlled all of radio; and Ted Shaker who controlled the television stations, the International Division, film syndication company, and television spot sales. Moore was to have news, sports, the television network, ABC International, and film sales. The latter two divisions would be taken away from Shaker, who was to assume greater personal responsibilities with Si Siegel in the area of corporate planning.

It all sounded good except that Elmer Lower, who headed ABC News, emphatically declared that he would not work under Moore, so news was deleted from the newly planned group domain. The television network, however, definitely would remain under Moore, and Moore would have the privilege of picking his own successor.

Tom Moore had been told all of this immediately after Leonard Goldenson returned from Miami on New Year's Day. At first Tom had been stunned because he had believed he was doing a good job at the network. His six years as President of the network had been marked, he thought, by definite contributions and there had been ample indications that his efforts were appreciated. In the area of sports, Moore had been an aggressive champion and advocate. It was his impassioned plea to Siegel seven years before that had saved *Wide World of Sports* from extinction after its initial thirteen-week trial. Ollie Treyz at that time had wanted to cancel the series because it was too costly and was not producing sufficient revenue.

In terms of performance in the crucial entertainment area, Moore also thought he was doing a creditable job. In 1963, for at least a couple of months, ABC had actually led in the prime time Nielsen ratings. Moore had been elected to the Board that same year. From every indication he felt that he "had it made." When the ITT merger was planned in 1965 he was one of the lucky five executives who had been "protected" by generous five-year contracts.

But the two-year limbo which ABC suffered from 1966 through 1967 affected the company in diverse ways. It was an enervating period. In addition, Moore's 1967 prime time schedule was not a success. He made the mistake of trying to "upgrade" the schedule. It was a critical success, but a ratings disaster. Neither *Stage 67*, a series of distinguished dramas, nor the four-hour prime time special on Africa, pulled the audiences they deserved. And several of the new series bombed. So now he had been told immediately after New Year's Day of 1968 that it was time to bring in someone "fresh" and move himself up to a higher level.

But whom to bring in, Moore asked Siegel and Goldenson. That was up to him, they said. He quickly came up with two candidates. The first one he suggested was John Gilbert, who had experience both in station operations and in the network. When little enthusiasm was shown for Gilbert, Moore suggested Jim Duffy, who also had years of experience in both the radio and television networks. There was nothing wrong with Jim Duffy, he was told. Duffy was an excellent man. But then Goldenson had asked:

"How about Elton Rule?"

"Elton Rule?" Tom Moore seemed surprised. Then he said, "I have nothing against Elton. He's a fine station manager. It's just that he has no network experience as both Gilbert and Duffy have."

"Well, it's your choice, but we think you ought to talk to Elton."

Tom Moore got the message. He knew he would have to have some convincing arguments as to why Rule was not the man, because they apparently had already decided that Rule was their choice. Still, Moore had to admit that his bosses were not being heavy-handed, or dictatorial. They seemed to be honestly leaving it up to him to be satisfied that Rule could do the job. So Moore had said:

"All right. I'll talk to Elton. If Elton really wants the job, if he will really be satisfied working for me, and is willing to report to me, then I'll have no objection to putting him in the job."

That's the way it had been left, and that's when Tom Moore picked up the phone and called Los Angeles.

◇   ◇   ◇

Elton Rule checked into the Hilton that Friday night, and the next morning was whisked to Tom Moore's home in Darien. The affair was cloaked in secrecy. Jack Gould, ace television writer for *The New York Times,* had heard that something was in the wind at ABC. He tried to find Rule at several New York hotels, then called Moore and asked if he knew where Rule could be reached.

Elton was sitting right there at a lavish luncheon spread prepared by Mrs. Moore. Tom, with his usual gracious manner, and exuding courtly southern charm, explained to Rule the "setup"; the chain of command; how the whole thing would work. By now Moore had convinced himself that he was, indeed, in full command of selecting his successor.

Rule, on his part, had no other signals to fly by and was equally convinced that Tom was doing the picking. And he was immensely flattered that he was Tom's first, and seemingly only, choice. There would be clarification meetings later that weekend with both Siegel and Goldenson and that, Elton told himself, would be his opportunity to "clarify" certain points and conditions before he would ever fully commit to the job.

But at least on this man-to-man level the talks went well. Before the afternoon was over, Elton extended his hand, and said:

"Tom, I'm your man! What's the next step?"

"Great!" said Moore. "We'll have a meeting tomorrow with Si and Leonard. If they buy the deal I'd like to announce it at once."

"So soon? Why?"

"Jack Gould knows something is happening. I'd rather get the story out correctly than have it garbled by the press."

On Sunday at Goldenson's comfortable but unpretentious home in Mamaroneck, and with Si Siegel present, the deal was confirmed. Siegel and Goldenson both said they would be pleased to accept Moore's "choice" of Elton Rule, but not before Rule was able to get, in private conversation with the two company leaders, private assurances that he would not be "short circuited" in his management of the network. While he was willing to report to Tom Moore on the table of organization, he must also be able to deal directly with both Siegel and Goldenson when important decisions had to be made. Television is a fast moving game, and television network operation is the fastest game of all. Decisions involving millions of dollars are made hourly; to expedite this critical time element, Rule said he must be able to get prompt decisions from the top whenever they were required.

Those assurances were privately given, so before the weekend was over, Jack Gould was at his typewriter telling the world what had happened.

But almost immediately something went wrong. As Moore recalls it:

"The next day, in Jack Gould's story it came out not as clearly as it should that I would continue to report to Si Siegel. Either Jack Gould misconstrued what I told him, or maybe I didn't make it clear enough, but anyhow, when the story broke the next day I noticed a definite chill on the part of my friend, Si Siegel. No question about it, his nose was out of joint. Si is a very sensitive person. I don't blame him for feeling as he did. Right then I got the feeling that I had lost Si forever as an ally in the company."

From that point on it was downhill for Group Vice President Tom Moore. A week or so later he went to Grenoble, France to oversee the production of ABC's *Winter Olympic Games*. Moore had put his heart and soul, and three years of planning, into this sports spectacular. Tom knew that with Roone Arledge, newly appointed President of ABC Sports; producing the event, and Julie Barnathan providing superb technical assistance, these Olympic Games would add new laurels to ABC's sports dominance; nevertheless he wanted to be there in person to do what he could.

When he returned to New York two weeks later, he learned that Elton Rule had indeed taken charge. He had already replaced one key executive, Edward Bleier, who headed ABC's public relations, advertising, and promotion departments; and he was making other changes.

Shortly after that, Tom Moore, in a Board meeting, took an opposite view to Goldenson in a dispute concerning one Board member, who was in the process of being removed from the Board. Now Leonard Goldenson became as cool toward him as Si Siegel. Moore felt a growing sense of isolation. Soon he was a Group Vice President with nothing to do.

By mid-summer of 1968, Moore realized that his usefulness to ABC had come to the end. He went to Siegel in extreme agitation and asked, "Si, do you mean to tell me that in this whole large company there is no longer *anything* for me to do?"

Si murmured that yes, that's the way it was.

A settlement was worked out that Moore considered fair, although after his "resignation" he felt the deep sense of loss that all executives feel when they lose their corporate home. "I felt," he recalls, "like Bill Cosby in one of his famous monologues, when he uttered that great line, 'I came home one day and found that my family had moved.' "

Today Tom Moore has no rancor or regrets. He had played

the game as well as he knew how to play it. He knew the risks going in. When Ollie Treyz had been fired six years before, Tom Moore had been the first to rush into Siegel's office and say: "Si, now that you fired Ollie, I want to be the first in line for his job!"

The script never changes in the corporate arena. The game never changes. Only the players change.[1]

And now that Elton Rule was firmly in the saddle, and Moore gone, the stage was set, and conditions ripe, for the *real* power struggle that was to ensue between Rule and his former boss, Ted Shaker.

---

[1] Tom Moore accepted a top executive post with Ticketron Corporation. Three years later, he formed a production company called Tomorrow Entertainment with financial backing provided by General Electric. Later the company was reorganized and is now owned equally by Moore and Dancer Fitzgerald and Sample advertising agency. In 1977, Moore suffered a severe heart attack. He has fully recovered and the company he operates, Tomorrow Entertainment, is doing a thriving business as a supplier of television programs to networks and stations.

11

Howard Hughes and His Takeover Machine

THE SHAKER-RULE BATTLE was, like many classic corporate confrontations, not a head-to-head battle. Neither had anything to do with the other in a direct operating sense. Shaker was a Group Vice President to whom the five ABC television stations and the Sales Representation firm reported. (The International Division and the film syndication division, which he formerly had, were returned to him after Tom Moore left the company.) Elton Rule was President of only the television network. However, that was the single most important division of the company.

The battle had been brewing between them for years. In terms of personality, philosophy, and management style no two men could have been more unalike. Ted Shaker believed that it was his destiny to occupy the top rung of the ladder—even Leonard Goldenson's job if Goldenson ever retired. Shaker's good-sized ego permitted him to believe that he was, without question, the smartest man in the company. A few of both his friends and critics believed that perhaps he was. In reaching for the top rung, Ted Shaker wanted nothing to do with the television network job.

That was too dangerous; too perilous a route to take. He had a better plan; and at this point in the company's history, and his own career, his plan seemed to be working. He had built a strong power base, principally on the five important television stations which ABC owned in the cities of New York, Chicago, Los Angeles, Detroit, and San Francisco. Five of the six largest cities in the country, representing some 25% of the population.

Shaker believed that ABC should appoint a single executive in charge of all broadcasting, both radio and television. Euphemistically, the title within the company was known as that of "Mr. Broadcasting."

Shaker's most consistent supporter was none other than Si Siegel, to whom Shaker reported. Siegel had given tacit encouragement, not only to the "Mr. Broadcasting" dream, but to the idea of Shaker going on the Board. In every sense, at this time, early in 1968, Ted Shaker was riding high on the range.

Elton Rule, meanwhile, had his hands full in his new job. He gave little thought to the power struggle that was subtly shaping up. Considering the vulnerability of his job, plus the tremendous rebuilding task the entire company had facing it after the ITT fiasco, Rule considered his odds at succeeding in the neighborhood of 100-1. So the additional threat of Ted Shaker did not really mean much.

At the very top level, Goldenson and Siegel also had their hands full. As the smoke cleared after the ITT cancellation, the press and industry speculated on what had gone wrong. There were numerous conjectures:

ITT learned that Justice had something on them, hence the merger never would have been permitted to go through; so ITT had sensibly given up.

Lyndon Johnson had the fix in against the merger.

Lyndon Johnson had the fix in for the merger, but it had gone sour when he appointed a new Attorney General who had a deep grudge against ITT.

ITT had many skeletons in the closet and the closet was about to burst open.

For these, and other far out reasons, so the rumors went, the three-judge panel of the Court of Appeals had chosen to sit on the case figuring that either ITT or ABC would get the message and eventually dissolve the marriage.

The most sensible explanation, however, seemed to be the basic one of money. In March of 1966, ITT would have acquired ABC for about 366 million dollars based on ITT's then stock price of $68.12. On the first business day of the new year, 1968, ITT stock sold at 116, which would have raised the purchase price of ABC to some 620 million! On January 3 ITT rose to 116½, while ABC sank to a new low of 61, versus a 1967 high of 102. ITT already had run up its price-earnings ratio; it already had its desired "visibility." ITT was now known from coast to coast. Harold Geneen's name was a household word. Millions of dollars of free publicity had been written about the company. As Si Siegel said, Harold Geneen had already achieved his objectives without having to pay for the expense of an ABC merger.

As to the possibility of yet another merger, Leonard Goldenson weighed the matter carefully. Rumors were rife. Sears Roebuck and Transamerica were said to be sending signals. Others were in private conversation with Goldenson or his colleagues or advisers. Such companies as Walter Kidde Company, Glen Alden Corporation, General Electric, and Litton Industries were named.

The truth was that only *one* serious merger negotiation took place after ITT, and it occurred in January, 1969 with Monogram Industries, an aggressive California conglomerate whose stock had zoomed, in 1967, from 10 to 80. The deal was highly unusual in that ABC would have been the surviving company, thus hopefully avoiding regulatory questions at the FCC about transfer of control.

But there were negative aspects to this merger. John Coleman, the outspoken financial strong man on ABC's Board, was said to be strongly against such a merger. There were image problems also. Monogram Industries was the largest manufacturer of chemical toilets in the world. One could conjure up all kinds of disastrous gags linking ABC programs with toilets!

Other more pressing problems than a new merger cried for

attention, particularly in the financial area. Profits had declined by 25% over the preceding year. (13.5 million for 1967 versus 18 million in 1966). Drastic economy measures were taken. Fifteen million was lopped off ABC's news budget for 1968, which meant that coverage of that year's two upcoming political conventions would be severely truncated.[1]

A $50 million convertible subordinated debenture was arranged, which would make it possible to repay ITT's 25 million loan within six months. Then a solution was found to the vexing problem of how to pay for theatrical films. Some $120 millions worth of feature films were factored through Manufacturers Hanover Bank, enabling ABC to pay for them as they were played.

The costly switch to color continued at as rapid a pace as funds would allow. Twenty-five percent of the nation's sets were now able to receive color programs, so color had now really arrived. Belt tightening in daily operations became the order of the day. Use of xerox machines was carefully watched; pencils were again sharpened to short nubs. Long term construction plans for studios and production plants in Los Angeles and New York were deferred to some indeterminate future date.

By mid-'68, ABC could feel good about having come to life after its two-year hibernation induced by the ITT merger attempt. It had a sense of poise and confidence once again, and was moving forward with some vigor and determination. And then suddenly at mid-year an event occurred that brought the company's skies tumbling down once again.

Early on Monday morning, July 1, Everett Erlick, ABC's General Counsel and member of the Board, received an urgent call to come to Goldenson's office. There he found the President, and Executive Vice President Siegel, looking as grim as he had ever seen them.

"I just got a phone call," said Goldenson. "Howard Hughes has made a tender offer to take over ABC!"

Erlick was aghast. "You've got to be kidding!" he said.

---

[1] This was considered to be a highly sensitive image problem but it did not develop. The American TV audience accepted ABC's 90-minute nightly convention coverage with gratitude and cheers.

President Goldenson handed him a sheet of paper on which the high points were written: Hughes, through his company, Hughes Tool Company, was offering to buy 43% of ABC shares at a price of $74.25, considerably above the last sale that had been registered the preceding Friday at $58.75. The tender offer would be open for two weeks and would expire at 3 PM on Monday, July 15. If successful, Hughes would be paying 150 million for about 43% of the company; or 37%, assuming conversion of all the shares underlying the 50 million convertible debenture issue which ABC was offering that *very same day!* Thus, for the next two weeks ABC itself was in a status of registration with the Securities and Exchange Commission and this placed it in a severe limbo position vis-à-vis defending itself against the takeover attempt. Also, there was, right now, so much trading in ABC stock that the stock had not opened.

It was clear, from what Erlick read, that the Howard Hughes Takeover Machine was functioning with stunning and diabolical efficiency. "Incredible!" said Erlick. "And today marks our first day in registration of our debenture issue."

"Are we able to speak out and defend ourselves?" asked Goldenson.

"I don't know. It's an unprecedented situation," said Erlick.

The news, while shocking, should not have come as a total surprise to ABC, for it had been foreshadowed the previous October when Gregson Bautzer, one of Hughes' attorneys, had called Leonard Goldenson and told him that Hughes Tool was "ready" to step in if the ITT merger did not materialize. Goldenson had politely ignored the overture, but later two Hughes emissaries approached Goldenson and repeated that Howard Hughes was still "extremely interested" in "helping ABC." Would Mr. Goldenson go to Las Vegas and discuss the matter with Mr. Hughes "in person?" Goldenson declined again, despite a natural curiosity to have a personal visit with the legendary recluse.

But now Hughes had taken the gloves off and was brazenly out to acquire ABC, with or without ABC's cooperation.

By sheer coincidence, ABC's Board was scheduled to meet

that same day. So the planned agenda was cancelled and the entire meeting devoted to working out strategy plans to combat the tender offer.

The Board required very little time to come to an unanimous resolution to fight the tender offer in every legal way that was possible. First of all it was an unfriendly takeover attempt. Second, no one wanted anything to do with the enigmatic and eccentric Hughes. Third, the offer was far below the intrinsic value of the company and therefore not in the best interests of its stockholders. Ev Erlick was charged with gathering together ABC's heaviest legal artillery to plan a specific legal battle plan. So he called Herb Berkson of the Washington antitrust firm of Berkson and Borkland. He called Jim McKenna of ABC's own FCC counsel, McKenna and Wilkinson. He called David Hartman of the New York firm of White and Case. Jim Hagerty, ABC's vice president of the Washington political scene, was asked to fly to New York at once.

With Erlick at the helm, this powerful tactical force came up with a plan. ABC must go to Federal Court immediately and try to enjoin the tender offer. At the same time they must commence proceedings at the FCC, for this was an attempt by Hughes to circumvent the FCC by taking over control of a broadcasting company without going through the established procedures of a public hearing to ascertain if the transfer of control of 19 radio and television licenses was in the public interest.

Said Erlick: "Either Hughes thinks he can ram this through the Commission, or else his attorneys are naive, or haven't done their homework."

At the same time, Erlick realized, the Securities and Exchange Commission presented a problem. How far could ABC go in publicly fighting the tender offer while the company was in two weeks of registration of its own debenture issue? The public relations firm of Hill and Knowlton was asked to prepare the copyline for ads for the New York press so ABC could let the world know that it wanted no part of Howard Hughes.

The next day, with a sample of a prepared ad in their hands,

Erlick and his men, accompanied by President Goldenson, paid a visit to Manny Cohen, then head of the SEC. Erlick's argument was simple:

"This tender offer, coming at this time, puts us in an untenable position. It will be unfair to our stockholders if they can hear only one side of the question. We've prepared this ad. We'd welcome any suggestions you have . . ."

Cohen studied the ad, said finally, "I'm not here to approve or disapprove ads. You go see my chief assistant. He may have some comments."

Erlick did. The assistant made one or two comments, asked a few questions to clarify some points in the ad, and wished Erlick good luck. With that base covered, Erlick's battery of legal advisers went to the U.S. Southern Distirct Court in New York where they filed for a temporary injunction with Judge Dudley B. Bonsal.

At the same time that this was going on, Jim McKenna, in Washington, was at the FCC asking for clarification of this "back door" attempt by Hughes to take over ABC. The FCC was sympathetic. On July 3 it voted 6-0 to notify Hughes that "public hearings would have to be held to examine Howard Hughes' qualifications to hold a controlling interest in one of the three major networks."

After that, the pace quickened. The battle of newspaper ads began. Siegel and Goldenson began getting calls from attorneys they did not know. Si Siegel recalled that, "every caller began with the line, 'I just came from seeing Mr. Hughes. He wants me to tell you . . .' " It began to seem like a joke, all these people claiming they had just seen Howard Hughes, and here we were, the company he wanted to take over and we had never seen, or talked to him!"

Greg Bautzer flew in from California to make an impassioned plea for "peace." "Hughes only wants to *help* ABC," Bautzer said.

"This kind of help we do not need," Goldenson answered coldly.

"Look," pleaded Bautzer, "you said you needed 90 million dollars and Mr. Hughes is willing to give it to you. You said you needed new facilities and Mr. Hughes is willing to build them for you. We see no reason why you shouldn't accept Mr. Hughes."

Mr. Bautzer was told to return to Hollywood and not waste any more of his time. In the meantime Leonard Goldenson was working on another strategy—a sudden merger with *another* company; one that would have the effect of blocking the Hughes tender offer. Earlier that year, Goldenson had held casual talks with L. Walter Lundell, President of C.I.T. Financial Corporation about a possible merger between the two companies. Now these talks were revived and intensified. The scheme was a daring one. Lundell had, at first, suggested that C.I.T. make a friendly tender offer for ABC's shares, but Goldenson was reluctant to make any deal in which ABC would not be the surviving company. Now Goldenson counter offered 1.2 billion in convertible debentures to C.I.T.'s stockholders in return for their shares, which were then worth about 800 million. If converted, these debentures would give C.I.T. shareholders more than 75% ownership of ABC! This presumably would avoid the transfer of control issue at the FCC.

Feverish negotiations went on over the weekend of July 6–7. An agreement was reached on Sunday between Goldenson and Lundell. On Monday both boards met to ratify the deal. ABC's board approved it in less than an hour, then sat around drinking coffee, and waiting for word that C.I.T. had also approved the deal that would, in effect, cut Howard Hughes off at the pass.

The morning passed and no call came. Shortly before 1 PM, Mr. Lundell did finally call. He was very sorry, he said, but C.I.T. had *not* approved the merger. He cited several problems that could not be resolved at the present time. But undoubtedly it was the confusion caused by Howard Hughes that served as the principal deterrent in C.I.T.'s decision.

On July 10 Judge Bonsal denied ABC's plea for a temporary injunction. ABC immediately filed for a permanent injunction. That also was denied. However, Bonsal ruled, all shares tendered must be kept in a bank of Hughes' choosing, and ABC could seek whatever action it deemed proper through the FCC.

Time was now becoming a critical factor. The Hughes tender

offer would expire on Monday at 3 PM. Press speculation favored Hughes' chances to gain the 43% of stock that he required to gain control of ABC. Then an extraordinary series of events occurred. Everett Erlick recalls them vividly:

"Following Judge Bonsal's denial of the injunction, we went upstairs to another judge to ask for a stay pending appeal. By 'we', I mean the Hughes lawyers, and our own. We found a judge and expected from him only a procedural discussion. But one of Hughes' attorneys turned it into a substantive discussion. The next day, Dave Hartman called me. He said we were in luck. Instead of a mere procedural hearing, the court had set a *full* hearing before a three judge panel of the U.S. Court of Appeals! This was extraordinary, because, despite the importance of the case, we did not expect to get this kind of hearing for several weeks."

Two days later, after intense preparation by both sides, a two-hour oral argument was heard by the three judge panel headed by Judge Henry J. Friendly. But the day was Monday, July 15th! The day of the deadline of the Hughes tender offer!

After counsel had presented their arguments the panel retired to deliberate. Again with surprising speed, they returned after little more than an hour, and rendered their verdict:

The injunction was again denied. However, it was denied in such a manner that it gave ABC much comfort. In effect, said the court, had ABC *not* gone to the FCC to ask that it take jurisdiction, the court would indeed have been disposed to grant the injunction sought by ABC. But since ABC had already gone to the FCC, the court would continue to *keep* jurisdiction pending the FCC's action. The court also encouraged the FCC to resolve the matter quickly in view of its significance.

Erlick ran to a phone and called Rosel Hyde, Chairman of the FCC. Hyde was not in. He asked to be transferred to General Counsel, Henry Geller. He told Geller that, in effect, the Court of Appeals was putting the burden squarely on the back of the Commission, and that expenditious action by the FCC would be of great importance to ABC.

Now it was the FCC's turn to show that it also could, on rare occasions, act with remarkable dispatch. Geller obtained a copy of the decision, and before the day was over attorneys for both parties were advised that a hearing would commence immediately and that, without question, Mr. Hughes could not expect to take control of 19 ABC broadcast licenses without first going through the procedure of a full public hearing.

Did this mean that Mr. Hughes would have to appear in *person* at such a hearing, a Hughes attorney asked.

Yes. Mr. Hughes definitely would be required to appear, was the reply.

That ended the threat of the Howard Hughes Takeover Machine! By 3 PM of that day some 1.6 million shares of ABC stock had been tendered by shareholders—400,000 shares less than the 2 million shares Hughes wanted to meet his goal of 43% of the outstanding stock of ABC.

However Hughes was still in a position to take over the company had he wanted to do it. All he had to do was to extend his tender offer until he obtained the necessary 43%. And there is little doubt that he could have succeeded in this effort in probably two weeks time. But the FCC's edict about appearing in person had changed his mind because the eccentric billionaire took only another 24 hours to withdraw his offer. Laconically, he said, "If Leonard Goldenson doesn't want me in ABC, I don't want any part of ABC."

So ended another bizarre adventure in ABC's turbulent history. This one inspired one board member to say, "We are an extension of Murphy's Law: If anything can happen to us, it will!"

There were some lessons to be learned from this experience, however—plus one important legal fallout that had significance for the entire broadcast industry. To begin with, in retrospect, it is clear that Hughes' attorneys were guilty of either naiveté or brazen ego, for thinking that they could actually take over a major network by circumventing the FCC. As Ev Erlick, who so deftly masterminded ABC's legal strategy, put it: "They really did not do their homework. The spectre of a man with a green eyeshade pulling strings from his penthouse in a gambling casino in Las Vegas simply did not make sense when it came to taking over a major broadcast company."

Yet the Hughes attempt was a "midnight raid" that conceivably could have come off if, after the tender offer, sufficient Hughes influence could have been brought to bear on the FCC. Some speculate that Hughes would not have mustered a single vote at the seven man Commission. Others say he could have mustered a 4-3 vote. Whatever the outcome it would have created incredible confusion for stockholders and for ABC. It would have sent ABC into another depressing limbo of legal suspension in which it would have slipped further behind its competitors. Credit in this case must be given to the swift legislative process that took place—particularly, the prompt actions of the U.S. Court of Appeals, and of the FCC.

The real fallout of this episode is that the tender offer route is probably foreclosed forever in broadcast ownership situations. Indeed, the converse is probably true. The results of the Hughes takeover attempt may encourage those corporations who think they are vulnerable, to go out and buy at least one lonely little FM station, say in West Branch, Iowa, to foreclose corporate marauders.

12

Mayhem in the
Executive Suite

As 1968 WORE ON, Ted Shaker saw, to his surprise, that Elton
Rule was "making it." This complicated his own scenario, which
had it that Rule would discredit himself by doing an ineffectual
job; and thus Rule, the only one inside the company whom he
now considered major competition, would be eliminated. Even if
Rule did an "ordinary" job, it would be acceptable in Shaker's
scenario because that would not thwart him from achieving his
ambition—to become the Jack Schneider of ABC, or "Mr. Broadcasting" as the hypothetical job was called within the company.
Ted Shaker had been selling this concept to both Siegel and
Goldenson on the oft-used argument that if it was good enough
for CBS it certainly was good enough for ABC. And there was
merit to the plan. Under one executive there could be stronger
cohesion, greater unity, and better implementation of direction.
Such a person, of course, would report to Siegel as EVP, and
Leonard Goldenson as President.

But as the weeks wore on, it appeared that Elton Rule was
looming larger as Shaker's main stumbling block. Shaker grew

more critical of those who reported to him. In May of 1968 he
raised eyebrows by firing his head of ABC's five owned television
stations, James Conley. Conley had been *his* man in every sense
of the word; a dedicated loyalist; one of his closest friends; an executive Shaker had brought with him from CBS when the ABC
TV Sales firm had been formed in 1961.

According to *Variety* magazine, Conley's resignation was
ascribed to a difference in philosophy as to how much autonomy
ABC's five owned television stations should have. Conley wanted
more and Shaker wanted less. But that was not the real problem;
the question of autonomy had been settled years ago—Shaker's
way—when he had ousted three of the five station managers in as
many years. A fourth, Dave Sacks in San Francisco was also on
Shaker's "hit list" and would be forced to resign early in 1970.[1]

The real story of Jim Conley's forced resignation was an old
story—Ted Shaker's inability to get along with his key executives
for any length of time. Conley learned quickly in his job that it
was almost impossible to please his boss; also that he was little
more than a glorified messenger boy; that anything he did, or
tried to do, had to be cleared with Shaker beforehand. When
Shaker began to burrow in and "build a file" on some hapless executive, Jim Conley was expected to help build that file whether
he agreed with his boss or not.

Yet with all of Shaker's personality problems, no one dis-
puted the fact that he was possessed of a brilliant mind, and that

---

[1] This author left ABC in 1964 as General Manager of ABC's Chicago station,
WBKB (later renamed WLS-TV), as a result of irreconcilable differences with
Shaker. Autonomy was indeed the main issue. I saw the company moving away
from a basic philosophy that I thought gave ABC a strength and uniqueness that
distinguished it from CBS or NBC stations. Our concepts of how to operate in
the "public interest, convenience and necessity" differed widely. I was not fired
from the company, although it was clear that I could no longer remain as manager in Chicago. Both Siegel and Goldenson urged me to remain with ABC, but
in a different capacity, with my headquarters to be either New York or Los
Angeles. I preferred to remain in Chicago, hence resigned on terms that I considered fair and amicable.

Jim Conley went on to head the Meredith television station group and has
been eminently successful there ever since he left ABC. Conley still maintains
friendly relations with Ted Shaker, but admits that he would not "enjoy" working for Shaker again.

he had done a superb job for the company. In terms of sheer ability he had, some said, the equipment to one day head up the company—if only he could overcome his personality problem. As one executive put it: "If Ted ever learns that you cannot rule by fear alone, and that you must let your troops have some semblance of human dignity, he'll be a great executive."

Ironically, in a different sense, Ted Shaker was as much of a maverick in the ABC hierarchy as Ollie Treyz had been. Except that Shaker disliked individualism. He prided himself on being a conformist; the perfect organization man. His philosophy of operation could be summed up in a few words: *Do it the way CBS does it, but do it better.* When he formed ABC spot sales to represent ABC stations in major cities he staffed it predominantly with CBS people. "Why not?" he boasted. CBS was the acknowledged leader, so how could one go wrong by emulating CBS, or acquiring its best people? Perhaps to give his organization some semblance of balance, he added one lonely NBC executive. Ironically, Ted Shaker had left CBS because his career has been blocked in the network sales area by, some say, the smiling Cobra, James Aubrey.

Soon after that he was given authority over the ABC television stations. He expressed horror at the highly individualistic style of the managers he inherited. He didn't like the way they dressed, talked, walked, or acted. He vowed to his ex-CBS colleagues that, in a short time, all of these station jobs would be theirs. A battle royal erupted between the old line managers, and Shaker, over the issue of autonomy and management style. Shaker insisted that local autonomy was ridiculous. Control must be centralized. Control must be firmly held in New York. That was how CBS did it. CBS, he was fond of saying, had class and style. He soon had his colleagues dressing like CBS—or more specifically, like Shaker himself. In the short career of James Aubrey at ABC the CBS patina had never rubbed off. The same could be said while Tom Moore was there. But with the advent of Ted Shaker it grew increasingly clear that, like it or not, ABC had bought a "piece of the CBS rock"—the solemn black skyscraper referred to in the trade as "Black Rock."

The only manager to survive Shaker's "shakeup" was Elton Rule, then General Manager of KABC-TV in Los Angeles. There were many who believed that Rule also would have been ousted if Shaker could have had his way. But Elton Rule was doing an exceptional job, and in addition he was held in high esteem by Siegel and Goldenson.

In contrast to Shaker, Elton Rule had a style that relied on rapport with his staff. His style was warm and informal. He knew, as most good executives know, that, while people may be motivated to work by fear, hope for advancement, and a desire for economic security, there is an additional element that is needed. If people *want* to work for you, if they trust you and believe in you, then you have a much stronger relationship going. Both Si Siegel and Leonard Goldenson, despite their differing personalities, had this quality in abundance.

Elton Rule demonstrated how much of these qualities he had very quickly in his network assignment. Rule was a good listener, a good judge of manpower, and a natural leader. One of his strengths was the fact that he did not have a special predilection for any one phase of the business over another. He saw them all as parts of a whole and dealt with each with patience and pragmatism. However, Rule was not having an easy time of it in his new role. No matter how difficult he had expected his new job to be, the reality of it was even worse. It was on-the-job training, while at the same time he was called upon to make financial decisions of a magnitude far beyond any that he had to make as a station manager.

Rule's only pleasant surprise was in the high quality of Tom Moore's staff. Jim Duffy was excellent. Rule learned that Duffy had been one of Moore's choices for his own replacement, so he knew that Duffy had to be deeply disappointed. However Duffy was a realist. He knew that he was doing a good job and that a new man like Rule would need his experience and talents. Also he had to be pleased that the top network job had gone to an "insider," to a company man, and not an outsider. Moore's other choice, John Gilbert, resigned in May to take a prestigious job with another broadcast company.

Another executive impressed Rule very much. His name was I. Martin Pompadur, administrative VP of the network. Four months after Rule took over, he gave Pompadur the title of General Manager of the network. A token improvement to be sure, but it gave Pompadur a signal that he was in favor.

That signal came just in time, because Pompadur was thinking of resigning. He was confused by the whole sudden change. He was torn by his loyalties to Moore. He had worked for Moore for 1½ years and now he wondered where his boss really fit. Was Moore being kicked upstairs? More importantly, where did Marty Pompadur fit in the new scheme of things?

Oddly enough, Pompadur had never met Elton Rule, though Rule had been a station manager since 1960. But as the first weeks passed he found that he was drawn to Rule's style. Rule was cool; unflappable. Moore only seemed to be that way. Rule actually seemed to *know* that he was in command. He listened. He seemed to epitomize the ideal of "grace under pressure" in those early hectic months when Rule was subjected to an ungodly experiment of well-intentioned purpose called "committee management." A dozen executives would sit around a conference table once or twice a week—Ted Shaker was one of them—and they would try to "help" Elton Rule run the television network. It was a ghastly failure. If anyone did manage to come up with a good idea some other committee member shot it down. Pompadur felt sorry for Rule but admired his cool during these time-wasting sessions.

Gradually Pompadur could see where Elton Rule was "taking them." He was taking them away from the panic and haste of making "crash decisions." Miracles, he said, were not expected. Progress takes time. We must develop a plan. A five year plan. We can't climb the mountain in all seven dayparts in one season. We will take them one at a time, starting with prime time. *One night at a time.* Five percent progress each year will do nicely, thank you . . .

Marty Pompadur thought it wonderful to hear such common sense. He wished he had had the opportunity to manage a television station as Rule had.

Then Rule espoused a cash management system. The network had never known where its money went. Now there would be separate cost centers. Research. Planning. Programming. Sales. Promotion. Public Relations. Engineering. No more totally amorphous "Administration" accounting.

In addition Pompadur saw that Rule enjoyed credibility and good will amongst affiliated stations, and this was something Tom Moore never had. Moore distrusted affiliates and they suspected him. The affiliates were a polygot lot, filled with the biases, prejudices, and political differences of the nation itself. Moore was a genuine "Southern gentlemen" and he simply did not understand affiliates, especially northern ones. Elton Rule, on the other hand, was accepted by them. He had been one of them for eight years. The managers of the affiliated stations had gotten drunk with him. To them Elton Rule was "one of the boys."

So when Rule offered Marty Pompadur a modest title improvement four months after the upheaval, Marty had no problem at all in keying in on the rising star of his new boss.

By late 1968 the battle lines were so clearly drawn between Shaker and Rule that everyone in the executive suite began taking sides. A year ago the betting "line" had been: How *soon* would Ted Shaker take over all broadcasting within the company. Now the "line" read: *Who* would it be—Shaker or Rule?

Following Jim Conley's forced resignation in May of that year, John Campbell was appointed by Shaker as head of the station group. Campbell, originally a sales executive for Elton Rule, had moved up the ladder rapidly. After a sales manager's stint in Chicago he had been made manager of WXYZ-TV, Detroit, replacing John Pival who had been third on Shaker's hit list, and then Campbell had been sent to Los Angeles to fill Elton Rule's post at KABC-TV.[2]

Everyone was pleased with Campbell's appointment. Si Siegel was convinced that Campbell was such a genial, levelheaded fellow, so well-liked by everyone that Shaker would be satisfied.

Campbell, however, had reservations from the beginning.

---

[2] John Pival died a year later in a freak boat accident in Florida.

He had seen enough of Shaker's style by now to know that his life would not be a pleasant one. Yet Shaker's methods continued to produce results. He brought the ABC station group from a poor third to a point where they were now getting a larger share of revenues than the CBS or NBC owned stations. There are 15 total network owned television stations. Nine of them are owned in the common markets of New York, Los Angeles, and Chicago. The other six are owned in differing markets, but taken in total, the market size of each network is about the same. By 1968 Shaker had raised ABC's share of this 15-station "pie" from 24% in 1964 to the impressive share of 34%.

In the meantime, while Elton Rule was making strides with the network, overall progress was being made on other fronts within the company. Profits increased by 10% in 1968.

Late in the year rumors spread that the decision had finally been made to appoint a "Mr. Broadcasting," and that it was now just a matter of tossing a coin to see who got the job—Shaker or Rule. Elton Rule admits that he was asked about the possibility of taking on this increased responsibility, but at that time he showed little interest, saying that he still had much to do to get the network on the footing he wanted.

Shaker also discussed the matter with Si Siegel.

What happened next depends on whose version one wishes to believe. One version had it that Ted Shaker was in fact selected to be "Mr. Broadcasting," and that he was so delighted with the news he ordered a case of champagne to celebrate the event with his closest friends.

However, a hitch suddenly developed. One executive was not consulted about this decision, and that was Elton Rule. According to this version, Leonard Goldenson, in agreeing to the new structure, is reported to have said to Siegel, "Does Elton know about this?"

Siegel is said to have replied, "I haven't talked to him yet, but I will."

The next day Siegel is said to have broached the matter to Rule: "Elton, what would you think if we made that 'Mr. Broadcasting' appointment."

"Si, you know how I feel about that job."

"Well, we've decided that's what we're going to do."

"Oh? And just who is this 'Mr. Broadcasting' going to be?"

"Ted Shaker."

Rule took a long pause to be sure he had Siegel's full attention. "Si, the day you make Ted Shaker 'Mr. Broadcasting' is the day that you can start sending my checks to California—because that's where I'll be."

"You must be kidding," said Siegel.

"I was never more serious in my life."

If that version is true, that is the day that the threat ended forever of Ted Shaker taking over ABC's vast broadcasting operations.

In January of 1969, the word went out that Elton Rule would be appointed to the Board of Directors. This news came as a crushing blow to Shaker since he also had been promised a position on the Board.

Whether this affected Ted Shaker's behavior or not is a matter of conjecture, but one thing is sure: John Campbell's relationship with his boss began to deteriorate.

"I could do nothing right," Campbell recalls. "He drove me up the wall."

Most humiliating to Campbell was Shaker's penchant for calling him into the office and then ignoring him. "Sometimes I could not even find out what was annoying him. When I would get up to leave, he'd say, 'No, sit there.' Then he'd turn his back on me and stare out the window." Things got so bad that on one such occasion the burly Campbell, who was an ex-Marine and twice Shaker's size, almost gave in to an impulse to seize him by the necktie, lift him off the ground and shake him like a rabbit. Though Campbell kept his self control, his blood pressure now began to rise dangerously. His doctors warned him to take a vacation or change jobs.

Dick O'Leary, who managed ABC's Chicago station, was also having personality conflicts with Shaker, despite the fact that he was doing a fine job. O'Leary had replaced Tom Miller, a Shaker loyalist who had tried desperately to manage the Chicago station precisely the way Shaker wanted it managed. After two years, Miller had grown disillusioned and resigned. O'Leary knew, of course, that his relationship with Shaker was going to be a "high decibel" one, because, "that's the only kind you can have with Ted." When O'Leary went to Chicago he told his wife that he figured he had security for "about two years," because Ted would have to wait that long before he could go to Siegel and say that he wanted to make still another management change in Chicago.

But in that two years much happened for O'Leary and it was all good. He began experimenting with a new format for local news, one that took an opposite approach to the establishmentarian methods of the other two network-owned stations in Chicago. O'Leary took his cue from the times. The world seemed to be coming apart in the late 'sixties. All societal values were being questioned. WLS-TV began experimenting with a more open, more contemporary approach to news. This format succeeded beyond all expectations and soon came to be called "Happy Talk" news. The format was parlayed, not only on to the other four ABC owned stations, but was adopted by ABC affiliates and other stations all over the country. The format has been criticized by news purists, but there is no doubt that it succeeded because O'Leary had properly evaluated the mood of the country at that time. WLS-TV, within two years, reached the top in ratings, news acceptance, and profits, so that, by 1968, Dick O'Leary was relatively safe in his job. Or, as he puts it, "As safe as anyone can ever be working for Ted Shaker."

O'Leary found Ted Shaker to be a fascinating study in character, so different from Elton Rule that it was like "walking from day into night."

At the same time he is quick to say that Ted Shaker was "bright, bright, bright!"

"He could glance at a rating book and get a pattern faster than just about anyone I know. He could identify problems, bring energy and effort in the short term better than anyone. His drive, his impatience, were qualities that I could understand and appreciate. But at the same time Ted was sadly lacking in his *people* relationships. In the long run, this became divisive and destructive. He was suspicious of everyone, trusted no one. He tired quickly of people, no matter how good they were. He created an environment of fear that is counter productive."

By the end of 1969, Shaker's frustration mounted to the breaking point. Something had to happen. His scenario had gone sour. He had been denied the "Mr. Broadcasting" title because the one man he had hoped would fail as the President of the network was succeeding. Shaker had been bypassed in favor of Rule for a position on the Board. His relationship with Si Siegel remained outwardly good because his Group was still performing as well as ever. But there were signs of strain even in that relationship. The gut in this tight bow of tension finally snapped in February of 1970, and the triggering mechanism was none other than John Campbell.

On a Tuesday in the first week of February, Campbell barged into Siegel's office and said two words:

"I quit!"

An astonished Siegel tried to calm Campbell, but it was no use. John's face was flushed, his jaw clenched.

"Si, I can't take it anymore. I can no longer work for Ted Shaker."

"What are the problems? Maybe we can straighten them out," said Siegel.

"There's only *one* problem and that's the man himself. He's got me up the wall so bad that my health has become involved. My doctor tells me my blood pressure is registering off the scale. I've talked it over with my wife and she agrees with me. If I'm going to live awhile longer I've got to get out of this job—like right now!"

Campbell's resignation made a profound impression on Si Siegel, especially since he had been the one who had fostered Shaker's career at ABC for the past 8 years. If John Campbell could not get along with Shaker, perhaps it was time to take a closer look at the entire situation. He tried again to get Campbell to reconsider.

"I'll stay as long as you want me to stay, until Ted finds another man," said Campbell. "But as for me, Si, I've had it! I'm going back to California to recover my health and my sanity."[3]

---

[3] John Campbell resigned effective March 13, 1970. He returned to the company in 1972 to head up ABC's Leisure Attraction Division and ABC's Entertainment Center in Hollywood, a position that he holds today.

On the heels of this unsettling event, Siegel was treated to another crisis. Shaker came in one afternoon to announce that he was going to fire another key executive: Donald W. Coyle, who headed ABC's International Division. Coyle had been its first President when the division had been formed in 1960. ABC International had not fulfilled the dreams the company had for it, but this had never been considered to be Coyle's fault. Changes in attitude by some 18 foreign countries with which ABC had dealt were the principal reason the division had been cut back in recent years. An increasing sense of nationalism in foreign countries, plus currency ratios and political factors mitigated against any resounding success by American companies in foreign media. Don Coyle, it had been assumed, was a solid executive, well-liked, earnest and hard-working. But Shaker had now soured on an executive who had been with the company for 20 years. Coyle was not a good business man, said Shaker, He must go. As to a replacement, Shaker had the "perfect guy," *another CBS executive!*

Siegel blanched at that. Every time Shaker went outside for executive help he seemed to come up with another CBS man! Siegel listened with growing disenchantment to Ted's recital of all Don Coyle's imperfections, and how much better a job his "close friend" from CBS would do. It was a melancholy experience for the Executive Vice President, and it would not be much fun explaining to the Board reasons why Ted Shaker wanted to replace yet another long-term ABC executive. If Ted had his way, he thought, there would eventually be no long-term people left.

Nevertheless Siegel did interview the new candidate, found him to be an impressive fellow who, no doubt, would do a good job. But that wasn't the question. Should Don Coyle really be fired after 20 years?

Shaker then left on a skiing vacation in Colorado, convinced that the matter had been settled and that the Board would approve the change on February 13, while he was gone.

Siegel began to have other ideas. Coyle had planned a trip to South America on business and pleaded that it would be embarrassing to the company to suddenly call off an important sales meeting he had planned for months. Siegel agreed and said Coyle could go. Shaker protested vehemently, saying why should Coyle go on such a trip when he was being fired.

Siegel overruled Shaker. "He isn't going to be fired, at least not until he makes that trip."

"But Si . . ."

"Forget it for the present."

Shaker stiffened. For the first time that he could remember, his boss was telling him he could no longer hire or fire as he pleased. "Si," he said, "we've already agreed that Coyle is being fired. I've already told Tom that he has the job."

Si Siegel sat there immutable and stony faced. He was not accustomed to being challenged this way. Shaker said something else:

"Si, if this change doesn't take place, I guess . . . you've got a problem with me."

Siegel looked at him. *No, you have a problem with me,* his eyes said. Shaker had pushed his luck too far. He was challenging the gray eminence of Si Siegel and was in danger of being hoist on his own petard. Yet Shaker had won all his battles in the past. It was inconceivable to him that he could lose this one. Siegel needed him. He felt he had Siegel's "number." But by now too many bodies had been buried. Ted Shaker had gone to the well once too often. The game was over.

"Yes, I guess you do have a problem with me," said Siegel in his guttural monotone. "Perhaps you'd like to settle this with Leonard."

An hour later Shaker met with Goldenson. After listening to the problem Goldenson called Siegel into the meeting. Shaker again recited the details that brought him and Siegel to such an impasse. Goldenson listened impassively and was of scant comfort.

"This is a matter between you and Si," he told Shaker.

"In that case I offer my resignation."

"Your resignation is accepted," said Simon B. Siegel.[4]

---

[4] Ted Shaker took a year off and travelled Europe with his family. Upon his return he accepted a job, which he holds today, as President of Arbitron, one of the industry's two major television rating services.

Thus ended the stormiest executive personnel battle within the ABC executive suite since the days of the Kintner-O'Brien dispute back in 1956. No longer was there any doubt about who would become "Mr. Broadcasting" within ABC.

The television industry has drawn eccentrics to it the way flowers draw bees. ABC had more than its share of characters and among these, Theodore (Ted) Shaker must surely occupy a place near the top of that list.

When his name is mentioned, even today at ABC, eyebrows are raised, quizzical looks are exchanged and half-smiles appear. Depending on whose gored ox you perform an autopsy on, Ted Shaker becomes a blessed saint or a bloody butcher.

Despite the high marks given him by some, there were others, like this author, who thought Ted Shaker was one of the more destructive and over-rated executives in the business. When it came to judging programs, news or entertainment personalities, public service campaigns or programs, his opinion was the kiss of death. If Shaker disliked a program or personality, that program or personality was usually sure to succeed. He was so locked into his own rigid notions of what he liked he never could accommodate his personal likings to those of the public. Since he had come from CBS, nothing could succeed unless it "looked like" something CBS might put on the air.

In the early sixties WABC-TV, New York, and Howard Cosell, produced several highly successful sports specials. Shaker disliked them and predicted their failure; *ergo* the public liked them and the critics hailed them.

In the turbulent sixties, when the world seemed to be coming apart at the seams, Shaker insisted that news personalities on ABC-owned stations wear identical blazers; their hair must not be too long; backgrounds of sets must be blue—all because that was the way CBS did it.

Shaker seldom was known to have an original idea. He was not an innovator. On the other hand, if research proved that he was wrong, or if a competitor did something worth copying, Shaker was quick and nimble in making adjustments. As a station manager himself, he would have been a failure.

Some thought Ted Shaker was Captain Queeg out of "Caine Mutiny." Others said he was Captain Bligh out of "Mutiny On The Bounty." Richard Beesemyer, another of his former CBS loyalists whom Shaker was about to fire as General Manager of WABC-TV shortly before Shaker himself walked the plank, said that Ted Shaker was great at "straightening pictures on the wall."

"He was loaded with hangups, internal problems, quirks . . . without them he could have been a real leader. But he destroyed himself."

That perhaps sums it up as well as anyone can sum up the riddle and puzzle of Ted Shaker. A man of brilliant mind, ineffably charming, as complex as any character in fiction, but too prone to "straighten pictures on the wall."

At any rate, after eight years ABC had cast off its last vestige of Shaker-induced CBS influence. CBS had been handed back its "piece of the Rock." As for the performance of the ABC-owned television stations, Dick O'Leary, who was an individualist in the true ABC maverick mold as much as Shaker was a conformist, not only matched Shaker's excellent record, but made it look somewhat pale by comparison. In the next eight years of O'Leary's regime, the ABC-owned stations increased Shaker's share of the 15 network stations revenue "pie" from 34% to an incredible share of more than 50%—which means that, in 1978, ABC stations were estimated to have made more than 100 million dollars profit, while the station groups of CBS and NBC made about 49 million dollars each.

ABC began to learn now that it was more fun, and more profitable to do their "own thing," in their own style, rather than to imitate others.

This realization, among other factors, also represented a turning point in the company's fortunes.

Part Four

Getting the
Act Together

13

Welcome
to the 'Seventies

TERE WAS NO LONGER any doubt about who would become "Mr. Broadcasting." The only question remaining was: how soon would it happen?

The announcement was not long in coming. On March 23, 1970, less than one month after Ted Shaker's resignation, Elton Rule was made President of all ABC broadcasting. He was nominated to the Board of Directors and continued as a Group Vice President along with two other Group VP's: Samuel H. Clark, in charge of all nonbroadcast operations; and Everett H. Erlick, General Counsel in charge of Washington affairs and corporate legal matters.

James E. Duffy, vice president of TV Network Sales since 1963, was elevated to President of the TV network.

I. Martin Pompadur was named vice president of ABC to "work closely with Rule in all operations."

While Rule still would report to Executive Vice President Simon Siegel, all broadcast divisions would report to Rule: ABC Sports; the owned television stations and radio stations; the radio network; ABC News; the television network; TV spot sales; ABC syndicated films; ABC International; Western Division operations; broadcast operations and engineering; ABC Public Relations; broadcast standards and practices; and ABC merchandising.

In addition, the week before, Richard A. O'Leary was named President of the five owned television stations; and Ellis O. Moore's television network public relations responsibilities were broadened to cover the entire broadcast division.

It was the most drastic realignment and consolidation in ABC's history and its implications within the company were far reaching. Despite this significant move the fact remained that after 15 years ABC still remained in third place. After 15 years of frantic peregrinations and determined effort, despite occasional flashes of success, the company still nestled securely, but uncomfortably behind NBC and CBS. It had to be a galling, chafing, and frustrating experience.

CBS still remained the undisputed leader. In the Foreword of this book I quoted a friend of mine who, in metaphor, described CBS as "a beautiful girl from the finest finishing school, but in your heart you know she's a whore." I asked that friend, Lester A. Weinrott, a veteran broadcaster, advertising man, and industry watcher, why he described CBS in that manner when, as far back as 1955, it was the pace-setter in the industry. Weinrott replied:

"By the late 'fifties, CBS indeed had its act together. A network must wear more faces than a pantominist. It has to be all things to all people. CBS definitely was not a whore in the public's eyes. It was a leader in news and public affairs. In terms of industry leadership it had the handsome, urbane and very capable Dr. Frank Stanton who represented the industry before Congress, and made statesmanlike speeches on issues. But CBS also had a Jim Aubrey who did the grubby work of making increasing sums of money with the less-than-classy entertainment schedule. In this regard he actually had a lower assessment of the U.S. television common denominator than did ABC or NBC. CBS thus performed a delicate balancing act, managing somehow to keep that part of its corporate personality a secret. It is in that sense that the 'whore' metaphor applies to CBS."

"How about NBC?" I asked.

"NBC always had to live in the shadow of mighty RCA. Because of that situation, because of the lack of clear-cut understanding and communicaiton between the two divisions, NBC, out of a sense of self-defense, has had to build layers of bureaucracy within its ranks as it tries to conform to RCA's notions and perceptions of how NBC should operate. Because of these layers, and the resultant committee style of operation, NBC finds it difficult to move quickly; to make the swift decisions that are endemic to the business. There are some who think that the technique of deniability was invented, not at the White House, but at NBC. And of course NBC was not helped by the ineffectual leadership of Robert Sarnoff for many years."

But my friend also agreed that all past assessments of NBC's style of management must now be ignored with Fred Silverman's appointment as President. With Silverman, NBC probably will never be the same. The question is: will Silverman get bogged down in the quicksand of NBC's entrenched bureaucracy?

"In some ways," Weinrott said, "changing NBC is going to be like changing the ways of the U.S. Post Office."

Maybe so. The real question with Silverman perhaps is not whether he can cut through the bureaucracy, but whether Silverman, after a couple of years, will grow bored or frustrated and suddenly ask himself the question: "What the hell am I doing here? This really isn't my bag."

But despite their differences in style, CBS and NBC at least had clear-cut and separate identities established by 1970. ABC did not. It was still considered a tag-along, "me too" network when in reality the opposite was true. ABC in its first 15 years was a flexible, sometimes recklessly innovative company. It plunged deeply into international television. It cracked the Hollywood program barrier. Its willingness to gamble on wild ideas like the four radio network concept marked it as a company willing to try anything. Yet, for some reason it was considered a network that followed and did not lead; a network that *reacted* to others; a network that stepped up to bat and always tried to hit that grand slam homer. It seemed to others to be inconsistent in purpose, unable to make up its mind about what kind of company it really wanted to be. In only one area, sports, had it fashioned a strong and unmistakable identity. In this area, both in concept and execution, it became the leader under Roone Arledge. In news, with the addition of Elmer Lower as chief executive, and with the acquisition of Harry Reasoner from CBS, and the expansion to a nightly thirty minute news show, it was making a serious bid for ascendancy.

Despite this, as of 1968 ABC was still searching for its identity, still trying to forge a sense of identity out of hard experience. But that identity was not yet delineated or articulated. Perhaps this was because the company was 25 years younger than its rivals. Its executive hierarchy was still young. Some corporations are like people who must learn everything the hard way; who cannot be told, but must experience everything first hand. ABC was such a company.

It also remained the butt of cruel humor. ABC, it was said, stood for the "*A*lmost *B*roadcasting *C*ompany." And: "If you want to stop the Vietnam War, put it on ABC—it'll be over in 13 weeks." Later, when Patty Hearst became a national figure, the jest went: "If you want to find Patty Hearst look for her on ABC's schedule on Saturday nights. That's where she'll be hiding."

Even ABC's shiny new skyscraper on the Avenue of the Americas came in for jibes. The building was rented, not owned. A candy store occupied space on the ground floor. Two blocks away stood the rather grim building which CBS had built as a monument to its own perceived image. It was called "Black Rock" and ABC was called "Schlock Rock," or "ABC's Candy Store," or "the crate the CBS building came in."

No one doubted, however, that ABC was eager to be the first to try anything. One ribald story that expressed the attitude of the three networks had to do with the fact that the three networks had been marooned on a deserted island. To their surprise they found there was a beautiful girl living on the island. The three networks decided it would be appropriate to make love to her. But who should go first?

ABC jumped up and said without hesitation: "I'll be first." With that ABC proceeded to ravish the beauty unashamedly in plain view of the other two networks.

When finished, CBS said he did not like being second to anyone, especially ABC, but he would also make love to the girl. However, CBS excused himself and took a walk to the other side of the island. When he returned he said to the girl, "I'll be next, but come with me to the other side of the island where we can have privacy."

After CBS returned it was NBC's turn. NBC said he was also anxious to make love to the girl. "But first," he said, "I've got to call New York and see what they say."

◇ ◇ ◇

Now that ABC finally had its "Mr. Broadcasting," the reaction within the company was one of enormous relief, not only because of Elton Rule's personal popularity, but because the long intra-company battle for power was over. It was a feeling of: "It's about time. Now maybe we can get our act together."

The company had made reasonable progress the preceding year. Net profits had reached a high of $16.7 million (versus CBS with well over 60 million). Martin Starger had replaced Leonard Goldberg as head of television network programing, and his efforts had already slightly improved ABC's third place standing. Elton Rule, the previous summer, had boldly declared that ABC was no longer going to be content with its cellar position:

"Morning, noon and night," he had told affiliates the previous June in San Francisco, "across the board in every time slot—against any competition, we have a single goal . . . we're going to win them all!"

Such flamboyant promises had been made in the past, Rule admitted; indeed this had been ABC's big fault—promising too much and delivering too little—but things were different now, Rule insisted. Because ABC had a well thought out plan; there would be consistent incremental progress from now on. Yet Dick Beesemyer, in charge of keeping affiliates on the team and persuading them to clear for programs, had to reach for the Excedrin bottle every time he looked at the clearance percentage for Friday nights. It was only 68%! His competitors goaded him. ABC, they said, was the "DB Network," meaning "Delayed Broadcast Network." They delighted in extolling ABC's lavish multi-media presentations which were made to affiliates. "There is only one problem," they told Beesemyer. "ABC's presentations are better than their programs!"

As far as the industry was concerned, in 1970 it was decidedly more paranoid than usual. Of course the broadcast business is always paranoid about its problems—but not without some justification. It is the most visible, most dominant, and most emotion-engendering medium of all. As an example, the year 1967 had actually been a poor year financially for the industry. Network television time sales dropped 1.4% for the first time in history, registering 609.6 million versus 616.7 million in 1966.

By contrast, 1968 was a much improved year. Network TV sales for the industry were up 4.5%. Yet *Broadcasting Magazine* logged 1968 as a "dark year full of paradoxes." It was a year, said the magazine, that was a "nightmare in which broadcasters were pilloried for allegedly provoking violence, and for almost all other happenings of a disturbing nature." Broadcasting concluded: "The unvarnished fact is that broadcasters are in a state of emergency."

But 1969 saw the industry's paranoia take a deeper plunge. For the first time, a major market· VHF television channel, WHDH-TV, Boston, lost its license after 25 years of FCC litigation. This, alarmists predicted, put 3 billion dollars worth of licenses "up for grabs." Nothing could have been farther from the truth, for the Boston case was strictly *sui generis*—one of a kind—born of a set of circumstances; and it can safely be predicted that another 25 years will pass before another major market TV station is taken away from present owners. The immediate fallout of the Boston case, however, was a rash of license challenges by those who naively believed that lightning can strike twice in the same place.

In addition, attacks came from another quarter. As *Broadcasting Magazine* put it, "Broadcast newsmen and TV-radio licensees were battered in 1969 by one of the worst storms of protest and criticism ever directed toward the media."

The catalyst in all this was the Nixon White House, and the spearhead in the well orchestrated campaign was Vice President Spiro Agnew who launched two major blasts in November of 1969, the most telling of which came in a speech in Des Moines. Agnew criticized the networks for having an eastern elitist bias and this speech was the forerunner of a year-long campaign to discredit television generally and its news policies specifically.

Television violence also came in for its share of attention. Senator Pastore became an "autumn friend" of the industry when he espoused a full scale probe by the U.S. Surgeon General into the causal connection between television violence and antisocial behavior. The assassinations in 1968 of Robert Kennedy and Martin Luther King had caused a national commission on violence to be formed and that group now indicated the networks for contributing to violence in America.

But the severest blow of all was to come in 1970 and that was one that would affect the industry's "bottom line." Before the end of that year, the industry would lose its desperate battle to retain cigarette advertising. There were not adjectives enough in the dictionary to describe the effect this had on the industry; but in crass dollars it came to a staggering $236 million!

Broadcasting Magazine grimly predicted: "Only an optimist would say we're headed for nothing worse than a recession."

Nevertheless, ABC could afford to be optimistic as 1970 began, because by mid-January, in the first week of the second season, ABC improved its Nielsen network ratings by four points over the preceding year: 19.7 for ABC versus 20 for CBS; and 22.4 for the then leader, NBC.

CBS, as usual, remained confident. Robert D. Wood, President of CBS network, said that CBS was going after its 15th consecutive year of prime time leadership; and the 16th year as the leader in daytime. The lead had narrowed considerably between the two leading networks, but there were few who doubted that

CBS would again win the ratings race for another year, although by a narrower margin than in the past.

Such were the conditions when Elton Rule took over the leadership of all ABC broadcasting in March of 1970.

◇   ◇   ◇

A peculiar psychology takes over in the executive suite whenever a major promotion occurs. A feeling of: *Well, that happened as it was expected to happen (or was not expected to happen), but now what next?* In other words, what does the latest promotion mean in terms of the future, and the very top management?

At ABC, the next upheaval would certainly involve the men at the very top: Simon B. Siegel. Leonard H. Goldenson. Or both.

Both men were 63 years of age. In two more years they would reach the age of mandatory retirement. However no one believed that either one would retire at 65. Goldenson could stay on at the pleasure of his Board, and there was little doubt that, if he gave the sign, the Board would give him that "pleasure." Siegel's continued service was a different situation. He would have to be "invited" by President Goldenson to stay on, but the general feeling was that this invitation would be forthcoming, since the two men worked so well together. In any event, both men had to at least be "thinking" about succession, and there was every likelihood that they would want to consider, if not retirement, some slowdown in the pace of their strenuous schedules.

The oddsmakers began to analyze the Rule promotion in terms of who would be the favorite candidate to become "heir apparent." Elton Rule certainly had to be considered such a candidate, insiders said. But there were others. Two in particular who had much going for them.

One was Everett Erlick, the smooth, sophisticated General Counsel of the company. Erlick had been on the Board since 1962, a Group Vice President since 1968. His domain was the tricky one of Washington politics, plus all legal matters of the company. He had handled his duties extraordinarily well. Under his hand ABC had never really lost a skirmish at the FCC. Erlick was increasingly becoming the visible spokesman for the company in issue-related matters that required a public stance. Erlick also had a solid background in advertising, having come to ABC from Young & Rubicam advertising agency back in the Ollie Treyz era. The network had then been an administrative mess and Erlick had been asked to come in and "tidy things up." His reputation had grown steadily since then and he was said to be held in high personal esteem by Goldenson himself. Ev Erlick also gave ABC a touch of class in that he was one of two members of Phi Beta Kappa in the top executive echelon. The other was the redoubtable Julie Barnathan.

The other candidate was Samuel H. Clark whose career was on the line this year as never before. Indeed, this year would be crucial for Clark if he was to continue to be a candidate for one of the two top jobs in the company. If 1970 turned out well he could, in fact, be the top candidate.

Clark had a domain as large as Rule's. He was in charge of all nonbroadcast operations of ABC. These included ABC's 434 theatres (owned outright and partially); ABC Records; two scenic attractions in Florida: Weekee Wachee and Silver Springs: ABC Marine World, an undersea exhibition located in Redwood City, near San Francisco; ABC's publishing operations, which consisted of three agricultural publications in Chicago, Des Moines, and Racine, Wisconsin.

Sam Clark was also a Group Vice President—had been since 1966. He had been elected to the Board in 1965. His reputation had been founded in 1955 when he launched ABC's record company.

Everything Sam Clark touched seemed to make a profit—at least the 20% pre-tax return on investment which Leonard Goldenson considered the minimum acceptable criterion for any enterprise ABC owned. The record company had made as high as 35% return on investment before taxes. In 1964 he was given command of ABC's theatre division. With the excellent help of Harvey Garland this division kept pace with the changing times.

Between 1965–68 marginal properties were divested. Some 150 new screens were built. ABC's management of its theatre portfolio was considered to be a model of efficiency in a declining business.

In 1966, Sam Clark was rewarded by being given command of all the company's nonbroadcast activities. In 1967 he had reached a conclusion that drastic steps had to be taken to meet the problem of dwindling supply of motion pictures. Distribution costs had risen from 35 to 47%. Some major studios had made colossal blunders in production. Twentieth Century Fox had written off 60 million dollars on "Cleopatra" and other pictures. Warners had taken similar losses. The lack of product badly hurt the theatre division. Sam Clark told Goldenson:

"We've got to meet this problem head on. We've got to get into theatrical production ourselves."

Leonard Goldenson not only agreed, but was even more enthusiastic than Clark. CBS had announced that it, too, was going into the production of feature films. And CBS owned no theatres. Certainly ABC had every reason to enter the field.

The announcement in 1967 caught the industry by surprise. How could ABC, in the face of its consent decree two decades ago, dare to make its own pictures? No one had bothered to look at the fine print in that consent decree; but the language clearly permitted then-UPT, now ABC, to produce motion pictures, not for its exclusive benefit, but for general distribution to the industry. Goldenson was proud of that victory with the Justice Department, and his stubborness on this point had delayed the final consent decree by several months.

Now, in 1970, Sam Clark's theatrical efforts were well under way. Two subsidiaries, Selmur Productions, headed by Selig Seligman, and Palomar Pictures, headed by former motion picture agent Martin Baum, were turning out pictures at an impressive rate. The first, "For Love of Ivy," starring Sidney Poitier, was released in 1968. Several others followed: "Candy," starring Richard Burton, Marlon Brando, and Ringo Starr; "Shalako," with Sean Connery and Brigitte Bardot; "The Killing of Sister George," produced by Robert Aldrich.

Seven more pictures were slated for release in 1970. Sam's old contract had been torn up in 1968; a new one written for $100,000 per year, plus deferred compensation, and a term that would expire at the end of 1973.

So Sam Clark, as the seventies began, was riding high. All other elements of his extensive division seemed to be flourishing. When it came to listing candidates for top management succession, Sam Clark's name had to be high on the list.

◇   ◇   ◇

Another hallmark of the new decade concerned radio. *FM radio.* 1970 would go down as the year that AM radio's poor cousin would finally come out of the closet and come into its own. By February of that year, FM stations in six major markets (Boston, Philadelphia, New York, Phoenix, Washington D.C., and Houston) were at least even, or ahead, of their AM counterparts.

This progress had not come quickly or easily, but was a slow, painful evolution dating back to the early sixties. ABC characteristically wanted to be the first kid on the block to demonstrate its FM know-how. It became the first of the three networks to set up its own FM division entirely divorced from AM. Separate studios, staffs, cost centers, and call letters were established. A young man of 28, named Allen B. Shaw, was placed in charge. He was brimming with ideas. Why not create an indigenous service aimed at the counter-culture youth market—at those freaky young people who dared dream that the world could, and should, be a better place? The sound would be progressive rock, of course, built around local live personalities. All live with the exception of a two-hour taped talk show. "Let's let it all hang out," said young Shaw.

ABC agreed. By mid-year the new policy was off and running, somewhat to the consternation of the ABC Board, some stockholders, and a few members of top management. ABC's new FM "sound" ripped America's establishment to pieces in music, song, lyrics, and dissident oratory. America's young "new morality" would set the country free. Studios were acrid with the fumes of pot. Psychedelic drugs inspired performers. Free wheeling disc jockeys with long hair, beards, jangling beads, told America where it should go.

At first the underground press did not "buy" the act. They found it incredible that one of the three establishment networks could be sincere in allowing such freedom to reign. ABC's AM rock and roll stations, they said, consisted of "utter exploitation"; ABC's FM stations were involved in "controlled exploitation." But gradually the youth press turned around and supported the new sound. ABC, with a record of conservatism in the past, suddenly found itself the favorite network of the spaced-out hippie culture.

The young new FM division had its finest hour on Independence Day of 1970. The three AM networks that day presented 5½ hours of "straight" entertainment starring such celebrities as Bob Hope, Dinah Shore, and Red Skelton. Bill Greeley, in a classic story in *Variety*, labeled it "Honor American Day"—"HAD."

But ABC's WPLJ-FM that day, presented an hour-long special program called "Self Evident Truths"—"SET," which it ran four times on the Fourth of July. Greeley wrote:

"There are two nations, the TV Nation, and the Radio Nation. And they are as far apart as Abbie Hoffman's Woodstock Nation and Judge Hoffman's Chicago Nation." The polarity was perfectly exemplified by the way the two electronic media celebrated Independence Day.

"The Radio Nation," wrote Greeley, "had skilled performers and a shock value in its forcefully articulate dissident stance that the big show (on the TV Nation) thoroughly lacked."

How odd it was, he mused, even inexplicable, that ABC had, on the one hand, its TV network which was "pegged as the Agnew web (for its conciliatory news posture)," and on the other hand its FM stations were making "the strongest kind of anti-administration statement."

A week late Greeley wrote that, while Metromedia was in the vanguard of the militant dissent movement on radio, ABC was really the company that puzzled him. "ABC believes that the best answer to the increasing polarity between American TV and radio audiences is a schizoid programming policy." He doubted that the policy would work, but regarded it as a most curious phenomenon, one to be closely watched to determine its outcome.

ABC's brass were watching, too. Some of them preferred to forget that the daring format even existed. Mounting financial losses added to the anguish of Hal Neal, ABC's overall radio boss, who had backed Allen Shaw. But Neal was a veteran pro and knew that fresh formats do not always catch on quickly. And some do not catch on at all. He had personally earned his spurs by turning *two* ABC AM stations around—in Detroit and New York, and he had the patience to back Allen Shaw all the way. To the credit of top management Neal was never pressured to change or cancel the format. Not even on the memorable day in Detroit when Elton Rule and his top aide, Martin Pompadur, decided to pay a surprise visit on their FM station.

The two had difficulty in finding the studio. It was located in a poor section of town and was housed, not in a building, but in a trailer! When Rule opened the door he saw a collection of debris that looked unlike any radio station he had ever seen. To make matters worse, a huge German Shepherd dog leaped out and bit him on the leg! The dog's owner, a spaced-out disc jockey, congratulated his dog for doing his duty and told ABC's President that visitors were not allowed in the trailer! Rule and Pompadur beat a hasty retreat.

A few weeks later the two execs were in Chicago and decided to try their luck again. They would drop in unannounced on the Chicago FM station. At least it was located in a downtown office building.

The scene that greeted their eyes was one they would not soon forget. Elton Rule is a tall, handsome fellow with ramrod erect posture, impeccably dressed and with the face and manner of a semi-benevolent Marine Major. Marty Pompadur looks like a Marine Captain who could also be Rule's first cousin. They stepped into a conference room where they saw, sitting around the table, a group of half-dressed staff members slumped in chairs, smoking illegal cigarettes and gazing serenely into space. The air was blue and pungent. The program director glanced benignly at his two New York visitors and offered them a "joint." Rule declined, tried to say something hip, like, "No thanks, I just put one out," and again the two beat a hasty retreat. They decided that the less they knew about Allen Shaw's FM stations the better off they'd be. In fact they visited no more FM stations that year.

"Maybe," said Rule to Pompadur, "if we just pretend we have no FM stations they'll just go away."

All radio formats, alas, must stand on their "commercial legs." To the dismay of Allen Shaw, Hal Neal, and the underground press, the hippie format had no commercial legs.

By July of 1971, after two rating books had come out, the rating were lower than they had ever been. The youth culture simply was not interested in such a far-out format. Maybe they had heard it all before and were beginning to seek other sounds, other ideas. Shaw and his innovative program expert, Rick Sklar, came up with a new one, a structured play list of "controlled progressive rock," and the ratings climbed quickly. The only criticism came, predictably, from the underground press, which charged that ABC was "selling out." The *Village Voice* said that ABC had been intimidated by the FCC.

Nothing was farther from the truth. The wildest FM experiment in radio history simply had not attracted enough listeners. But no one could accuse of ABC of not trying. In retrospect, the experiment brings back fond memories to Allen Shaw. And some disillusionment, too:

"The jocks were hypocrites," he recalls. "They were more gung ho to improve their wallets than they were to improve society. They were kids from middle class, or wealthy, families; a part of the disillusioned generation that had everything, but were looking for something else. However, looking back at what was later to come—like Watergate—I think history has proved them to be more right than wrong. So perhaps we should be grateful for the signals they sent us."

Elton Rule has since developed a slight aversion to German Shepherd dogs. As for Marty Pompadur, his brief encounter with the sub-culture would stand him in good stead when he became deeply immersed in ABC's record company two years later.

As for ABC, the paradox of the FM experiment, contrasted with the conservatively tabbed television network ("Agnew Network") is worth examining in a later chapter dealing with ABC News.

Allen Shaw continued his stewardship of the FM division and was rewarded in 1976 when he was named President of the division, which, like its AM counterpart, is by all odds, and all criteria, considered to be the most successful FM division in broadcasting today.[1]

---

[1] ABC FM owned stations are: WPLJ, New York; WRIF, Detroit; WDAI, Chicago; KAUM, Houston; KSFX, San Francisco; KLOS, Los Angeles; WRQX, Washington, D.C.

14

"All Humans Have Taken Nature for Granted"

FOR THE BROADCAST INDUSTRY, 1970 lived up to the predictions made for it: "A dismal experience." U.S. corporate profits fell by 9–10%, and in the knee-jerk reaction that always follows, advertising budgets were trimmed accordingly. Total television revenues amounted to 3.2 billion, a gain of 4.2%, considerably below the 11% gain registered the year before.

"Now we can admit," said Richard Doherty, a respected economic consultant for the communications business, "that 1970 was a true recessionary year." The economy, he said, "may get out of the 1970 valley, but only part way up the mountain."

ABC avoided the economic shoals in decent fashion that year, and managed to equal the 16.7 million profits before taxes that were made in 1969. But if one subtracted capital gains and non-recurring losses or gains, the year-end profit came only to $15.9 million.

In general terms, the company made respectable progress. The television network improved its ratings; most notable was the long-time franchise it established on Monday nights with professional football. The addition of Harry Reasoner as co-anchor man with Howard K. Smith strengthened ABC News. The five owned television stations, under Dick O'Leary, began a spectacular rise in profits and ratings, catalyzed chiefly by the success ABC was having with its informal, highly personalized format of *Eyewitness News*. In radio, the four network concept finally broke even. Performance in nonbroadcast areas was satisfactory with the exception of the adventure in theatrical production. Three of seven feature films were written off as losses, but there were high hopes riding on another half dozen films that would be released in 1971.

The outlook for 1971, however, was another matter. It definitely was not good. If not grim, it surely was not sanguine. Cigarette revenues were to disappear on January 2. The economy generally was expected to continue soft. On the plus side, there was the acceptance by all three networks of the thirty second spot which would open the medium up to many new advertisers. Of particular benefit to ABC would be the FCC mandated introduction, in the fall of 1971, of the "prime time access" rule which would result in the reduction of some 500 hours per year of network production. This meant a cost saving of some 60 million per year to the three networks. NBC and CBS vowed to exhaust every legal remedy to bring about the demise of this one year test, but ABC quietly, and gratefully, supported the ruling.

Retrenchment became a password among the three networks as the year began. ABC, as usual, made headlines in this area long before its rivals. In February word leaked out that 300 of its 15,000 employees were being laid off. Ironically the news came the same week that ABC had some startling news via the national Nielsen ratings. For the week of January 18–24, ABC outrated CBS and NBC and placed five of its entertainment programs in the "top ten." (ABC—21.3; NBC—21.2; CBS—20) This sudden, but only temporary surge, stung CBS. The mood at "Black Rock" grew more somber a few days later, when William Paley ordered a 15% cut in budget.

Coming up soon would be ABC's annual meeting of stockholders. At best, Leonard Goldenson looked upon these meetings as ordeals; he looked forward to this year's meeting with the same enthusiasm with which one faces a bout with flu. The first two quarters were running behind the previous year. The company was closing the ratings gap, but any financial benefits from this would not show until next year. Lawrence Welk's program had been cancelled after 15 consecutive years and this had evoked a storm of viewer protests. He expected tough questions from stockholders over that matter. In addition the motion picture losses were increasing far beyond expectations. "Lovers And Other Strangers," and "Song Of Norway" were doing okay, but "Last Valley" was a bomb. Still, Sam Clark had high hopes for five other pictures that were scheduled for release later in the year. They were: "The Touch"; "The Grissom Gang"; "Kotch"; "Straw Dogs"; and "Cabaret." Goldenson, with his experienced eye for successful films, held out little hope that any of them would be the kind of blockbusters that ABC needed to save its theatre division from utter disaster.

So on May 18 when the annual meeting was called to order in the ABC large studio on 66th Street, Leonard Goldenson had reason to be unhappy. In addition, he did not look well. He had ample reason for not looking well. The simple fact was: he was exhausted. His schedule the preceding fortnight was one that would have exhausted a conditioned young athlete.

Two weeks before, he had flown to Denver and spent four days and nights in meetings on behalf of United Cerebral Palsy. At the end of that week, on Saturday, he had returned to New York—not to go home, but to stop off on his way to Europe. At Kennedy Airport his secretary took two hours of business dictation between planes. Then it was on to Stockholm. Despite the eight hours difference in time between Denver and Stockholm he plunged at once into conferences with Ingmar Bergman, who was doing his first English language picture for ABC Pictures entitled "The Touch," starring Elliot Gould.

Then he went on to Munich where he held more conferences with Cy Feuer who was producing "Cabaret," starring Liza Minnelli and Joel Gray. The picture was a joint venture between ABC and United Artists.

With virtually no sleep, he flew to London for another two

days of meetings with Dan Melnick who was producing "Straw Dogs," starring Dustin Hoffman. Finally, after almost two weeks of 18-hour days, and little sleep, compounded by jet lag, Goldenson returned to New York on Saturday morning. Instead of closing out the world and getting some rest, he played several sets of tennis in the afternoon because tennis was something he did every Saturday and he was a creature of habit.

On Sunday, one would think that any allegedly sensible 65-year-old man would surely have rested, but no, Leonard Goldenson did nothing of the kind. The annual meeting of shareholders was scheduled for the following Tuesday. He had a lot of "homework" to do to prepare for the meeting. So he convened a number of his staff at his home on *both* Saturday and Sunday to prepare for the annual meeting.

Hence, on Tuesday, May 18 the wonder of it seemed to be, not that Goldenson looked tired, but that he had managed to get there at all! Somehow he got through the meeting without too much difficulty. He turned on his broad smile, psyched himself up to almost his full level of enthusiasm, and answered difficult questions from the audience. The Lawrence Welk fans were every bit as indignant as he had expected. Yes, he admitted, stringent cost saving measures had been put into effect. When would the economy improve? He did not know. Yes, it was true the record company's earnings were not up to those of the preceding year. Theatre operations were also running at a lower rate than the year before, and he regretted that this would probably continue throughout the rest of 1971. As for theatrical production he drew a gasp of surprise when he said that, effective July 1, 1970, "We reduced our budget for the production of new pictures, and we expect this reduction to continue for the year beginning July 1, 1971."

Sam Clark, who was there, smiled and pretended he had not heard. Sam had high hopes that "Cabaret" could equalize past losses and vindicate his judgment. In the volatile picture business it only took one hit to "make everyone well."

There were probing questions from astute stockholders about the financial report; about programing. Why was *Dark Shadows* cancelled? ("A decline in audience levels.") Why were so many programs repeated? ("Economics of the business dictate the practice, although we do introduce some new programs during the summer rerun season.")

How about children's programs? Violence? When will dividends be increased? How often does the Board meet? Why do Board members hold so little stock in ABC? . . . On and on. Facing stockholders at an annual meeting can take on all the aspect of an inquisition.

Finally, bone weary, but still smiling, Leonard Goldenson wished them all good luck and said he hoped to see them again next year. Same time, same place.

Maybe.

For, a few days after the annual meeting, Leonard Goldenson was struck down by a heart attack.

◇   ◇   ◇

Si Siegel and Elton Rule heard the news on a Saturday morning. Goldenson, they were told, was in Harkness Pavilion of the Columbia Presbyterian Medical Center. Dr. Dana Achley was attending the patient. The prognosis, as is always the case in the first hours, was guarded. However the patient was resting well and not in discomfort. The first 48 hours usually tell the story. The press was told that the coronary was "mild." Goldenson's excellent physical condition and remarkable stamina would probably pull him through. Physical exercise had always been something of a fetish with him. Though short in stature he had played basketball in high school on a team that had won the Pennsylvania state championship. His tennis game was considered far above the average for a man of his age. He was diet conscious, did not smoke, and only on the rarest of occasions ever took a sip of wine.

By the end of the first week Dr. Achley was able to assure family and friends that the patient was making a remarkable recovery, although there would have to be a prolonged recuperation period at home. After three weeks in the hospital, he was permitted to begin a strict regimen of rest at his home. And perhaps, Dr. Achley suggested, it was time for Leonard Goldenson to take a good look at his life and his schedule. Two weeks of sleepless conferences in various parts of the world, was clearly idiotic for a man of his age. Goldenson ruefully admitted that he had been pushing too hard. His own reaction to the attack had been one of shock and astonishment that something like this could happen to him. "I should have been able to pace myself better," he realized. He promised that, yes, from now on things would be different. He would begin to live as though he were as mortal as the next man.

But after a few weeks at home his restless nervous energy returned and he began "climbing the walls." Goldenson is not the philosophical or contemplative type. He is strictly a man of action. His mind must have problems to solve. He likes to read, but reading alone is not enough. Nor is television or movies; or conversation. Goldenson was not an exemplary patient. He called the office daily, involved himself in major decisions just as though he were on the scene. He admitted he was a bad patient, but added plaintively, "I can't stand having nothing to do."

His wife, Isabelle, bore the brunt of her husband's impatience. She grew nervous herself watching him pace the floor, tense with boredom. One day she came up with a sudden idea:

"Why don't you paint?" she asked.

Goldenson looked at her. "Paint what?" The house was in no need of paint. Besides that would be too strenuous.

"I mean paint like an artist paints."

"Me? You must be crazy. I have no talents in that direction."

"How do you know unless you try? Judge Davis says anyone can paint if they make up their mind to try."

He remembered a visit recently to his friend, State Supreme Court Justice Erwin Davis. An oil painting had been propped on an easel in a corner. "Who did that?" Goldenson had asked.

"I did. I'm taking up painting," the judge explained.

"You?"

"Of course."

"I can't believe you did that, Judge."

"Well, I did it. I study each week with Alton Tobey."

Goldenson admired the still life and Davis added, "Leonard, that's something you ought to try."

"Me?" Goldenson laughed. "That's the last thing I could ever do. I don't have any talent."

"How do you know until you try?"

That visit had been a week ago. Now Isabelle was telling him the same thing the Judge had said. It sounded like a conspiracy.

"I'm going to buy you some paints," she said. He laughed at her. "Honey, you are absolutely out of your mind if you think I could ever paint!"

Isabelle Goldenson is as determined as her husband. Something in his voice told her that he *might* just try . . . A few days later, she surprised him with a set of quick drying acrylic paints plus brushes, canvas and all the paraphernalia required by a budding amateur artist.

"Now," she said, "go out to the garden and *paint!*"

Goldenson did as he was told. He worked for several hours and returned holding a colorful splash with impressionist overtones which, he said, rather horrified him. On the bottom was the inscription: "If this is my contribution to art—poor art!"

Isabelle praised the effort. At least for a few hours her husband had been totally distracted from his boredom. He admitted, too, that for those few hours he had been able to "shut the world out." From that time on he became a dedicated amateur artist. Like his friend Judge Davis, he began to take lessons from the noted Alton Tobey in Larchmont. Şince 1971 Goldenson has created an impressive body of work. He has painted more than fifty large canvases which have been exhibited in the Palm Springs Desert Museum and elsewhere. His work tells much about himself—insights that could not be revealed in any other manner. His work has evolved from nostalgic memories and still lifes to personal communications. He now insists on trying to "make a statement." He has chosen to depict the lesser streets of New York in all their grim squalor. One sees vendors, derelicts, and prostitutes—somewhat reminiscent of the photographic documents of New York by the famous Weegee.

Leonard Goldenson paints with vitality. He likes to paint

people. He is prone to bright, vivid colors. He is better with people than with still lifes. His scenes invariably say something about man, his environment, the human condition. In Goldenson's gallery one will see the spiritually disenfranchised, the homeless, the lonely; their condition often magnified, or contrasted, by the magnificence of Manhattan's skyline, or a backdrop of opulent luxury. One of his favorites is a man walking along a New York street passing a pile of garbage that stands taller than himself. The plastic bags of rubbish look more like jewels as they glisten in the afternoon sun. Behind the man looms a modern skyscraper. On the street next to the garbage lays an empty box that bears the label: "Tiffany & Co." Goldenson obviously was impressed at one time by a New York garbage strike; but he is trying to say something more:

"Here is man, with all of his accomplishments; yet he is in danger of being engulfed by his own garbage."

In another painting, labelled "Geriatric Set," Goldenson shows a group of elderly people all dressed up but with no place to go.

"They are still eager for companionship," he explains. "But they don't know where to find it. They have nothing to do. There is a loneliness in their eyes. It is pathetic that they cannot find something more important to do with their lives than sit on a park bench in Central Park . . . some way to make a contribution. If we don't have a feeling that we are *contributing something* . . . all the meaning goes out of our lives."

When Goldenson was pleased enough with his art to no longer keep it a secret, he wrote a letter to his 90-year-old mother in Florida. That letter reveals much about the man, and is worth repeating here:

"I guess my heart attack on May 28, 1971 really changed my attitude. One day, in July, after I had returned to our home, Isabelle brought me a painting kit and said that I really ought to try my hand at it. Rather reluctantly, I went down to the golden deck of our house, from where I could see the small pool, some of the bushes and flowers. And I tried to paint what I saw. Frankly, it was a miserable attempt as you can see from the copy of what I did—it's the first one in the album. And it made me more convinced than ever that I wasn't a latter-day Picasso, Andrew Wyeth or even a male Grandma Moses.

"But by October, faced with the boredom of not being able to play tennis on weekends, because of orders from the doctor, I realized that I should be doing something to occupy my mind and my time. And, much to my surprise, I finally decided to try to paint. I called Judge Davis and arranged to meet him on a Saturday morning in order to take lessons from Alton Tobey. In the album I have enclosed a photograph of each painting I have made since then, in progressive order, if one can call it progress.

"I am now an ardent, if amateur painter and find it extremely fascinating and exciting. In attempting to analyze my involvement, there are, I think, three reflections that stand out in my mind at the present time. They are:

"1. I now look at objects with a completely different point of view. I look at them from a color standpoint; how they relate to each other, and what impact the sun may make on an object in the sense that it reflects reds and yellow, that it might not do so on a dark day. I look at other objects which reflect the blue sky without the sun and the impact it makes after such reflection. As an example, I always thought the bark of a tree was grayish black or brown, but in the sunlight, if you look closely, you can also see reds and yellows.

"2. I find tremendous excitement in trying to mix colors. As an example, one may paint a tree where the leaves are naturally green. At the time you select the green, you may feel you are absolutely right in that color selection, but then when you relate that green to the other objects in the painting, you see the green you have selected has changed compared with the other colors, and you have to go back and re-evaluate the green you originally picked.

"I suppose all humans have taken nature for granted and I probably more than anyone. But now I watch flowers and trees and their relationship to each other, so that, in the back of my mind, I am building up a storehouse of knowledge I should have started 40 or 50 years ago.

"3. I have always taken objects for granted without determining their exact proportions or exact peculiarities. For example, when it came to painting coconuts, or coconut trees, I thought I knew their shape and color but I had never observed enough to be sure of their exact shape or color. I had to work from a picture of these objects. Now I hope I will be able, in the future, to paint objects, their shapes and dimensions, etc. from previous knowledge, without consulting pictures of them.

"In my first painting, which is an apple and plum, and which I did under Alton Tobey's direction, I attempted to relate size as well as color to each other. I found in drawing a plate that, if I had remembered my elementary math, it would have been easier, but I never related it to painting.

"When Alton Tobey pointed out that I had done this in grade school, I immediately said what a dunce I had been in not reacting to other things in life other than the math course at that time. In other words, painting does cause one to open one's eyes to things around one.

"I started on fruit and you can read in the back of the painting an explanation of what I hoped to accomplish in that particular attempt. After finishing some fruit, I started on scenes, the first of which is a scene in Japan and the second in Ireland. Both were taken from post cards.

"I am now moving on to humans but, as Alton Tobey properly said, I should only do one person at a time because there is a required knack in painting an individual human face and body before you relate each person to the other. Being a gambler, I painted a photograph we had taken in Martinique, over the Memorial weekend. Although the faces are not a true image of either Isabelle or myself, it did teach me a lot from which I will profit in the next painting. The scene in Martinique is reasonably good and reflects the real background in the snapshot.

"Foolish as it may sound, I find that after I finish each painting, even though it is not very good, I will say, 'Did I do that?'

With the full realization that one is very amateurish in one's approach, it does give one a strong urge to discipline oneself to do something better. Accordingly, when I learn more about painting humans (in a very superficial way, of course) I intend to paint animals (horses, dogs, cats) and then get into the depth of painting flowers.

"So, as my endeavors unfold, I hope you will follow the development of a *young* artist whose desire it is to put on canvas what pleases and fascinates him, who hopes that he will be able to develop enough confidence in himself and his work eventually to embark on doing something in his own style, whatever that may be."

◇   ◇   ◇

As of this writing Leonard Goldenson's mother is still alive. She is more interested in her son's development as a "young" artist than his business career. After all, he has already achieved success in that field. This is something new. Her son is now an *artist!*

15

Who's On First?

On January 17, 1972, Elton Rule was appointed President and Chief Operating Officer of American Broadcasting Companies, Inc. This was the final event in a string of events that were triggered by Leonard Goldenson's heart attack.

After chafing under several months of forced inactivity by doctor's orders, Goldenson knew that, for him, retirement was out of the question. A condition to be abhorred and ignored. At the same time he was willing to accept the fact that he must make some kind of adjustment in his lifestyle. He must let go some of the reins yet still retain the challenge of overall responsibility for ABC.

The company, as of that time, had no chairman. President Goldenson had purposely left that title vacant, thinking that one day he might assume that title himself and pass the Presidency on to Simon Siegel or someone else.

Now that time had apparently come. But what kind of chairmanship would he fill: active or inactive? After three months of convalescence he was bursting with nervous energy; he knew that the chairmanship role he would recommend to the Board would be one in which he would remain as chief executive officer, while the newly appointed President would become chief operating officer.

Having made that decision, the next question was: who should be the President? Si Siegel was the nominal and logical choice for that job, but Goldenson's heart attack had set off a chain reaction in Siegel's mind culminating in his decision to retire. This came as a distinct shock to many. There were those who believed then, and believe to this day, that Siegel was bitter over the fact that he had never been appointed President; that he had hoped to become President for at least the final year of his career—the year in which Goldenson suffered his heart attack; and that he was still further disappointed that Goldenson did not urge him to remain active beyond sixty-five.

None of these stories are true. At least both men swear that they are not true, Siegel, according to Goldenson, *was* urged to remain after retirement age. "I wanted very much to have Si stay on," says Goldenson. "We wanted him to become vice-chairman of the company with Elton Rule reporting to him. But Si insisted on retiring."

As for a successor, both Siegel and Goldenson were in full agreement that there was only one logical candidate for the job and that was Elton Rule.

Sam Clark's chances had diminished greatly in the wake of increasing losses in the motion picture division. By mid-year they still were mounting with estimates that the total losses incurred by the two producing entities, Selmur Pictures Corporation and Palomar Pictures International, Inc., would reach as high as $40 million. In addition, the President of Selmur, Selig Seligman, had died of a heart attack earlier in the year. All future picture production had recently been cancelled. After some thirty pictures ABC was writing off the experience and Sam Clark's career had been seriously damaged as a result.[1]

---

[1] The decision by ABC to abandon theatrical film production was aided by the fact that certain elements of the broadcast industry filed an antitrust suit against the company.

As for Everett Erlick, his strength and value to the company had not diminished in the least; but it seemed illogical to switch Erlick from an area where he was invaluable, into a line position where Rule had already gained the necessary experience and had proven himself. The logical thing to do with Erlick was to keep him where he was; make him senior vice-president of the corporation; continue to benefit from his long experience and sound judgment. Furthermore, if Erlick were moved into the senior line operating role, who would replace Erlick?

So, as 1971 wound down, Elton Rule remained the only logical candidate for the Presidency.

The third event was triggered by Si Siegel's announcement of his retirement. Goldenson appealed to him to remain, and offered Siegel the position of vice-chairman of the company with full operating responsibilities as before. Siegel said, no, he had been doing a lot of thinking since his friend's heart attack. The two men were the same age (Siegel being three months younger than Goldenson). The time had come to "hang it up." "If I were vice chairman," said Siegel, "it would be my nature to tell Elton what to do, when really he's qualified to do it without me. If I stayed on it wouldn't be fair to him." Goldenson reluctantly accepted Siegel's decision, but not until he extracted a promise from his longtime associate to remain on the Board; more importantly, to remain on the five man Executive Committee that reviewed and approved all major expenditures and policy decision.

The question now was Rule himself. Would Rule accept the increased responsibility? Did he really want it? Elton Rule, in all

---

Many of ABC's theatrical films were critical as well as boxoffice successes and are still producing revenue; hence the 40 million loss estimate may be too high. ABC films were made in the budget range of 2½ million dollars, although some went much higher. Biggest hits were "Cabaret," "Charly," "Lovers and Other Strangers," "Straw Dogs," and "For Love of Ivy." Production was divided about evenly between the two producing companies.

The two biggest boxoffice disasters were made with budgets of 6–8 million dollars. They were: "The Last Valley," an epic drama about the Thirty Years' War starring Michael Caine and Omar Sharif; and "Hell in the Pacific," starring Lee Marvin and Toshiro Mifune. Sam Clark believes that, if it had not been for these two "disasters," the theatrical film division would have been self-sustaining.

his years with the company, had exhibited a curious kind of independence. He never seemed to be over-eager for any job. At times he appeared downright disinterested. On more than one occasion he piqued Siegel with his semi-facetious remarks about how little it would take for him to return to his beloved California.

Several times during the fall of 1971 Siegel cautiously explored the matter with Rule. "How would you feel, Elton, if the top job were suddenly placed in your lap?"

And: "I just may decide to retire next year. You know where that would place you?"

Rule was usually as diffident as Siegel was wary. These thrusts and parries became a little game between them: Siegel dangling the golden carrot and Rule ignoring it by saying, in effect: I don't know how I'll react. Try me and see.

In December Siegel held a more serious conversation with Rule. As usual, the latter fended the matter off. Siegel persisted.

"Look, I'm serious. Let's stop kidding around."

"Who's kidding?"

"I want to know the answer."

"What answer?"

"Would you like to be the President of this company?"

Rule frowned. These hypothetical questions about some distant future annoyed him. "Si, we've gone over this before."

"I know we have. But I need some answers."

"What kind of answers?"

"Reassurances."

"What kind of reassurances?"

"I want to know if you will pledge your life to ABC and stay here in New York—you talk so much about going back to California I never know if you're kidding or serious—I need answers because, I'm telling you, this definitely could happen . . ."

Rule shrugged his shoulders. "I've heard all this before. If this is supposed to happen, tell me, just *when* is it *going* to happen?"

Siegel's face remained an inscrutable, almost Oriental mask. At moments like this, one thought that he had missed his calling.

He should have been the U.S. representative across the negotiating table from Russia's Molotov. Then he said:

"Would next month be too soon?"

"Next *what?*"

"Next month. January. I plan to announce my retirement on January 11, to become effective two months later, April 7, so I can qualify for some stock options that come due by then. I will remain on the Board and on the Executive Committee. A week later, on January 17, Leonard will announce you as President. He will become Chairman and remain chief executive officer. You become the chief operating officer and will also go on the Executive Committee."

A slow grin spread over Siegel's face as he enjoyed Rule's look of amazement. Finally, he thought, he had broken through Elton Rule's famous "cool." "Do you believe it now?" he asked. "Is that soon enough for you? Or would you like it done tomorrow? If so we can probably arrange that." Siegel laughed. For once Elton Rule had no reply.

◇   ◇   ◇

Reaction to the Rule appointment was generally favorable. *Variety* magazine said that under the new chain of command ABC would become "the least topheavy and bureaucratic of the three network corporations, and managerially the most informal."

ABC division presidents now would deal directly with the top, whereas CBS "continues to increase its layers of management, while NBC tends to favor a hierarchy of committees."

Regarding the new President, *Variety* said, "a new era" was now in the offing. One that would be marked by the company's projection of a "new, more glamorous, and more assertive personality."

"Siegel," said *Variety*, was "a most able administrator, an introverted leader who avoided public view and was scarcely known outside the ABC executive suites. Rule, on the other hand, has attributes of the politician—a coolness and savvy sociability—and looks straight out of Central Casting . . . He is an apotheosis of the TV sales exec who went all the way up—suave, likeable and quietly forceful. Moreover he has the glow of a winner."

Rule's ascendancy occurred four years to the week since he had come to New York in 1968. He had earned his spurs in the rough and tumble crucible that was uniquely ABC's *modus operandi*. He had walked that thin, narrow line that separates success from disaster. And, just as Simon Siegel had put his imprint indelibly on the company for a decade, now Elton Rule would do the same—in a year that was "hedged with optimism"; and a decade that, despite turmoil, had no other way to go but up.

◇   ◇   ◇

The broadcast business cannot exist without rumors. They are the oxygen support system for actual survival. Without rumors most broadcasters would wither away and die. They are also a function of the high degree of insecurity, the pervasive state of paranoia that are endemic to the business.

By mid-1972, the rumors about ABC were relatively good for a change. The company was doing well financially. Other than some unsubstantiated rumors about Elton Rule working on some "crazy new reorganization plan," there was little being said that was negative. There were not even any new ABC jokes being bandied about in Manhattan's media watering troughs.

Until one day in July when an agency account executive said to a CBS friend at lunch in Mercurio's, "Don't ask me why, because I can't prove it. . . ."

"Prove what?"

"I hate to admit it, but it looks to me as though ABC is finally getting its act together."

The CBS exec withered his friend with a glance. "You gotta be kidding."

"Why?"

"Haven't you heard?"

"Heard what? Did they raise their rates?"

"Worse than that."

"Nothing can be worse than that."

"It happened this morning."

"What happened this morning?"

"I mean . . . ABC, this time, blew it. They really blew it."

"For Chrissake, tell me . . ."

The CBS exec tamped, and lit, his new Sasieni pipe which he hated; he had only recently given up cigarettes and was appalled at how little pleasure there was in smoking a pipe. "I'm not sure I can explain everything that happened. I mean, it's so complicated, no one really understands it. But I'll try. . . . You see, today, ABC just announced a new organization plan. What a lulu! It's so unbelievable that it sounds like something out of 'Wizard of Oz.' "

"Get to the point."

"Remember that old Abbott and Costello routine about 'who's on first'? Well, that is what it's like. Jim Duffy, you see, is still President of the Television Network, except he's really *not*. Research and Programing are under two other guys. Duffy has now become more like a coach than a player. And does Duffy report to Elton Rule anymore? No! He now reports to a *radio* guy named Wally Schwartz!"

"What the hell are you talking about?" demanded the frustrated account executive.

"I'm trying to explain Rule's new organization setup which he announced this morning. It's the most cockeyed plan ever conceived. Even NBC couldn't come up with a cockamamie like this. It's supposed to increase efficiency, straighten out lines of authority, 'increase emphasis on certain areas of operational responsibility,' and a lot of other bullshit. Actually it has screwed up the entire upper echelon and has created another tremendous upheaval within the company. In fact I got a call from a guy just before I came here to meet you . . . he's certain that Jim Duffy is going to resign."

Thus the reaction to the most sweeping restructuring ever of a major network company, which was announced by ABC on July 17, six months after Rule took over as President.

Now there would be two "Mr. Broadcastings" within the company. Radio and television would be split. All radio would report to Harold Neal, but this was not a surprise. Neal's fine record of consistent performance made him the logical choice for such a post.

But in television, all divisions would report to Walter Schwartz who, until now, had been president of the highly successful four radio network concept. James Duffy, president of the television network, would report to him! In addition, two areas under Duffy—programing and planning were being pulled away and set up as separate operations. Programing would be called "ABC Entertainment" and would be headed by Martin Starger. "Planning and Development" would be headed by Fred Pierce. These men would also report to Schwartz.

The rumors that Jim Duffy would resign were not true. Duffy had no intention of resigning. But he was confused. Overnight his domain had shrunk by half. Considering the natural paranoia that afflicts all broadcasters it was natural for him to consider that this was a calculated attempt to downgrade his executive powers. To be president of a television network without the authority to select and approve program schedules, and to have little to say over long range planning and development, had to be a blow to his ego. Add to that the ignominy of having to report, not to Elton Rule, but to a *radio executive,* and it was easy to believe, if your name was Jim Duffy, that you were being passed over.

This however was not the case. Elton Rule was quite satisfied with Duffy's performance. The problem simply was that the job of running a network had grown too large, too demanding for one person. There was Sales. Station Relations. Research. Development. Planning. And, of course, the man-killing ogre of them all—programing; trying to keep up with the new pilots; providing a schedule that interfaced with all other network facets of operation. Rule had become convinced that the time had come to make a change in the old traditional structure of a network—a structure that had always imitated the structure of early radio networks.

Rule had worked on the plan for months. He knew it would create consternation and confusion within the company. Even

THE WINNING TEAM: Elton Rule, shortly after he was appointed President of ABC, Inc. in January of 1972, standing next to Leonard Goldenson, Chairman and Chief Executive Officer.

MAESTRO AUTHUR RUBINSTEIN: Talking to Rule and Goldenson on the occasion of an award he received on "Musical America" in December, 1975.

HIS "SECOND CAREER": Chairman Goldenson sitting before one of his canvases in 1978. Painting became an important therapeutic outlet after a heart attack in May, 1971.

FRED S. PIERCE: President of ABC Television since 1974 and considered the chief architect of ABC's network television success.

FRED SILVERMAN: His contribution to ABC's success catapulted him to the Presidency of NBC.

JAMES E. DUFFY: President of ABC's Television Network since 1970. He well remembers the tough going in the early days.

WILLIAM SHEEHAN: His ABC new regime gambled, and lost, on the controversial teaming of Harry Reasoner with Barbara Walters.

ROONE ARLEDGE: The flamboyant and brilliant executive who directs the destinies of both news and sports at ABC. No other executive has responsibility for so much programing on a single network.

RICHARD O'LEARY: President of ABC owned television stations, who created a super payoff amongst the three networks. His division leads CBS and NBC by a substantial margin.

EVERETT H. ERLICK: Senior VP and General Counsel since 1968, he led the company through its labyrinth of legal problems.

JOHN E. CAMPBELL: He returned to ABC after Ted Shaker's resignation, and now leads ABC's leisure attractions division.

MICHAEL P. MALLARDI: An important cog in ABC's management, he has been VP and Chief Financial Officer since 1975.

JULIUS BARNATHAN: He is ABC's man of many talents and, since 1976, has been President of the company's highly skilled operations and engineering division.

BARBARA MAKES HEADLINES—AND WAVES: When she joined ABC in July, 1976. Shown here at the announcement party with Chairman Goldenson, President Rule, and ABC's ubiquitous Howard Cosell.

HOMETOWN REVISITED: Leonard and Isabelle Goldenson standing in front of a sign at the edge of his home town, Scottdale, Pa. 1974. The town today has a population of 6200, two stoplights, and no theatres. Scottdale was larger when Goldenson was a boy, and had two theatres.

DEVOTION TO A CAUSE: Goldenson standing behind Cerebral Palsy poster girl, Carol Savage, in Chicago, 1978. To the left: Norman Ridley. On the right: John Ritter. Leonard Goldenson's fanatical devotion to the cause of Cerebral Palsy has earned him wide respect as a humanist.

NEW DIRECTIONS: Seth H. Baker presides over a division that represents ABC's highest priority in corporate diversification—publishing. Baker joined ABC in October, 1977.

LEONARD H. GOLDENSON,
Chairman ABC, Inc.

ELTON H. RULE,
President, ABC, Inc.

Leonard Goldenson found difficulty with it, and urged Rule to "go slow" in implementing it. But Rule was certain of his ground. After all, he had formerly occupied Duffy's spot. He knew precisely what a complex task it had become to run a modern network.

So the decision had been made and the change effectuated on July 17. Despite all his assurances, Rule could not persuade Duffy that the changes were really necessary; nor could he convince him that the new plan in no way reflected on Duffy's record or ability. Only time would be able to bring that truth home to Jim Duffy who now began to feel sorry for himself. His family life became affected. He began to doubt himself. As far as he was concerned he had done a good job in the four years he had headed the network; and look at the thanks he was getting!

Retaining perspective became Duffy's biggest problem. When he had to read in the *New York Times*, and trade papers, that his area of jurisdiction had definitely been "depreciated," it was hard to know whom to believe, or what to believe. He was proud of the sales organization that he had built at ABC since 1970 when he had been named president of the network.

Duffy was a veteran of ABC's "rugged years." He dated back to 1963 when he had switched from the radio network to the television network. He had helped ABC build credibility when it was known as the "bargain basement network"; when it got the left-overs from budgets that went primarily to CBS and NBC. Agency relationships needed a lot of "shoring up" in those days. "When you buy from ABC, get it in writing," the word went. "ABC is long on promises and short on delivery." Affiliates cancelled shows on the slightest prextext. Or delayed them to hours like Sunday morning, or after midnight. His roughest experience had been the time he had had to face a gang of surly affiliates at a meeting in the Virgin Islands; had to tell them that ABC must pass on an AT&T cable increase.

Then there was the year 1971, when all that cigarette business went out the window.

Yes, Jim Duffy had a lot to look back on. And now it was difficult to retain one's perspective; to avoid the feeling that he was being pilloried for doing a good job. Somehow Duffy hung on. He had been through rough times before, so as a true ABC stoic, he determined that he would, once more, "roll with the punch." It helped him to think of other battles he had won, such as the time in June of 1971 when he had called together all parties interested in improving children's programs. He had convened a "Children's Workshop." Clients, agencies, parent groups, and others had met for two days—some of them reluctantly—to hear Duffy expound on how childrens' program could be improved and de-commercialized. He remembered the hard stares, and the blunt questions put to him by skeptics. Was Duffy simply showboating? What good was going to come of all this?

Duffy said he frankly did not know what would come of it. "But we will feel the effects, and the results, for years to come, if we are sincere in our efforts."

And improvement had come. His critics later grudgingly admitted that Duffy had not been "showboating" after all.

Still, what did all that matter now, he asked himself, when Elton Rule's surgical scalpel had, in one swift cut, excised the most important part of his network domain?

Things got so bad that Jim Duffy almost "lost it." He felt the center coming apart. But somehow he hung on. Gradually he saw that progress was being made and that a lot of it was due to the new organization plan. There was more depth; cleaner organizational lines; specific target areas were better identified. He was able to give full, undivided attention to network affiliate relations, upgrading the station lineup, and to sales, advertising, and promotion.

Fred Pierce was able to quietly look ahead and plan, not just for one year, but several years. "ABC Entertainment," under Marty Starger, was able to concentrate on that kind of product that would meet the test of Rule's five year plan—not sensational overnight successes that would put ABC on top in one year; but steady, persistent incremental increases of 5% per year. Proof of that was already there. Average audience ratings in the past three years had increased 15–20%. Revenues in 1972 increased 15%

(869.4 million versus 756.4). In net profit the company increased a whopping 70% to 35.6 million (from 13.2 million in 1971).

Jim Duffy's "truncated" network, that year, had its best year in history. The movies on Tuesdays and Wednesdays were a hit. ABC Theatre, featuring 90 minutes and 2 hour original dramas and comedies, received critical acclaim. Elmer Lower's news division recorded a 50% increase in audience with its new anchor team of Harry Reasoner and Howard K. Smith. Overall ratings were the higest ever. Leadership in daytime was reached for the first time in ABC's history.

One other milestone was achieved: for the first time in its history ABC's network was profitable. It seemed a rather fitting way for the company to say farewell to its second decade.

But to the American public 1972 would always be known and remembered for the unprecedented 64 hours of coverage of the Munich Olympics. And though that event was marred by the tragic assassination of Israeli athletes by Arab terrorists, ABC's sports crew brought the horror of it all to viewers in the U.S. and the world with a dignity and daring that brought praise from around the globe including the President, Congress, and international press.

In terms of performance, this was probably ABC's finest hour; indeed the coverage of those traumatic events may go down for decades as television's finest hour.

And as for the ABC reorganization plan, while it suffered barbs for a long time after its original introduction, it finally did receive the highest accolade its rivals could pay: that of flattery by imitation. Five years later both CBS and NBC "borrowed" all, or most all, of the features of the controversial restructuring plan of ABC's entire company.

16

Derailed

IN SEPTEMBER OF 1972 Sam Clark took a phone call from Martin Pompadur, VP and executive aide to Elton Rule. Sam had been getting increasing calls from Pompadur of late and he found them irksome, to say the least. As senior VP of the parent company and head of all non-broadcast divisions, Sam thought he was entitled to report directly to new President Rule. He sensed that trouble was brewing. Pompadur's tactics convinced Clark that, despite his seniority, his career was not in the healthiest condition.

Today Marty wanted the latest figures on the record company. They were not "happy" figures. The record company, that year, seemed headed for a big dip in profits. Gross revenue was holding about the same, but with expansion to a new office in Atlanta, acquiring new record labels, getting new stars like Lefty Frizzell, Ferlin Husky and Billy "Crash" Craddock, plus the danger of excessive inventory, and a host of other expenses, Sam could see that the bottom line of this company was in serious trouble. Net profits in 1971 had been 6.3 million. The way things were going this year, ABC Records would do well to make one million. But Jay Lasker, Sam's President of the record company, had convinced him that expansion was necessary. ABC already had nine labels including Dunhill, Command, Impulse, and Westminster, plus distributing arrangements for other records. Yet the creative base of the company, Jay had told him, had to be made stronger.

ABC already had an impressive list of stars such as Jim Croce, Cashman and West, The Four Tops, Kracker, Gladstone and Steely Dan, B.B. King, Ray Charles and the Grass Roots. In the classical field, "Tales of Hoffman" featuring Beverly Sills had been released and it had been a hit. In the ABC Record and Tape Sales corporation, headed by Lou Levinthal, rack sales jobbing had been increased to meet the growing demand by new selling patterns in large discount and retail chains; and while this required over expanding inventories of product, Lasker and Levinthal believed, and Clark concurred, that this was necessary if ABC was to keep up with competition.

A few minutes later Sam received a call from his man, Jay Lasker, on the West Coast.

"Just got off the phone with Marty Pompadur," said Jay. Sam and Jay had an agreement that whenever Marty went over Sam's head and called Jay direct, the latter would report the conversation at once.

"Yeah? What did Marty want?"

"He wanted the figures."

"The figures? What figures?"

"The figures of the record company."

Sam felt the circulation increasing in the region of his neck. "I just *gave* him the figures!"

"Well, that's what he wanted."

A typical Pompadur stunt, thought Sam. He is playing one of us against the other. He knows Jay will tell me and that this will get my blood pressure up.

"Okay," Sam said wearily. "You gave him the figures. I gave him the figures. There can be no doubt now that he's got the figures. Keep me posted."

When Sam hung up he began doing some serious thinking.

The time had come when he must have a showdown as to exactly where he stood. The only place to find out was, not from Elton Rule, but from the Chairman himself.

Yes, that time definitely had come. Sam stewed over the matter for the next few days. The outcome of such a meeting would be absolutely crucial to the continuance of his career. He planned the scenario in the greatest detail. Leonard Goldenson was not just his boss. He was an old friend. They had seen rough times together. But despite their long personal friendship Sam knew he must approach Goldenson obliquely. No head-on confrontation. Goldenson deplored that sort of thing, thought it lacked style. Tact, diplomacy, and finesse were more to his liking. Sam decided to "position" his showdown meeting in terms of an informal chat. Drop into the Chairman's office, talk about unimportant matters for a few minutes, then let Leonard know that he was not entirely happy with the way the internal chain of command was working; then he would let it drop, almost as a spur of the moment observation: "Leonard, I've been doing some thinking. I've got only a few years before I reach mandatory retirement age. Maybe I should take an early retirement."

Then, hopefully, Leonard would say something like: "Oh, c'mon Sam, why would you want to do a thing like that? We need you here. You stick around till you reach full retirement."

Yes, that would be the way to handle it, thought Sam. And if Leonard answered in words like that it would decide the matter. He would know that the rug was not going to be pulled from under him. He would stick it out till he reached 65.

Sam Clark made the appointment a few days later and followed his carefully planned scenario. But when he said the actual words, "Leonard, I've been doing some thinking . . . maybe I'll take an early retirement," Goldenson looked at him with that benign, always pleasant, always considerate expression, and replied:

"Well Sam, that's a personal decision that you alone must make. I wouldn't know how to advise you on that."

Sam's heart fell. Goldenson was *not* urging him to stay; nor was he advising him to get out. What he *was* signalling, quite clearly, was that Elton Rule was the President and chief operating officer of the company; and if Sam was chafing over Marty Pompadur's methods, well that's the way it had to be.

Sam Clark, at 58, decided that the time had come to hang it up. He wasn't bitter. Disappointed, yes, but not bitter. The company had been good to him. He had ample stock options. There would be no tag days for Sam Clark. If early retirement became a bore he'd become active again.

So on September 11, 1972 Sam Clark announced his decision. He would remain till the end of the year to help with an orderly transition of his many responsibilities; he would turn in his stripes as a corporate officer and go off the Board effective September 29.

Sam was tendered glowing tributes from both Goldenson and Rule when he resigned on January 19, 1973. His careful nurturing of ABC's theatre portfolio through the difficult television era, and his launching of ABC Records, would go down as distinguishing hallmarks of his 17-year career and major contributions to ABC's emergence. His only Waterloo was the treacherous and volatile world of producing theatrical movies—a graveyard that is filled with the bones and dreams of some of the country's brightest and most adventuresome entrepreneurs.

◇   ◇   ◇

Shortly after Sam Clark's retirement, ABC's non-broadcast operations were set up as the ABC Leisure Group, and it came as no surprise to anyone when Martin Pompadur was appointed President and elected to the Board of the parent company.

Now Elton Rule's new team was in place. A feeling of optimism, even euphoria, spread through the executive hierarchy. In the hard-to-impress financial world there was also a feeling that, at last, ABC was ready to make its move to the top.

Pompadur's star, in particular, seemed to be in the ascendancy. He was considered a prime candidate for future succession, and in addition to having responsibility for theatres, records, scenic attractions, and publishing, Pompadur was charged with the job of seeking out other diversification opportunities.

ABC, like CBS, opted for the policy of trying to achieve up to fifty percent of its total revenues and profits from companies that were not directly related to broadcasting. Both ABC and CBS feared that the golden profits of broadcasting could not endure forever. All things move in cycles. Commercial broadcasting, especially television, was dead center in the eye of the hurricane. Despite the industry's formidable lobby in Washington, there were very real fears that growing public clamor among special interest groups could force Congress to dismantle, or diminish, the free enterprise system of broadcasting as it stood. In addition there were fears that technology would vitiate the system: cable interests had dreams of a "wired nation"; satellite transmission directly to the home was being talked about; new forms of home entertainment—video cassettes and disc machines—were emerging from the prototype stage; and there was always the haunting spectre of pay television.

So Pompadur was charged with broadening ABC's nonbroadcast financial base. *High Fidelity* and *Modern Photography* magazines were acquired in 1974 along with *Word, Inc.*, a publishing and record company based in Waco, Texas, which produced and distributed records, tapes, books, sheet music, instructional magazines, and a journal for "inspirational living."

ABC's farm publications, the *Prairie Farmer* in Chicago, *Wallace's Farmer* in Des Moines, and the *Wisconsin Agriculturist* in Racine, added health, accident, and life insurance to its list of services for subscribers.

Meanwhile, John Campbell's leisure attractions operations were expanded. In May of 1973, 280 acres of land were acquired in Largo, Maryland to build an educational wildlife preserve where visitors could observe the full range of animal life in a natural environment. The Historic Towne of Smithville, near Atlantic City, was acquired a year later. Consisting of 2,200 acres, Smithville was an early American crossroads town reconstructed from buildings brought from throughout the state. It also had its own museum of early Americana, plus a private airstrip and chartered airplane service. A joint venture was entered into to manage "Seven Seas," a major tourist attraction in Arlington, Texas.

Major renovations were made at Silver Springs and Weekee Wachee in Florida. A five acre island was created at Silver Springs and environmentally oriented, battery powered boats were introduced. At Weekee Wachee new restaurants, shops, and displays were added.

There was no question that both Pompadur and Campbell were on the move. The major fallout of this feverish activity came in mid-'73, when it was announced that a contract had been entered into (to be closed a year later) to sell 123 of ABC's theatres for 25 million in cash. These were theatres in what was known as the "Northern Group," located principally in the large industrial cities which were feeling the pressures of social change. Nine theatres were acquired and 37 others (besides the Northern Group) were divested in 1973, leaving a balance of 266 in the "Southern Group." Theatre business had reached a plateau. Revenues had hovered in the 57 to 64 million range during the past five years, with profits ranging between $7 and $9 million. The wheel had come full circle. The two decade cash supply by ABC's vast theatre holdings had served its purpose, and the sale of the Northern Group foretold the eventual sale of all of ABC's remaining theatres in 1978 for $50 million.

◇　◇　◇

Like Marty Pompadur, ABC's other rising star, Wally Schwartz, was also elected to the Board in 1974. As President of ABC Television, Schwartz had his hands full. As bright, energetic, and dedicated as he was, it was not easy stepping from radio into the awesome responsibilities of all television divisions. And it was not easy to "learn from the top."

The greatest responsibility was that of having to "sign off" on ABC's fall network television schedule for the '73–'74 season. Martin Starger, who as head of "ABC Entertainment," the program division that had been stripped from Jim Duffy's jurisdiction, was as qualified as anyone in the business, yet the final authority to say yes, or no, rested squarely on Schwartz' tall, slender frame.

A network television schedule is not put together by guess-work, or at random. There is a reason for every program being in a certain position on the schedule. Each script, each star must help move that schedule toward a goal dictated by one factor: *Research*. Within that framework, all kinds of hunches can be played. Stars, writers, directors, even producers, can be juggled; but research remains the all-pervasive god in network planning. At ABC, research had dictated that the direction the schedule must take must unequivocally be the younger family demographics of those between 18 and 49 years of age. The previous year, 1972, had been a good one in terms of ratings. Real audience gains had been made. But now, in discussions for the fall schedule, new goals began to be discussed. The argument went: we have securely anchored ourselves with the 18–49 households. Why not expand our base? Add further dimension to that base. Why can't we keep what we have, yet add programs that will appeal to more mature audiences—not necessarily mature in age, but mature in intellect? Or, translated more simply: add a touch of class.

If there was a quality of *deja vu* to this argument (harking back to 1967 when Tom Moore had tried it), no one commented on it.

It could be done, said Martin Starger. It could be done subtly, deftly, without sacrificing the audience base ABC already had.

Wally Schwartz agreed.

In addition, there were persuasive arguments in favor of this change of direction. Conditions were different than they had been in 1967. Roone Arledge's sports division was then only beginning to make its reputation. At the time ABC Sports, under Arledge's brilliant leadership was unquestionably the network leader in sports. In 1967, ABC News was still floundering. In 1973, Elmer Lower had pushed ABC News into a definite competitive position. The Reasoner-Smith anchor team had actually, for a few weeks that year, tied for the ratings lead. In 1967, the five ABC owned television stations were doing well under Ted Shaker; but now Dick O'Leary had pushed the stations into positive local audience leadership in New York, Chicago, Detroit, San Francisco, and Los Angeles.

Therefore, was it not time for ABC to assert itself in a bid for a new kind of leadership? To reach for the stars with solid mass audience appeal programs, and yet give the public something more? It was a beguiling argument; a titillating proposition. Marty Starger was convinced it would work. Barry Diller, head of prime time programing, agreed. Elton Rule and Leonard Goldenson listened and were willing to be convinced. But the final decision had to be made by Wally Schwartz, who said, *yes, let's go.*

So ABC's schedule for '73–'74 debuted with its "touch of class." The *ABC Theatre* hosted a distinguished list of quality drama: Eugene O'Neill's "Long Day's Journey Into Night," starring Laurence Olivier; Edward Everett Hale's classic, "Man Without A Country" starring Cliff Robertson; "The Glass Menagerie" with Katharine Hepburn; "Wedding Band," the first of Joseph Papp's New York Shakespeare Festival dramas; and "F. Scott Fitzgerald And The Last Of The Belles."

For nature and history lovers there were specials such as "The Primal Man"; "Jane Goodall's Africa"; "Texaco Presents The American Heritage"; National Geographic specials, and a continuation of Jacques Cousteau's specials.

In new series programs a number of shows premiered, all oddly enough containing the letter "k," so that they became known as the "K series": *Kodiak, Kolchak, Kung Fu,* and *Nakia.*

The·results that year could not be called a success. In fact, they appeared more like a disaster. ABC ratings slipped that fall and winter. The gains of the previous three years vanished. ABC fell to a poor third. Year-end net profits were not affected, however; in fact they actually increased from $35.6 to $47.2 million. But this did not alleviate the concern of the program schedule; bottom line is never affected until a year later, when lower ratings command less advertising dollars.

In the second half of the season, the winter of 1974, the ratings continued downhill. Feverish plans were made for the '74–'75 schedule. For Wally Schwartz, it was his "do or die" year. Stomachs became tight in top executive echelons. Leonard Goldenson demanded to know *what the hell is going on?* Elton Rule waited nervously for the start of the fall season and began preparing his backup plan in case the ratings dropped any lower.

When the first week's Nielsens appeared, the world knew what company executives feared would happen: ABC's new schedule was an unmitigated disaster! None of the new shows appeared to have a chance to make the top thirty competitive list. Variety predicted that six "freshman entries" (*Kodiak, Night Stalker, The New Land, Sonny Comedy Revue, Paper Moon, Texas Wheelers*) were "headed for the boneyard by January." Four other new shows (*Harry O, Get Christie Love, That's My Mama,* and *Nakia*) were of "marginal status."

To make matters worse, two ABC holdover shows, *Six Million Dollar Man,* and *Kung Fu,* were in "deep jeopardy." The entire Friday night schedule was ripped out and replaced with movies.

"ABC is clearly up against the wall," said *Variety,* "and scrambling at this juncture to buy a little time with Friday night movie preemptions while it tries to line up a crash program of replacement shows and possible schedule moves."

ABC's troubles were both short range and long range, said *Variety.* "There is nothing on the shelf right now that it can throw into the breach." ABC needed more situation comedies and "a couple of strong hour dramas."

The ratings disaster quickly parlayed its devastating effect upon the five big-city owned television stations. The network lead-ins played havoc with their evening local news ratings. In New York the Nielsen overnight ratings had ABC's channel seven "looking like a New York independent." Bill Greeley, *Variety*'s ace reporter, put it succinctly in the lead of one of his stories: "The new season rating disaster is shaking the corporate system to its nerve-ends."

And clearly it was. In the fifth week of the Nielsen season, the scorecard showed: CBS first with 20.9; NBC 19.9; ABC 16.9. There could be no doubt that the five week trend was definitive. ABC's top ranked show, *Streets of San Francisco* placed 15th! In the top third of the 63 shows that made up the three network competition, ABC had only three! Only six shows in the middle third; and an even dozen in the bottom third!

Action had to come, and it came swiftly. Less than two months after the season started Wally Schwartz was moved out of his position into the Leisure Group division.

Fred Pierce, who had quietly been watching the debacle from his position of Senior Vice President under Schwartz, was named on October 22, 1974 as President of ABC Television.

Martin Starger drastically revamped his entertainment division. Barry Diller, the prime time program chief, had already left the company to become head of Paramount Pictures; he would not be replaced. Edwin T. Vane was given the administrative burden while Starger began spending full time in Hollywood. Michael D. Eisner and Brandon Stoddard were moved up.

The shakeup was sweeping and drastic. ABC had, in the short span of one year, plummeted to a new low. All dreams of moving to the top were gone. All of the steady, incremental progress that Elton Rule had plotted was for naught. Leonard Goldenson was furious. Sparks flew in the executive suite. Oddly enough, because of the delayed reaction effect, ABC's bottom line was not affected that year of 1974. Profits actually increased from $45.4 to $49.9 million.

But ABC was in deep trouble and knew it. What was more galling, the entire industry knew it.

The network of mavericks, despite its progress in recent years, had not yet gotten its act together.

17

Miracle on Sixth Avenue

WHAT HAPPENED NEXT comprised the most incredible admixture of events ever to befall any network. It was as though fate was mixing some witches brew of triumph and disaster in the same cauldron. It remains today a turn of events that still has industry analysts shaking their heads in disbelief.

On the well built shoulders of soft spoken Fred Pierce lay the burden of 1) trying to figure out what had gone wrong; 2) putting together a new schedule; 3) arresting the downhill ratings slide in a matter of weeks. The latter, of course, was impossible. Once a network begins to decline in ratings the turnaround takes, not weeks, or months, but years. The reasons for this long lead time are complex and subtle. It takes the best brains in a company to figure out what actually went wrong; one cannot rush in pell-mell and begin changing programs without knowing what went wrong. When the reasons for the slide are finally known, it takes another year or more to put into production the kinds of shows that will turn the ratings around.

In ABC's case, the new President of ABC Television had no

doubts about what had gone wrong. Pierce had come up through the ranks and had developed impressive credentials. He had started in 1956 as an analyst in the television network research department under Julie Barnathan and Ollie Treyz. He had shown his analytical strength as head of planning and development for the television network in 1972. In January of 1974 he had been promoted to senior vice president of ABC television. For years Pierce had been considered the company's "super think tank"; a one man Rand Corporation when it came to knowing what would, and would not, work for ABC's program schedule.

In the midst of all the program failures Fred Pierce remained calm. He had an eight word statement for what had gone wrong:

"We simply took our eyes off the ball."

"We made the mistake of trying to emulate CBS. We have tried that in the past and it never worked. We're a different network. We have a different kind of audience. Different demographics. Our audience perceives us differently."

In his role as second in command Pierce had smelled the trouble that was brewing. Wally Schwartz, new in his job, had been pushed and tugged in various directions. His program chief, Marty Starger, had gone off on some tangents that were time-consuming and distracting: a children's circus; a rock concert; an investment in a Broadway play. Barry Diller, who was Starger's prime time program expert, was more interested in making movies than he was in developing series programs. As a result the series form, the staple of all networks, became somewhat neglected; and with all of that ABC's program target had become diffused; enlarged and diffused.

Pierce restored the old target, the one that had worked so well in the past. Working closely with Michael Eisner, head of series development in Hollywood, ABC rushed six new series on the air in mid-season, January of 1975. The new programs struck hard at ABC's proper target: they were big city oriented; had strong, colorful personalities; they were fast-moving and contemporary. Three of them, *Barretta*, *S.W.A.T.*, and *Barney Miller* made an immediate impact on the ratings. The effect on morale was strong. Hitting three winners out of six in mid-season is sel-

dom accomplished. Pierce proved his point: the problem had
been that ABC, indeed, had "taken its eyes off the ball."

The company also needed more situation comedies, but
Pierce had none ready. In spring, yes; next fall, certainly; meanwhile the ratings decline was halted. In fact, before the '74–'75
season ended, ABC gained back some of the ground it had lost;
but not enough to change its dismal third place standing.

As 1975 began, Elton Rule knew that this would be the year
in which the company would have to "pay the financial piper."
And the price would be shockingly high—higher than anyone
dreamed. Adding to the problem was the condition of the general
economy. The inflation-recession spiral of '73–'74 looked as
though it had one more rousing year of negative performance
before it would level off. It was time to batten down the hatches,
so Rule put out a belt-tightening edict: No new employee could
be hired at any level without the *personal* approval of the President!

In addition to all the other bad news, Marty Pompadur informed Rule that the record company was piling up inventories at
an alarming rate. Considering the slow economy it would take a
miracle to stem a loss of several million dollars.

In January of 1975, Pompadur replaced both Jay Lasker and
Howard Stark, president and executive vice president, respec-
tively, of ABC Records and named Jerold H. Rubinstein as president.

Pompadur had other problems. The cost of operating ABC's
lavish new office complex in Century City in Los Angeles made it
clear that most of the Leisure Group division would incur a red
ink situation beyond past projections. Hence, for Elton Rule, as
1975 dawned, he had twin battles to wage: one was the battle of
digging out of the ratings cellar; the other was to avoid an utter financial calamity. Another year like this and he could see himself
back in Los Angeles managing a local station!

In May, a much needed boost to everyone's morale came
when Fred Pierce announced that the CBS *wunderkind*, Fred Silverman, would leave CBS to become President of ABC Enter-

tainment, the network program division headed by Martin Starger.

The Silverman coup electrified the industry. Silverman's achievements as head of CBS television programs since 1970 were well documented. Under Silverman's sagacious direction, CBS had dominated the three networks. His program "touch" was considered uncanny. He knew what the mass audience wanted and gave it to them. Yet he had been chafing under CBS' restraints and constraints; particularly he resented certain "attitudes" that he perceived were held against him. In short, Fred Silverman felt that his contributions to CBS were no longer being properly appreciated.

Pierce sensed the problem when he chanced to meet Silverman at the "21" bar in New York at Christmastime in 1974. The two were hardly strangers. They had met when Pierce had been a research neophyte back in the Ollie Treyz era and Fred Silverman was doing his masters thesis on television programing as a graduate student at Ohio State. Silverman's thesis had dealt with ABC, and Pierce had cooperated by giving Silverman the information he needed.

"He was a bright young guy who, I knew, would make it big once he hit the job market," Pierce recalled.

Upon graduation, Silverman hooked on with WGN-TV in Chicago. His success in positioning theme movies for that station led him to New York where he went to work for WPIX-TV. There only six weeks, he had been lured to CBS where, at the young age of 25, he had been given a position as director of daytime programs for the CBS network.

Frank Swertlow, in an article in *New York Magazine*, recalled that memorable Christmas meeting:

Fred Pierce: "I wasn't concerned with what his relationship was over there (at CBS), but I assumed that it was not totally in sync or I wouldn't have gotten the vibrations that he and I were, so to speak, on the same wavelength."

Swertlow quoted a certain CBS source: "Freddie was appreciated, but never accepted (at CBS). He wasn't a classy guy. He

needed to be controlled or he would destroy you. They treated
him like the 14-year-old child he programs for."

Also Silverman was not the "Ivy League type" which is endemic to CBS. Wrote Swertlow: "He didn't buy his worsteds at
Paul Stuart or know the difference between the Dunhill Mon-
tecruz and Montecristo cigars. He also didn't carry Twinings tea
bags in his pocket, as one CBS exec did."

"In the eyes of many of his colleagues at CBS, television's
number one programing whiz was a baggy pants slob. And because
of it, he was denied the kind of salary he wanted and the perks
and recognition he deserved."

A modest raise, and the use of a limousine, might have kept
Fred Silverman at CBS.

Pierce's fortuitous meeting at Christmastime came at the
perfect time for ABC. Pierce got Silverman's message, which the
latter may not intentionally have been giving. At any rate, further
meetings followed. By May the deal was wrapped up. ABC "appreciated" Silverman to the tune of a three-year contract starting
at $250,00, a paid-up life insurance policy, stock options, housing
on both coasts, and unlimited expenses.

ABC stockholders "appreciated" the deal, too. ABC's stock
jumped two points (valued at 35 million) with the news of the
acquisition. Now suddenly ABC was said to have a "hot hand."
The new team, said the trade press, could certainly not be expected to work miracles overnight, but in two or three years ABC
very possibly would be a strong contender to the leader, CBS.

The two men went to work with a vengeance. The fall schedule for '75–'76 was already in place, Pierce had served as the
fundamental architect, but in Silverman he had a superb "fine-
tuner"; a diligent program "fixer" who read every script, exhausted every possibility to get the maximum out of each program
in each series, not merely in terms of the productions themselves,
but in terms of cross-pollination of stars, cross promotion, and
program spinoffs.

In their planning, the two Freds took advantage of what was
considered a new albatross around the networks' necks—the
CBS-inspired "family viewing hour" which called for "whole-

some" and "innocuous" fare in the first hour of network transmission: 8–9 PM in the east; 7–8 PM in the midwest. This change made it a brand new ball game for all three networks. ABC's strategy was to "throw away" the first hour—use it for new development projects; try out situation comedies; experiment with new forms, new talents; throw in the strongest programs at 9 PM (or 8 PM in the midwest), such as *NFL Football,* the *Rookies, Barretta, Streets of San Francisco, Starsky and Hutch,* and two weekly movies.

When September arrived, ABC had "retargeted" its entire prime time schedule and was ready to face the annual fall ratings mayhem. The results, beginning with the very first week, astonished the industry, surpassing even the fondest hopes of the two Freds. ABC's strength made itself felt from the very start of the Nielsen contest. The first week was called a fluke in the trade press. As soon as the new season settled down and viewers had a chance to "sample" all the new shows, CBS' long superiority would again assert itself.

But CBS never made its move. Neither did NBC. It was not a runaway, but by mid-season ABC continued to hold a slim lead; by the end of the year that lead increased. A startled industry asked how such a thing could have happened. And surely it would be a miracle if ABC could hold its lead for the balance of the season, through the winter and spring of 1976. If that happened ABC would truly have been said to have performed the impossible—jumping from a dismal third to network leadership in *one* year!

But while this good news was developing, bad news came from another sector. As 1975 came to its close, Marty Pompadur had to admit what company accountants had been logging for the past twelve months: ABC's recorded music operations would report a staggering loss of 27.3 million dollars! Excessive inventory was being returned. The bankruptcy of W. T. Grant stores was given as another reason; the general economy, another. But there was more to it than that. Clearly, previous record company managements had made some wrong decisions. ABC's management at the very top also had to take its full share of the blame, for somehow, they had let the volatile record business get out from under their control.

In addition, there was other bad news. The leisure attractions divisions, including the office building in Century City, posted a loss of 12.1 million!

In Largo, Maryland, ABC's Wildlife Preserve was doing so badly after two years of operation that it was simply shut down.

Add to this the lower revenues from the television network and it became clear that the day of reckoning that Goldenson and Rule dreaded was going to be much worse than they had expected. When it came time to add up the bottom line for the full calendar (and fiscal) year of 1975 the company was forced to notify its stockholders the drop in net profits would exceed $32.8 million!

The 49.9 million made in 1974 would drop to a mere 17.1 million for 1975!

No picture could better illustrate the extraordinary dynamics of the network broadcasting business, a game that someone described as "like playing with a nitroglycerine-loaded yo-yo."

◇　◇　◇

Yet hope springs eternal. The phoenix rose from the ashes. Sometimes a miracle does occur, and that is what happened to ABC when its financial fortunes were at their lowest ebb.

As the "second season" began to unfold in the winter of 1976, it became clear that ABC had no intention of relinquishing its lead. The two Freds continued their relentless planning and added new programs as the year began. *Donny and Marie* overcame the tough odds against live variety shows and became an instant hit. *Laverne and Shirley* were tested in a segment of *Happy Days*, then launched in their own situation comedy. Another hit.

Several other new shows were dropped into the schedule: *The Bionic Woman, Charlie's Angels*, and *Family*. All became hits.

The winter Olympics from Innsbruck, Austria, were carried, with strong misgivings that they would weaken the audience. Instead, they *added* to ABC's lead. An innovative advertising and on-air promotion campaign directed by Sy Cowles, began to palpably increase the tune-in.

ABC seemed to be able to do nothing wrong. As Fred Pierce put it: "Everything fell into place. All the parts fit." At the same time, a little luck also helps and Pierce admits that ABC began to have its share. A mini-series called *Rich Man, Poor Man* had been a favorite project of Barry Diller. Diller was now long gone from the scene, but the multi-sequence "novel for television" written by Irwin Shaw, had finally been completed for ABC by Universal Pictures. At the end of the football season ABC had a gaping hole in its Monday night schedule. *Rich Man, Poor Man* was dropped into that slot.

Presto! It ran away with the ratings. "We looked like geniuses," said Pierce, "but we really were not. We simply had that product ready and that was the place to put it."

A show that was just getting by, called *Happy Days* was turned into a hit when Michael Eisner suggested to Pierce that a relatively minor character named Arthur Fonzarelli—"The Fonz"—played by Henry Winkler, had star quality that would turn the series into a hit. The change was made and *Happy Days* jumped from 20 to 48 percent share of the audience.

In long form entertainment such specials as *Little Ladies Of The Night, Eleanor and Franklin*, the Emmy Awards, Oscar Awards and Tony Awards, added strength and variety to the schedule.

By March, ABC's leadership was definite and the miracle on Sixth Avenue was assured. Its average rating of 18.7, and share of 30.7, equated to an improvement of 13% over the preceding year.

After two decades and three years of dogged effort ABC had vaulted to the summit in the incredible span of only one year!

One of the heads of another network said that the likes of such a happening might never be seen again—and that, for the good of the industry, it might be well that it never happen again. When asked why, he simply commented that there would be implications and repercussions caused by ABC's ascendancy that would be felt for years to come.

A prophetic statement indeed.

18

A Flash in the Pan?

As the fall of 1976 neared and the '76–'77 program schedule was made ready, the industry waited to see if ABC could repeat its success. The big question: was the previous year's success a fluke? A flash in the pan? Many thought so. There were as many skeptics as believers. CBS and NBC, they said, would not sit still; adjustments would be made. ABC would be strong, yes; but CBS would regain its position with a dozen new shows and by mid season would narrowly be in the lead, while ABC and NBC fought it out for second place. At the end of the full season in the spring of 1977, CBS would again have demonstrated its leadership. To industry conservatives it was unthinkable that CBS would place second for two years in a row.

Others, however, disagreed. Herb Jacobs, veteran industry prognosticator with an excellent track record, believed that ABC had settled in too strongly to be dislodged. By the end of 1976, or midway in the season, said Jacobs, ABC would have a 20.3 rating and would still hold first place. Second position would be held by CBS with a 19.1 rating. NBC would bring up the rear with 18.0.

Meanwhile the team of Pierce and Silverman, along with their Hollywood staff, worked with great precision.

From the start of the new season, the skeptics were proven wrong. ABC jumped to a narrow lead in the first week and never relinquished it. By December 19, Herb Jacobs' prediction about ABC was proved correct, except that his predicted lead of 20.3 turned out to be a 20.9 rating. CBS was *not* second as he had predicted, but third with an 18.7, while NBC placed second with 19.6.

The continued slippage of CBS astonished a lot of advertisers and their agencies. The skeptics disappeared. ABC's rise to leadership had not been a fluke. If there were any doubters, they changed their mind at the start of the second season, when ABC pulled a coup that astonished everyone in the industry. The eight-day mini-series, *Roots* began on January 23 and attracted the largest audience in television annals. Some 130 million Americans (about 120 million of which were white) watched for 12 hours on 8 consecutive nights, giving *Roots* an astounding 44.9 rating and a 66% share of the audience. ABC's rating for the week was 35.5 and its share 52.1%, the highest ever achieved by any network.

Nothing like this had ever happened before. Television, the most criticized medium of all, had given Americans a program that they not only watched in unprecedented numbers, but a program that drew virtually all raves and no criticism.

Roots was a phenomenon in more than one sense. After the first night viewers throughout the country began to rearrange their schedules for the next seven nights so they could watch the program. There was a genuine sense of loss when the series ended. Alex Haley, author of the book, David Wolper, producer of the series, and ABC had not the slightest idea the series would be viewed by so many people, or that it would have such a profound effect on the country. Bars without television sets closed early. Bars with sets also suffered because viewers wanted to watch *Roots* in the privacy of their homes. Restaurants also suffered. Motion picture theatres suffered the most. With it, ABC had a stroke of luck, for in the northern part of the country it was the coldest week of the winter; yet in warmer regions the viewer-

ship of *Roots* was equally high. Sales of home video cassette recorders zoomed. To the surprise of some, and perhaps the disappointment of the KKK and other bigot groups, the series did *not*
generate a reaction of violence in schools and communities. William Greider wrote in the *Washington Post:* "Assume that these
TV people know what they're doing, if not as artists or historians,
as packagers of massive audiences, as manipulators of images that
draw people to their TV sets."

Greider was only partly right. No one at ABC, including the
two Freds, or Brandon Stoddard, or Mike Eisner had any idea
that *Roots* would "go through the roof" as it did. On the contrary,
they considered *Roots* a high risk venture. For that reason it was
"thrown away" in the schedule, so to speak; inserted at the end of
each evening with the hope that the regular fare each night would
build a "lead-in." If *Roots* failed miserably, at least it would not
destroy ABC's schedule for the week.

The genesis of a project like *Roots*—the largest ever attempted by any network—was an adventure in itself, fraught with
peril and vicissitudes. One has to marvel at the fact that *Roots* did
manage to survive the complex system of checks and balances
which affect and control the creative process in television program production.

Roots was born because David Wolper, a long-time successful producer of documentaries, believed in it. He became interested in the manuscript even before author Haley had finished
it.[1] Wolper approached Barry Diller, who was then in charge of
ABC prime time entertainment. Diller assigned Lou Rudolph to
read the unfinished manuscript. Rudolph liked it and recommended to Diller and Brandon Stoddard that the rights be purchased. ABC network sales executives, however, had no great enthusiasm for a period piece that dealt with slavery from the
viewpoint of the slave. Advertisers were apt to be nervous about
such sensitive material. But Alex Haley's own charismatic personality swept everyone into a mood of enthusiasm. *Roots*, he con-

---

[1] In 1972, David Wolper heard about Haley's "work in progress" and tried to
buy it, but was told that Columbia Pictures had an option on the property. This
option eventually expired. Wolper paid Haley $50,000 for the rights.

vinced them, could be a breakthrough of fantastic proportion if properly handled.

Not until August of 1975 was a contract signed. ABC won the rights despite a last minute bid by producer David Merrick. But it remained a "step deal," with many steps remaining to be taken before production actually began.

In mid-June of that year, Fred Silverman joined ABC. The next "step" in the planning process would be his to take or not take. Silverman liked it. A commitment was made for six hours of programing for 6 million dollars.[2] There were the usual disagreements between producer and network, but the project moved forward.

In September of 1975, before actual production began, David Wolper suffered a heart attack which was so serious that it resulted in heart bypass surgery. He remained off his feet until January of 1976.

During those months Wolper's on-set producer, Stan Margulies began shooting at Savannah, Georgia, where all the major location shooting was done. (Contrary to general belief, none of *Roots* was shot in Africa.)

Early in 1976, Fred Pierce found himself being confronted by a jubilant Fred Silverman, Brandon Stoddard, and Mike Eisner. The subject: *Roots*.

"Look," they said, "this material is so fantastic we think it should be expanded from six hours to twelve hours."

Fred Pierce laughed. "You're not serious."

"We sure are."

"What are you guys trying to do, get me fired?"

"Wait till you see the rough cuts of the first two hours."

Pierce looked at the footage and had to agree with his colleagues. *Roots* was not merely "good," it was "superb." It was also "dynamite." Therein lay the problem. Where could they schedule such a potentially controversial series? Pierce recalled:

"There was a very real concern that it might turn off a large segment of white America. Also it might antagonize young blacks.

---

[2] ABC's investment eventually reached $8 million.

None of us really knew what it would do. Would whites and blacks reject it for different reasons? Would there be a backlash? We simply had no way to know, or to find out. So Fred and I agreed that we couldn't insert it into our regular schedule. We could only schedule it at the end of the prime time evening. Frankly, we were worried about what might happen. We were already over budget by a million dollars. We knew we could not recoup our losses from advertisers. We were warned about the possible reaction of some affiliates. If the press reaction was bad at the start, would the public reject the rest of the series? All of these concerns gave us nervous stomachs . . ."

The rest, of course, is history. There was no backlash. Middle class America was "ready" for the lesson of a black man searching for his roots in a white dominated world of slavery and oppression. The timing had been right. Advertisers got the biggest bargain in history. By the time the final night had played, Sunday, January 30, *Roots* had become the most watched show in television history, surpassing "Gone With The Wind." *Roots* captured eight of thirteen places in the all-time television audience contest.

More importantly, *Roots* left a different America, a country that was groping for new meanings, new definitions, new and better solutions than had been provided by the past.

And so, as 1977 began, there could be no question that ABC was on its way to a second year of leadership. And the good news for the year just ending, 1976, was *all* good. The meager profits of 17 million for 1975 jumped 320% to 71.7 million! ABC's broadcast revenues for the first time exceeded one billion dollars.

As the '76–'77 season rolled to its close in the spring of '77, the company's lead grew larger. Full season statistics showed that the lead was even larger than anyone had dared to predict: A 21.5 Nielsen rating for the entire season compared to 18.7 for CBS, and 18.1 for NBC. The first four of the top ten shows belonged to ABC; seven of the top ten carried the ABC banner. CBS, which had been the premier network since the early fifties, placed only two shows in the top ten. NBC, the perennial runner-up had only one show in the top ten.

As *Time Magazine* put it: "There is no parallel in the history of broadcasting—and few in any well-established industries—to ABC's sudden rise. It is as if, in the space of two years, Chrysler had surged past General Motors and sent Ford reeling back to Dearborn. Or—to stretch the truth only a bit—as if China had discovered some mysterious all-powerful Z bomb and in victorious glee ordered both the White House and the Kremlin dismantled and shipped, boards and nails, to Peking."

The irony of ABC's television network leadership lay in the fact that the most important symbol of its strength, its television network, was only *now* catching up with other company divisions which had long since achieved supremacy over their counterparts at the other networks.

The five owned television stations, under the leadership of Dick O'Leary, had been at the top for the past five years, not only in audience, but in profits.

The radio division under Hal Neal had been the leader over NBC and CBS for an even longer term. Under Neal the four radio network concept, managed by Ed McLaughlin, was the "only game in town" in terms of network radio. The four networks of ABC now had 1,500, affiliates, more than all competitors combined.

The AM station division, managed by Chuck DeBare, had for something like ten years been the most listened-to, and most profitable stations in the country.

The seven ABC owned FM stations, under Allen Shaw, also had established clear-cut peer leadership in terms of audience and profits.

Another measure of the company's leadership, or rather, the impact of that leadership, lay in the synergistic effect it had on ABC's affiliated stations. These stations rose to leadership in ratings in almost every city. This in turn had a "snowball" effect that was to dramatically increase both the quality and size of ABC's network.

The reaction within the company was one of pride mixed with incredulity. Had it *really* happened after 25 years? Was this reality, or some kind of dream? And—how long would it last??

Such introspection gave way to euphoria. Lapel buttons and badges began to appear. No one knows where all of them came from, although some, certainly, came from the Promotion Department:

> "We are still #1—Things may
> never be the same."

> "After all these weeks of
> sustained industry leadership
> it would be rather osten-
> tatious to have a button with
> a #1 larger than this." (Printed
> on a very large, very ostentatious
> button!)

Others were home made, or typewritten inserts super-imposed over other copy:

> "What does #1 mean?"

> "If it's so easy why did
> it take so long?"

Only Leonard Goldenson was qualified to answer that question. Surely it was a painful memory that he would never be able to forget. The road to the top had been filled with 24 years of potholes. Friends had come and gone. Colleagues had won and lost. Some had been handed the baton, others had been discarded. It is the inexorable corporate system. Goldenson called his top staff together and expressed his feelings:

"We must not change. We must continue to be grateful and gracious, keep alert, and continue as we are. Above all we must never forget the days when we were *not* number one."

Goldenson is not a sentimentalist. He seldom indulges in reminiscences. He does not like to look back. But he was in a mellow mood one day after ABC's second year at the top. Ironically, on that same day a major shakeup was occurring two blocks away in the stern facade of CBS' "Black Rock."

Was it perhaps true, he was asked, if ABC's success had come as a result of things that ABC did, or a result of things that the other networks did *not* do? Such things as errors of judgment; slippage in executive quality; complacency; etc.

Goldenson would not comment. He had only compliments for CBS, and particularly its brilliant leader, William Paley.

"All I know," said Goldenson, "is that we must be gracious, friendly, and as open as we have been in the past when we were not on top. We must never forget where we have been." Then he flashed his wide smile. "I'm not so sure it wasn't more fun back in 1953 when we were just getting started; when we were getting our ears pinned back. Those days were fun, too, because we had so much to learn, and because we had to fight so hard . . ."

Goldenson always did relish a good fight. He still does. As far back as 1969 *Fortune Magazine* wrote of him:

"The frustrations in news, and the general non-progress of his company in recent years, have been rough on Leonard Goldenson. He is a proud man and has made it quite clear in the past what he wants ABC to be. 'No. 1,' he has said. 'I will never be satisfied with less.' Some of his detractors, and there are many to be found, regard that goal as completely unreachable, at least in Goldenson's time, and as posing a considerable threat to the company. 'He's got an emotional hang-up.' one Wall street analyst says. 'He wants to stand four-square on the podium with William Paley on one side and David Sarnoff on the other. Great, except that his wanting that has cost the company millions. Isn't it possible that he could concentrate for now on being a better third?' "

Anyone who could think that Leonard Goldenson *ever* could be content to be less than number one, or that he could be seduced by such weird logic, should be a candidate for a psychiatrist's couch. One can perhaps make a case that having an obsession to be first in any field of endeavor is wrong; but if it is wrong, so is the national psyche of the nation wrong, for being first still seems to be the favorite goal of all Americans.

And who can say that Goldenson has not now qualified himself to step up on that podium with the mythical David Sarnoff, and the legendary William Paley?

In any event, no novelist would ever dare cast Goldenson as one of this century's titans of communications, despite the fact that his stature as such a titan now seems assured—for the fact of the matter is, Goldenson is remarkably unpretentious in his personal life and business style. He prefers to be called "Leonard" rather than "Mr. Goldenson." He is always accessible to his "team" and his "players." He prefers talking about them rather than his personal accomplishments. His life has been touched by personal tragedy, and he still spends vast amounts of time on the affliction that took the life of one of his three daughters (cerebral palsy). He is as capable of enthusiasm today as he was decades ago. He loves to tour various divisions of his vast company, and will give as much time to the FM stations division, or a new publishing acquisition, as he does the television network.

The big question now is: *Will success spoil Rock Hunter?* Will complacency set in? Will ABC become overconfident?

Fred Pierce, for one, will not be affected by that syndrome. He is too busy to worry about the past, and the future does not unduly concern him. His smile is a little broader these days and he appears to be more relaxed than in the past. But then Pierce always seems relaxed. He is the epitome of the modern broadcast executive, highly disciplined, and utterly unflappable. His personal achievements since he assumed the Presidency of ABC television, have been slightly phenomenal, yet he seems to have no interest in taking bows. Others can do that if they prefer. Pierce is an intensely quiet man who likes to work in anonymity. He prefers dealing with his executives on a one-to-one basis. Meetings are held to a minimum. Position papers, reports, and long memos are unheard of, other than a meticulous poring over of research reports, a subject he knows so well. He knows that he enjoys the loyalty of his colleagues, not only because he works as hard as any of them, but because he has, to as great an extent as is possible, taken the "fear syndrome" out of a business that is filled with hobgoblins of fear, tension, crises, and the unexpected.

Jim Duffy is also too busy to look back, although he has been in the eye of the storm as much as anyone. He can remember when ABC had dreams of only reaching parity with CBS and

NBC; when affiliates cancelled, or delayed, the feed of ABC shows with impunity. Like Ev Erlick, he can remember when every ABC executive had to do the job of four or five men. Like Julie Barnathan, he can remember when a set of color cameras had to be moved from one studio to the other, and then be hauled off to a sports event.

In 1977, when ABC had been the leader for two years, Duffy could revel in the fact that "his" network had finally achieved parity with the other two networks. Now Duffy had a daring plan to *exceed* parity.

"No question about it, we're going to do it," he said. "Just give us two more years. That's all it will take."[1]

Elton Rule, in his President's office adjoining that of the Chairman, also exuded the cool, quiet confidence that typifies his style. Would success spoil ABC? Would overconfidence, or complacency set in? Rule did not think so. The indelible past, he reminded, was only "yesterday"; besides, there was still much to do to make ABC the leader in all areas in which leadership counts. In the broadcast area ABC was, as of 1977, still not the leader in daytime. In late evenings it was not number one. In news it clearly was not the leader. News leadership remained the most elusive and baffling problem of the company, a real enigma. The challenge to make ABC number one in news, said Rule, was a commitment that both he and Leonard Goldenson felt deeply about and were determined to carry out, regardless of cost or effort.

In the non-broadcast area ABC still had to find a way to establish a profitable niche for its beleaguered record operations. The hemorrhage of losses from its recording and record distribution activities was stemmed somewhat in 1976 with a loss of only 6.5 million; but in 1977 another whopping 29.8 million loss had to be taken. Only the leading network could afford to take such

---

[1] In 1979 NBC had 212 affiliated network stations, CBS 203, and ABC 199. But sheer numbers are no longer that important. It is the *strength* of affiliates that count. In the past three years ABC has snared 29 affiliates away from its competitors and is now credited as being at least as strong, and probably stronger, than NBC or CBS.

losses with equanimity. Nevertheless profits for 1977 reached 109.7 million dollars!

"Complacency will not be our problem," said Rule in 1977. "There will be other problems, but complacency will not be one of them. Our memories are too long. And our Chairman has the longest memory of all."

Another conviction that Rule and Goldenson share is their strong sense of the responsibility that leadership entails. Such a position goes beyond profits or ratings; the kind of leadership they envision is one of a larger dimension, one that is sensitive to, and responsive to, the social issues and forces of our time.

Roots can be said to be an example of that conviction. While *Roots* was conceived as an entertainment program, and succeeded beyond wildest dreams, it was considered a high risk venture when conceived. The company actually lost money on the initial showing. Rates were charged for a nominal share of audience, of 30–35% of the audience. If it had achieved only that modest, average share, the company would have been satisfied because the program represented a social commitment that it felt obliged to make.

Elton Rule says there may be too much emphasis on the fact that one company or another is in first place. He also says that in the future there will probably be no great degree of dominance by one company over another. Each will have its own degree of difference, its own strong points, deficiencies, and vulnerabilities. But all three networks will prosper. ABC will strive mightily to remain the number one network, but if it slips behind in the next few years, that difference will be relative and not nearly as significant as leadership has meant in the past.

It is often said that it is more difficult to stay on top than to reach the top. In 1977, when ABC completed its 25th year, Chairman Leonard Goldenson began to face that new test. Surely it would be an adventure both novel and esoteric, both demanding and even intimidating, but also an adventure that ABC would welcome as it remembered the past and faced the future.

Part Five

ABC Today

19

Debits and Credits

In 1979 ABC was enjoying its third consecutive year of television network leadership. In other phases of broadcasting—TV, AM, FM owned stations, and the four radio networks—ABC's leadership had also increased. In *Fortune Magazine*'s 1977 directory of the 500 largest industrial corporations ABC jumped from 170 to 152 and was expected to advance another dozen points in the 1978 rankings.

In 1978 ABC's profits on continuing operations were $127,510,000, or $4.60 per share, on gross revenues of $1,783,985,000. Assets at the end of 1978 were $1,101,000,000, and the company had 9,400 employees.[1] In terms of profit, revenue, audience, or virtually any other criteria one chooses to use, ABC is the leading broadcast company in the world today.

How long it will remain the leader is a question no one can answer. Success, like failure, runs in cycles. One fact, however,

---

[1] These assets are drastically understated, because ABC values its 18 owned television and radio stations at cost. The difference between cost and market value of ABC's five television stations would be at least 500 million.

remains clear: ABC's success, now in its third year, cannot be considered a fluke. Three years of steadily rising ratings and profits have convinced even the strongest skeptics that ABC's success is solid and likely to continue. Indeed, the cycle could be a long one.

Yet its remarkable leap from third to first in one year gives hope to its rivals, particularly NBC, which has "magician" Fred Silverman (now President of NBC) who played a significant role in ABC's miraculous rise. Considering the volatility of the television network, business positions can be reversed in a single year. From a practical standpoint, however, the odds of either NBC or CBS duplicating ABC's feat in such a short time are probably slim. ABC's success resulted from, not only its own agility, initiative, and fine tuning of the mass audience, but from mistakes that NBC and CBS made. ABC is not likely to make mistakes that stem from managements that have grown inbred, overconfident, diffuse and multi-tiered.

The more successful and dynamic a company is today, the more problems it is bound to have. If one were to list ABC's major problems (and challenges) the following would comprise such a list:

—*News Leadership.* This is ABC's most pressing broadcast priority and is fraught with complications, not the least of which is the unorthodox management style of Roone Arledge who is a classic maverick, a gifted sports impresario, and the new head of ABC News.

—*The Human Factor.* Morale. Executive suite succession. Complacency. Overconfidence. All of the complex human problems that exist within any company. These problems become more critical when a company achieves leadership.

—*The Silverman Syndrome.* Has Fred Silverman's defection to NBC had a deleterious effect on ABC? How much did Silverman do, or not do, for ABC? How much credit should he get, or not get, for ABC's success?

—*The Burden of Leadership.*

—*New Dimensions of Leadership.*

Before examining these problems and challenges it might be

well to run down certain other areas of operation that need not be considered as matters of concern.

ABC's priorities can be simply stated. Maintaining leadership in broadcasting is obviously the company's first priority. A second is to "catch up" in its physical broadcasting plant. Vast sums are being invested in brick, mortar, and equipment, deferred for more than a decade, and intended to make ABC's operating plant the finest in the country.

Another priority is to improve ABC's non-broadcast properties and operations. In this connection the company took a surprising step in 1978: it bowed out of its theatre business entirely! In October of 1978 it sold its remaining 272 theatres to Plitt Theatres, Inc. for 50 million dollars. Reasons given were that theatre profits had reached a plateau—4.8 million pre-tax profits in 1977, down from 7 million in 1976. Film product continued to be scarce and increasingly costly; more importantly, the buyer-seller balance had grown lopsided in favor of Hollywood suppliers. Movie producers dictate terms that are onerous and there appears little likelihood that this imbalance will change in the foreseeable future. Therefore ABC unsentimentally exited from a business that had been its source of cash in the early fifties when it was building its network.

Another reason, not stated, but implicit in the sale of theatres, should give a chill to theatre operating companies everywhere. ABC has its own crystal ball to tell the future, and that crystal ball is telling ABC that the proliferation of technologies and services of the future will make the in-home television set much more important than ever in the past—which augurs poorly for theatre attendance in the coming decades.

Another drastic cutback has occurred in ABC's International Division, a daring idea that became only a memory of the bright hopes held for it in the sixties. At its peak ABC held minority interests in stations in six central American countries, plus the Philippines, Australia, Canada, Colombia, Ecuador, Chile, Argentina, Japan, and Lebanon. Once these stations were linked with others in an international consortium called "Worldvision." But a growing sense of nationalism in foreign countries, plus other problems militated against the success of this bold venture. Today ABC owns small investments in two stations in Japan, and one each in Guatemala, Panama, and Bermuda. But the company still provides program services for various foreign stations. In withdrawing from international activities ABC has actually made a profit from all of its situations except Argentina where it incurred a heavy loss. Today, because of its connections in countries where it has operated, ABC enjoys a rather unique advantage which has helped give it quick and exclusive access to programs for its sports division and news stories for its news division.

ABC's Leisure Attractions Division, which owns three outdoor parks—Weekee Wachee Spring, Silver Springs, and The Historic Towne of Smithville—plus the lavish Entertainment Center in Los Angeles, will probably not be a target for further expansion. This division adds only $30 million to ABC's gross revenues of $1,783,985,000 and the company is said to be no longer enamored with the leisure field.

Smithville, because of its proximity to the new gambling center of Atlantic City, was expected to be a success. It was not, despite improvements made to the site. ABC sold Smithville in 1979. Nevertheless, as a real estate investment the sale was enormously profitable. The $7 million purchase price in 1974 almost tripled when it was sold five years later.

ABC's eye-catching Entertainment Center in Century City on the west coast has given the company an expensive lesson in real estate and building management. It probably will never be profitable, but as a symbol of influence and prestige in the impressionable film capital, it may be worth its 80 million dollar investment.

High on the list of ABC's problems today would certainly have been that of its record operations. This was a division that has lost some 70 million dollars in the past six years causing many within the company to say: why don't we get out of this business. In 1979 ABC did exactly that, selling to MCA, Inc. for an estimated 35 million. (In the summer of 1978 the company sold its distribution centers for records and tapes for an estimated 16 million dollars).

The company's highest priority in terms of expansion and diversification is unquestionably the field of publishing. Taking a cue from its rivals, CBS and RCA/NBC, ABC has quietly but intensively been adding to its publishing division. ABC's success with its early fifties' fortuitous acquisition of three *Prairie Farmer* agricultural publications make this decision a logical one. Since then the company has put together a large, unsynergistic, but profitable array of magazines and special interest publications under the direction of a brilliant new executive named Seth Baker, who is said to be one of the company's hierarchic super stars and a sure candidate for further advancement within the company. Unlike CBS, Baker is not looking for glamorous or well-known publications where the competition is strong, but for those that have a well established niche in their field, such as those ABC currently owns: *Los Angeles Magazine*; NILS Publishing Company, publishers of various annotated legal services; ABC Leisure Magazines, which include *Modern Photography, High Fidelity,* the Schwann music catalogues and various satellite publications; Word, Inc., a diversified religious communications company; ABC Farm Progress Publications, which include *Prairie Farmer, Indiana Prairie Farmer, Wisconsin Agriculturist, Wallace's Farmer,* and the Wallace-Homestead Publishing Company; Miller Publishing Company, specializing in agricultural magazines; Hitchcock Publishing Company, whose magazines include *Infosystems, Quality,* and *Assembly Engineering;* and in 1979 ABC Publishing division made an agreement to buy R. L. White Company, a real estate communications firm which includes *Homes Magazine.* Also in 1979 ABC acquired 51.6% of Chilton Company, a publisher of specialty magazines, books and related marketing and research services. A tender offering will be made for the balance of shares.

ABC has learned somewhat ruefully that there is a real price to pay for television leadership in the U.S. today. It is a price of pain and scathing criticism that flows like hot lava down a mountainside, from a very free and very vocal American press.

When Gary Deeb of the *Chicago Tribune,* one of the most severe critics of media, wrote in 1977: "ABC is sick of being told that its programing and corporate ethics are a gross insult to viewers," one can understand how easily paranoia is generated.

Deeb was setting up Fred Pierce for a solar plexus blow after Pierce had decided that he, and ABC, had had enough of the press's ill-tempered criticism. Pierce decided to go on the offensive. He took on the press in a bizarre confrontation and suggested that ABC personnel might have to do their own stern evaluation of the media, namely the press.

Someone asked if Pierce was thinking of something like a "truth squad," and Pierce acceded that this was the general idea. Gary Deeb, and others, mounted the hustings. Wrote Deeb:

"What ABC must learn is that intimidation, harassment, and counter offensives rarely work anymore. Giant corporations don't scare people quite as easily these days, and the consumer movement has taught us it's sometimes possible to embarrass a big company into correcting a few wrongs."

Other critics took equally virulent aim at ABC simply because ABC had found a way of beating its competitors at their own mass audience game. ABC merely learned how to "fine tune" the mass audience a mite better than its rivals.

Robert Wussler, while head of CBS-TV, labeled ABC's schedule as "junk." Shortly after that he was removed from his job, not necessarily because he was wrong, but because he had violated the cardinal principle of the network game: do not criticize your competition for doing better what *you* would like to be doing best.

Paul Klein, head of television programs for NBC, had better luck. He castigated ABC for "programing for kids and dummies," but managed to retain his job.

There are arguable answers to these charges, but they go deeper than ABC's role on center stage at the present time. They go to the very heart of the American soul and deserve to be treated as a separate phenomenon in a later chapter.

The pain of leadership for ABC is real, and it will continue indefinitely. As one ABC executive described it: "The pain is most bearable financially, but in other ways it can be a royal pain in the ass!"

Another problem on the debit side of the ledger must be mentioned briefly, and that concerns sports.

Yes, ABC, of all companies, has a problem in sports. On the surface this sounds like the contradiction of the decade, for ABC has been the acknowledged leader of network television sports for the past 15 years. It has won every award, every accolade from a grateful public and a begrudging press. Under the brilliant guidance of Roone Arledge, ABC sports has built itself into a dominant position on ABC's schedule. His fellow maverick, Julie Barnathan, has managed to fulfill every outrageous technical demand of Arledge. Howard Cosell has become the most versatile on-air star of all three networks, is the most highly paid, and has become the most sought-after spokesman of any network in history.

ABC Sports, under Arledge, is the envy of its competitors, and until recently, its large contribution to ABC's schedule has been as solid as the rock of Gibraltar.

But lately there appear to be signs of chinks in ABC's sports armor. The problem lies, not in ABC, but in sports itself. In oversaturation of sports. Cosell has been saying this for two years and he is probably right.

The leadership of the National Football League must come under scrutiny for it seems to be pressing its luck even more than baseball, basketball, golf, and hockey. The NFL has demanded further access to prime time schedules on Thursday and Sunday nights. ABC, fearful of losing the additional games to a rival, bought a schedule for 1978. ABC made a mistake. The public appears to be in a mood to reject this further incursion of pro football beyond Monday nights.

There are other signs that oversaturation has begun in televised sports. If this happens it is ironic that ABC will become affected more adversely than its rivals simply because it is the leader in sports on the tube today.

In summing up ABC's debits and credits one can conclude that the ledger is about as evenly balanced as it ever will be in a company that depends primarily on broadcasting—and that explains why ABC is as intent on diversification as its older and already highly diversified rival, CBS.

Two problems however remain. One concerns ABC's intense desire to achieve leadership in news. This remains ABC's last broadcast mountain to climb.

The other concerns the effect Fred Silverman's defection to NBC has had on ABC.

Both are deserving of special attention.

20

News— ABC's Mega-Problem

LEADERSHIP IN NEWS has been, and remains today, ABC's biggest problem. Over two and a half decades, the company has made numerous "new commitments" to excel at news. It remains ABC's Achilles heel, and now under Roone Arledge the company has made still another "new commitment."

What these chances for success add up to, may better be assessed if we take a look at past efforts. Five men have led ABC news. John Daly was the first (1953–61) and he worked against heavy odds. Station clearances were minimal and operating budgets were miniscule. In addition, Daly worked in disharmony with ABC executives after Robert Kintner left the company. Kintner and Daly both were newsmen so they understood each other. After Kintner left, Daly knew his days at ABC were numbered. Goldenson, he felt, had little understanding of news problems, or an appreciation of the importance of news. Si Siegel, he was certain, was even less knowledgeable. Siegel, on his part, had little sympathy for Daly's temperament. Siegel considered Daly a prima donna who turned every minor problem into a major crisis.

Siegel also faulted John Daly for playing the double role of star and chief executive, and for refusing to develop backup strength in the anchor role.

Nevertheless ABC, under John Daly, did manage to earn some grudging respect in television, but never as much as it had known in the earlier days of radio. In January of 1961, Daly tendered his resignation once too often and this time it was accepted.

James Hagerty came after that, but his career as News Director lasted only two years, from 1961 to 1963. Hagerty, despite his impressive credentials as President Eisenhower's press secretary, was not right for the electronic media job. He had no experience in the field. His style was autocratic and his manner austere. However he spent ABC's meager budget wisely. He improved coverage in Washington, D.C. and established news bureaus in London, Paris, Rome, and Berlin. One of the men he hired was William Sheehan who, 12 years later, would get his own chance at putting ABC news on top.

A variety of anchor men were tried after John Daly resigned: William Lawrence, Bill Sheehan, John Cameron Swayze, Al Mann, Peter Jennings and Ron Cochran who lasted the longest— two years.

In April of 1963, Hagerty was moved upstairs to a corporate post where his talents as a politically astute problem-solver, and his many contacts, served the company well until his retirement in the early seventies.

In 1963, ABC made another "new commitment" to news leadership. This time they decided to find the most experienced professional they could find, and they would support him with a budget at least tripled over previous expenditures. They zeroed in on Elmer W. Lower who served on Bob Kintner's crack NBC news staff. Lower was vice president and general manager of NBC news under William McAndrew and Julian Goodman; before that he had earned a reputation at CBS.

Lower had a low opinion of ABC news. When Ted Shaker called him to set up an introduction to Si Siegel, Lower replied: "I don't really want to be seen in that building." When

Shaker persisted, Lower agreed. "Well, if it's late enough in the afternoon, I guess I can take a chance."

Siegel unsmilingly told him that ABC was now ready to make a do-or-die run at news leadership. Funds would be made available to set up foreign bureaus which ABC badly needed. Instead of buying news film from UPI-Fox Movietone, ABC would now gather its own film reports.

Lower politely said he was not interested. But Siegel persisted. A few weeks later he found himself sitting on Leonard Goldenson's back porch in Mamaroneck drinking iced tea and eating cookies. Goldenson never served liquor. The Chairman reiterated his determination to spend whatever it took to make ABC number one in news. The commitment was "absolute."

Elmer Lower believed what he heard. It sounded like a golden opportunity to head up his own news operation, something that was not likely to happen at NBC because his two superiors were his own age. So he accepted the job.

When he came to ABC, however, the situation he found was not reassuring. The zeal and the determination seemed to be genuine, but the cash simply was not there. The news budget was a mere 4 million dollars, about a fifth of that of either CBS or NBC. Morale was low. Equipment was poor and limited. ABC's engineering department was not up to the standards he had known at NBC. He clashed quickly with Tom Moore, President of the television network. Within a few months he decided he had probably made a mistake and thought of resigning. He was forced to live with some incredible blunders of judgment. As one example, ABC's need for revenue was so great that it accepted a regional network late evening newscast in the time that traditionally belongs to local stations—11 PM in the east; and 10 PM in the midwest. Few affiliates would clear the program for Sun Oil Company. ABC's owned station in Chicago was forced to move its leading newscaster, Alex Dreier from 10 to 10:15 PM. As a result the station's competitive position slipped to a poor third in no time at all. Similar disasters occurred at other stations that were foolish enough to carry the network news program. It was the kind of silly, desperate decision that only ABC was capable of making at the time.

Nevertheless, Lower did build, slowly but persistently, a solid news organization. During his 11 years ABC came closer to the top than it has ever come since. But the progress was painfully slow. When NBC and CBS, in 1963, decided to expand their nightly newscasts from 15 to 30 minutes, Elmer Lower had to wait until 1967 before he felt that ABC was capable of filling a 30 minute nightly report!

By the end of 1967, ABC was budgeting the unheard of amount of 35 million for news and public affairs. But on New Year's day of 1968 Harold Geneen called Leonard Goldenson to tell him that ITT was calling off its merger with ABC. Three days later Goldenson ordered Lower to lop off 8 million from his news budget for the upcoming year. Lower did so by cutting back that year's political conventions to 90 minutes per night. Despite a drop in image in the close knit media enclave, the American public applauded the move because it gave them an alternative viewing choice.

In 1973–74 Lower found a new anchor combination that made ABC more competitive than it had ever been in the past. The Howard K. Smith–Harry Reasoner anchor team increased ABC's audience by 50%, and achieved for the first time, affiliate clearance by some 175 stations—in 1963 ABC's Ron Cochran had been seen on 95 stations; but seven different network feeds had to be used to accommodate the reluctant stations; and in the entire state of Ohio there had been no clearances at all!

During that period the Smith-Reasoner team came within striking distance of equalizing NBC's formidable John Chancellor, and CBS' leader, Walter Cronkite.

In 1973 Lower, contemplating his retirement in 1978, assumed a senior corporate post and handed over the reins to his hand-picked successor, William Sheehan.

Sheehan, restless for further success, began tampering with the Smith-Reasoner format. His research told him that Reasoner could do better if he became the solo anchor star. As a result of this move the ratings dipped slightly, then reached a plateau.

This prompted the controversial teaming of Barbara Walters and Harry Reasoner in July of 1976.

The Walters-Reasoner teaming, while fraught with risks, was not made for reasons of "show biz" razzle dazzle as many believed. ABC, along with other networks, was then contemplating an extension of its nightly newscast from 30 to 45 minutes. Affiliate resistance formed and the idea had to be abandoned; hence the two strong personalities were left to confront each other in a 30 minute format that was not long enough for either of them. The on-air chemistry became so obviously discordant that it soon became a question of which one would survive. Reasoner, in particular, was loathe to cooperate. As Bill Sheehan put it:

"Harry grew petulant and worked against his own best interests. Barbara turned the other cheek so many times she didn't know which way she was facing."

The new format, after an initial upsurge in ratings based mostly on public curiosity, soon slipped lower than its former level with the result that, once again a "new commitment" in news was called for.

◇   ◇   ◇

The present bid by ABC for news leadership is the most interesting of all. It involves an executive who, at the peak of his career, had grown restive and was seeking new worlds to conquer. Another network almost corralled him, offered him more than a million dollars a year, but Roone Arledge remained at ABC because ABC gave him *carte blanche* to make ABC news first in the industry.

The Arledge appointment was viewed with something like alarm by a press that is notably hidebound and suspicious of anyone who is not a member of its journalistic "club." After all, Arledge had no traditional journalism credentials. There were fears that his sports background and show business approach to television would spill over into ABC news. Gimmicks, it was said, would replace content; form would rule substance; tabloid journalism might result. ABC network news might become an extension of the "happy talk" format used by ABC owned stations with such success. In addition, Roone Arledge's lifestyle made some people nervous. His cherubic countenance wore a defiant, sometimes insolent grin; his bush jackets, cowboy boots, wild sports shirts, and unruly red hair did not fit the image of a network news director. After 17 years with ABC, ten of them as President of ABC sports, Roone Arledge, at 45, remains essentially the untamed maverick he always was. And it is difficult to envision him being as productive in the more disciplined environment of the other networks.

The jury still remains out on the Arledge regime at ABC news. There have been encouraging signs of movement, however. In one year ABC has moved from a low of 17% share of audience to a range of 19–21%. NBC remains in the 23–25% range; CBS about 26%.

No one can deny that Arledge has not tried some new ideas or that he has a rationale for those ideas. Having no Cronkite, Arledge decided to try to make a virtue of not having a star anchorman. Desks were established and manned by multiple anchor men in Washington, Chicago, and London, with special material coming from New York. Stories were passed around, or "whipped around" from one anchor to another; or one anchor to a series of reporters in the field. The pace of the program was quickened. More stories were covered. Reporting was personalized and more depth, color, and background were added.

Because Arledge is a colorful individualist, anything he does is prone to get attention. In the early weeks of the new format, ABC got more attention than it desired. Some of the reporting was over zealous; some of the commentary was shrill and strident; there were errors in journalistic judgment. But on balance, even ABC's worst critics concede that the new Arledge version of ABC news is somewhat livelier, crisper, cleaner, more technically proficient, and the reporting more aggressive.

Early fears of critics have not been justified. The four-way split screen was abolished, and the "whiparound" technique, while flashy, has not become a substitute for substance. ABC has not gone tabloid. The sacred cows of "journalistic integrity" have not been impugned.

Some viewers say that ABC's news sometimes seems to have too many elements in it, that it has a "cluttered" look, and the pace moves too quickly.

Arledge doesn't mind this criticism. It is this "differentness" that distinguishes it from the others. He uses the word "feel" a lot when he describes what he is trying to do. He wants the nightly news to have a different "feel," a different "texture."

"If one wants to talk about gimmickry, the present format of having a single talking head is a gimmick that was spawned by necessity. Newspapers have no single unity like a "talking head." Their front pages are crammed with stories written by various reporters from wherever the news occurs. Television, in the early days, could only do this in a limited way.

"When Frank Reynolds leads off with a story about a coal mine strike in Virginia we think it is perfectly logical to have him on the scene where he can have breakfast with the miners, talk to mine officials, and get his *own* story. The result is a story that has a different "feel" to it.

"When California has a devastating forest fire, why have Max Robinson lead into it from his desk in Chicago? Why not have him at the scene? The result, again, is a different 'feel.' That is what we are striving for."

In fact, Arledge hopes eventually to establish an anchor desk in Los Angeles so the western part of the country can be better covered. He admits that some nights the format "comes together" better than others, but in general he is pleased with the way it is evolving.

As a result of the Arledge effort, all three networks are now, for the first time, going in separate directions. NBC has changed its format to one in which its star, John Chancellor, is minimized in importance by the four basic segments of the present NBC format: a lead story; a rundown of important stories; "Segment 3," which is a five minute documentary; and a wrapup of all the major headlines. CBS, with its superstar, Walter Cronkite, stands pat with the star system.

ABC, with its multiple anchor format not only eliminates the star system but seems to skew slightly toward a younger audience —although Arledge denies this. When Elvis Presley died, ABC featured his demise as the lead story, while CBS used it later in its program. When Bing Crosby died CBS used it as the lead and ABC used it later in the program. As one court jester put it, if President Carter died, NBC and CBS would open with a portrait of the President etched in black. ABC would return to its four-way split screen opening. In one corner there would appear Rosalynn and her daughter, Amy. In another we would see Carter's mother, Lillian. In another corner we would see brother Billy brooding over a can of beer. In the top right hand corner we would see the face of the President smiling benignly down upon all of them.

More than content or technique, the key problem in ABC's success or failure lies in its basic sense of total commitment. Certainly the dollars are there. ABC is building a $20 million news center in Washington that will be the envy of all the other media empires. One aspect of "total commitment" is that of time. How much time will ABC be willing to give its present effort? In the past 17 years it has used 10 different formats, anchor men, or anchor combinations. Anything less than a two year test would be absurd, since news is not sought after by all viewers—indeed, some 25% of the total audience never watch news at all!

In 1977, President Elton Rule announced to ABC affiliates that it was pledged to become the nation's news leader. Roone Arledge, at the podium with him, said that CBS correspondent, Morley Safer, told him it would take ABC 7 years to achieve leadership. "John Chancellor," said Arledge, "told me it would take five years. Even Elton Rule told me we should not look for anything quick—it might even take a year."

The remark was made in jest, and brought a laugh from the crowd. But the underlying barb was well aimed; lack of commitment in terms of time has always been ABC's problem in the past.

◇   ◇   ◇

And what if the Arledge format does not work?

Another idea has been bandied about ABC for several years. Its time may be near. That is the idea of a network bowing out of the nightly news contest and becoming an electronic wire service for all affiliates, other interested stations, both commercial and public, and cable systems.

Some news experts, like Bill Sheehan, Arledge's predecessor, think that this idea is "just around the corner." He points out that local stations in the large markets have a more pervasive news image than their networks. A network electronic wire service (or D.E.F. as it would be called, which stands for "delayed electronic feed") could pollinate the local station's image with national and international news in such a manner as to make its popularity invincible.

Further, the network "star system" is a tortuous route to take. News stars are hard to come by. Cronkites and Chancellors come along infrequently. The network providing such a service would have an exclusive franchise on the idea because there would be room for one. The cost to the network would be less. Revenues would be higher. Profits would be possible. The network's own news and public affairs image would not suffer, because it would continue its coverage of elections, conventions, documentaries, specials, etc.

It is a fascinating, free-wheeling idea that ABC might be tempted to try as it keeps making "new commitments" to news supremacy. Certainly it is in the same bold league as ABC's four way radio network concept, and its *Wide World of Sports*.

Unfortunately, the progenitor of *Wide World of Sports* is not the likely person to push such an idea. Arledge thinks it has interesting possibilities, but doubts if stations would really accept it.

"They still expect a network to provide a total service." But he has a compromise in mind that he will try at once if stations are interested. The compartmentation of a local-only half hour of news, followed by a national-only half hour, is a hybrid system that baffles him. "I would like to have stations insert 6–8 minutes of local news, sports and weather in our network news, provided the stations would permit us to put 6–8 minutes of national and international news in *their* local news."

The idea is probably too logical ever to be accepted, considering the rigid mentality of the television news fraternity.

This raises the question: will Roone Arledge succeed? He is

pragmatic about his own future: "I would like to be judged on three counts: 1) Is ABC news better than a year ago? 2) Is news now better on all three networks? 3) Did ABC play a catalyst role in that improvement?"

If he does not succeed, will he remain at ABC? Arledge has been going through a difficult time. He has grown highly sensitive to criticism, a fact that probably surprises even himself. Until recently he had seldom experienced criticism from the press; his reputation as a sports impresario was sacrosanct. Then he was accused of lack of candor with the press in connection with the *20-20 News* special, the debut of which turned out to be a debacle. Arledge takes full blame for the disastrous first show and admits that he should have postponed the series for several months. "It was dumb of me not to hold up *20-20*. I had four new projects going at the same time. I went ahead against my better judgment. We did ourselves a lot of harm."

Arledge is showing signs of learning how to live with criticism and he is candid about his mistakes. If his bosses can recognize that no new news format can succeed sooner than two years there may be real hope for ABC to achieve success in its fifth news regime. Actually Arledge has two factors working in his favor; the remarkable upgrading of ABC's affiliate lineup will assuredly bring some improvement in ratings.

Secondly, star values may indeed build around ABC's anchor men, Frank Reynolds, Peter Jennings, Max Robinson, plus commentary by Howard K. Smith and special material by Barbara Walters. Each of them has his, or her own kind of star value. Furthermore, there is nothing to prevent ABC from returning to the single star anchor system. In the winter of 1979 ABC *did* return to the single anchorman concept. Frank Reynolds was given that role, although Jennings and Robinson remain prominent in ABC's nightly telecast of "World News Tonight."

On the negative side, there continues to be the worry that with ABC's complicated format, form *will* somehow get in the way of substance; that the cumbersome mechanism of having to "whip around" from place to place, from desk to desk, may be self-defeating.

Movement in news ratings comes with about the same speed that glaciers move, so with even the slightest improvement in the past year ABC has reason to be pleased. The total audience share of news viewers generally remains the same year after year, increasing only slightly in times of world stress (Cuban missile crisis); domestic scandals (Watergate); and wars.

Thus ABC must be patient. Roone Arledge need no longer consider himself as a kind of superman, and sufficient time must be given the format. Arledge has a contract that runs until 1980. But that would not stop him from getting out if he felt the job of running both news and sports was too big for him. In that event he probably would resign; his powerful ego would hardly permit him to return to the job of running sports only. After all, he has climbed that mountain. Roone Arledge never likes to climb the same mountain twice.

And if he did resign? He would then probably set up his own production company.

Then ABC would have to make a sixth "new commitment." This time it might decide to establish the first electronic wire service for the broadcast industry.

21

Silverman Syndrome

WITH LEADERSHIP COMES the usual grab bag of problems dealing with: morale; who's on first in the executive suite; succession to the throne; complacency; over-confidence.

These problems are predictable, but not insuperable.

Complacency and over-confidence can virtually be dismissed. ABC remembers too vividly its past to become a victim of these problems.

The power struggle in the executive suite is a more serious matter. Ambitions are beginning to show at ABC. Egos are going to be bruised as those in the top echelon jostle each other for power. They do not have to be told any longer that they have done a good job. They *know* they have done a good job. Now they want the recognition that goes with the territory. This will affect morale in various subtle ways. Some within the company say that morale within the company is not as high as it was when ABC was in third place.

As for "succession to the throne," Elton Rule, of course, has long been designated as heir apparent if Leonard Goldenson retires. But will Goldenson retire? Probably not. His present contract expires in December of 1981. He will then be seventy-five.

A corollary of that question concerns President Rule who, in 1981, will reach 65. Though Rule is in perfect health and looks many years younger than his age, there are those who predict that Rule may decide to take his pension and retire to his beloved California. If both Goldenson and Rule leave, two men would move up to the top.

Seven candidates, at least, comprise the elite inner circle known as the "Eligible Seven" within the company. They are, in alphabetical order: Roone Arledge, Seth Baker, Jim Duffy, Everett Erlick, Michael Mallardi, Richard O'Leary, and Fred Pierce.

In terms of general bench strength, however, Elton Rule is said to be less than satisfied with ABC's "depth" of executive manpower, which means that there could be plenty of room for others who can make their reputations in the next three years. And there is always the possibility that ABC will break its own rule and go outside for executive help.

However, there is a problem that overshadows these considerations, and ranks in importance with the record company and the challenge of news leadership; that problem was created by Fred Silverman's defection to NBC in 1978.

This problem has had a pervasive influence on ABC. It has created a peculiar kind of paranoia within the company that centers around the question: how much did Fred Silverman do, or not do, for ABC? How much credit should he get, or not get, during his two and a half years of active duty at ABC?

ABC is sensitive about Silverman's defection. At the age of 41 he was hoisted to the Presidency of NBC, even to his own amazement, not to mention the surprise of a blasé industry. On the day of that announcement ABC's stock dropped 1¾ points while RCA's stock gained more than one point and was the most actively traded stock of the day. Only ABC knows the real value of Silverman's contribution to ABC, and only Silverman knows how much he will be able to do for NBC.

But there is more to it than that. Some insiders think that

ABC did not have to lose the talents of Fred Silverman. A year
before his three-year contract was to expire in June of 1978, he
told his boss, Fred Pierce, that he felt he was "growing stale,"
and "getting a little tired." He wanted a new challenge. After five
years in programing at CBS and a year and a half at ABC, Silverman told Pierce he did not think he would continue in the same
job.

The two Freds made a great team together. Pierce has
always acknowledged Silverman's major contributions to ABC.
Silverman admits that ABC already had a sound program development plan when he joined the company. ABC also had a secret
weapon named Michael Eisner whom Silverman terms: "the
brightest program executive I ever worked with." Also, Silverman
was happy at ABC. He would have been willing to remain if only
he had been able to convince Pierce that he was serious about
making a change in duties. He said:

"Hell, I would have been delighted to get a shot at that news
job which they gave to Roone Arledge."

He admits that, from ABC's viewpoint, he did not have
much of a chance to get out of his program job because he was
doing well at it. But in retrospect he thinks that, had he ever
been able to discuss the matter with Leonard Goldenson or Elton
Rule, the results might have been different.

The circumstances of Silverman's departure also led to a mis-
understanding that has ruffled feathers on both sides. ABC has
stated that Silverman promised that he would never leave ABC
for any other network.

But Silverman insists that this is wrong. "I promised never to
go to any other network in the *same* program job. I never
dreamed that I would be offered the Presidency of a company like
NBC—and that is a job that is far different from that of programing."

Indeed it is. And now Silverman is talking about changing his
own rules of the LCD (lowest common denominator) game that
he played so superbly in the past. He sincerely thinks that the
time has come to upgrade programing.

"Times change. The public is ready for it. NBC is ready for

it. I have the full support of the Chairman, and the Board, of RCA. Our affiliates want it. I firmly believe that a good show can find its audience no matter where it is placed on the schedule."

As an example he pointed to a show that had then (in the fall of 1978) recently debuted, called *Lifeline*, a real life docu-drama dealing with doctors and their patients. Silverman was pleased with the early ratings. "I think *Lifeline*, in a few more weeks, will attain a 30% share. It may take longer, but I am convinced it will get there."

The results, however, turned out differently. Despite an all-out advertising and promotion effort, *Lifeline* did not reach the survival level of a 30% share and was cancelled a few months later. Despite his much quoted intention of "upgrading" programing, Silverman put his stamp of approval on a fall schedule for 1979 that, even before it debuted, drew criticism from television critics who charged that NBC, in the fall of 1979, would be as mass dominated as the programs of the other two networks.

Looking back at his two and a half years with ABC, there was another source of irritation that still rankled Silverman and that was Fred Pierce's contention that Silverman was good at scheduling, and good with talent, but weak in development. Fred Silverman bristles at this charge:

"I recently took a look at ABC's 1978 schedule and did a tally of the shows I had a hand in developing. For the most part they were new projects, and in one or two instances they were dormant scripts. *Charlie's Angels*, for instance, was a dormant script; it had been on a development report for one and a half years. My tally shows, *The Hardy Boys, Galactica, Operation Petticoat, Laverne and Shirley, Three's a Crowd, Taxi, Eight Is Enough, Vegas* (which I resurrected about a month and a half before I left), *What's Happening, Soap, Carter Country, Love Boat*, and *Fantasy Island. Love Boat* was a movie script that had been in development for a year and a half. That amounts to about 75% of ABC's schedule. *Family* and *Mork and Mindy* were the only two shows I had nothing to do with."

The "Silverman Syndrome" begs two questions:
1) how much will Silverman's defection cost ABC in terms of

his contributions? It is too early to assess that one because when Silverman left ABC the company was in such great shape it could literally coast on its own momentum for a year or two.

2) how much will Silverman's defection cost ABC in terms of personnel? Who will Fred Silverman seek to bring over to NBC?

The answer to the second question is: probably none. ABC, as a precautionary measure, signed new contracts with numerous of its key executives shortly after Silverman left; enough time has elapsed to consider the second question not to be a problem.

Finally, will ABC over-react to NBC and Silverman? Will it become hyper-sensitive to the moves of the 41-year-old commercial genius who has made two of the three networks a reflection of his own program talents?

And if Silverman truly changes NBC's direction away from the LCD formula, he may throw the entire industry into turmoil. If he goes back on his word, or does not really try, he will be called a hypocrite. If he tries and fails he will become a sacrificial lamb. New precepts, and impeccable timing, must go hand in hand if they are to succeed.

Just how Fred Silverman goes about his "new direction" in programing makes for a fascinating future chapter in the unfolding saga of this remarkable young man.

ABC will be watching with a wary eye.

22

A Company
at the Crossroads

ALL LEADING COMPANIES are at the crossroads. How to go forward . . . how to make certain adjustments to maintain leadership . . . these are the burdens and challenges of leadership.

It is clear that ABC rose to the top not only because of what it did, but because of what CBS and NBC did *not* do. CBS became a victim of its own atrophy and of William Paley's loss of touch in the sensitive, volatile broadcast field. CBS' new, unseeded broadcast team must go through a process of trial and error that may get worse before it gets better. NBC, under Fred Silverman, will never be the same. The committee style of management at NBC is already gone. The satellite-of-RCA syndrome is also gone—that is, as much as it ever will be "gone." The "sanctification-of-Fred" process goes on. Whether Silverman has a messianic complex or not, the fact remains that he is singularly talented and he just might lead NBC—and the entire industry— to the promised land of not-perfect television, but to a better quality level of programs.

ABC's biggest problem is not so much the burden of leadership, as it is the *delineation* of that leadership.

How should a new leader in the broadcast business act?
What *are* the new dimensions of that leadership?

Does it suffice to leap from six dollars a share, to eight, to
ten, to twelve dollars? Does it suffice to broaden, diversify, grow
into another super conglomerate? Is that all that leadership entails in the world's largest, most powerful broadcast company?

The answer is: of course not. And ABC knows it is not the
answer. ABC is searching for other answers, other dimensions, al-
beit inchoately, but the fact that it is *aware* of the need to delin-
eate new dimensions is a healthy sign.

Higher ratings alone . . . higher dividends alone . . . will
not suffice as they would for other companies. ABC is in a business that is integrated into the lives of 220 million Americans.
Television comes into our lives before toilet training. We expect
more from television. We certainly expect more in terms of
leadership from television corporations. As the song goes, "The
times, they are a-changin'." ABC must change with them as it
seeks out new dimensions of leadership.

◊   ◊   ◊

The time is 1978 and the scene is a podium in a private suite of
rooms in Chicago, a high level meeting of national leaders and
Chicago supporters of United Cerebral Palsy. The speaker is
Leonard Goldenson.

He bounces to the podium. A 72-year-old man who can still
bounce. Goldenson is euphoric today. Beaming smile. Friendly
nods. Today he is doing business at his "second store." Some say
he loves this store more than ABC. Goldenson and his wife
formed UCP as a national health agency (6th largest in the U.S.)
in 1950 after they learned that their daughter had cerebral palsy.
Since then he has contributed vast sums of money to the agency.
That is not important. Millionaires like Goldenson *should* give
away money to worthy causes. What is more important is the vast
amounts of time and energy that Goldenson has given to UCP.
His dedication amounts to passion. He covers the country regu-
larly, speaking and beating the drums, much as he did 40 years

ago. Funds to be raised? A telethon planned? National policy to be discussed? Goldenson has bag packed and will travel anywhere.

Today he is announcing that ABC will lend its facilities and personnel for a year-end network telethon. He gets so enthused that he loses his place in his prepared remarks. He gets ahead of himself. Screws it all up. To see the Chairman of ABC, and the lifetime Chairman of UCP, get so mixed up brings a good-natured laugh from the crowd. But there is no embarrassment. They have seen Leonard Goldenson do this before. He simply can't contain himself when he gets into the subject of cerebral palsy. Goldenson laughs at himself, makes a self-deprecating remark, and plunges on. . . .

Any assessment of ABC today should end, as it began, with one man: Leonard Goldenson. He *is* ABC. It is hard to think of ABC thriving without him, though of course it will.

ABC has been crisis-ridden, often accident prone, indomitably optimistic. In 25 years it has been tempered by hard knocks, good luck, bad luck, many mistakes, but always it has been dominated by the indefatigable spirit, zeal, and optimism, and the singular drive of Goldenson.

Said one CBS executive, "ABC has weathered more storms than Popeye, the sailor. It has blundered, bumbled, foundered, fought, clawed, and scrapped its way to the top mainly because of one man. It has had incredible luck when it needed it (cancellation of ITT merger); it is capable of bold moves (the four way radio network); it has done many things, but its greatest asset has been Goldenson."

So, what kind of man is Leonard Goldenson? Who is he? Strange though it sounds, there are executives who have been with him for 25 years who are still asking that question. Among other things, Leonard Goldenson is the following:

He has a smile as broad and ingratiating as President Carter, but the smile can disappear in an instant. He has a hearty laugh but does not really have a great sense of humor. He likes to be "sold." He appreciates flamboyance in others but is, himself, the most unflamboyant of men. He has a temper but it is so controlled that when he uses it one feels that he has prepared himself in advance for the outburst. He has a puritanical moral outlook and drinks perhaps two glasses of wine in a year. He never swears, he dislikes profanity, and abhors scatological humor. It has been said of him that the real reason he espouses autonomy as a management philosophy is that, if things do not go right, he can blame someone else.

He is generous of spirit, but can be hard of heart. He has known tragedy in his personal life and one senses this soon after meeting him. He dislikes personal confrontation, but can handle it if he must. He reads books, but not many. He is a high stakes gambler, plays tennis with a tenacity of style; he seeks consistency of play, tries to get his opponent to wear himself out; by contrast, in business, he has gone for the "kill" all of his life.

He is resilient, adaptable, yet in some circumstances can be absolutely inflexible. With all of his suddenly turned-on charm he remains oddly colorless. Despite his success he remains the most unpretentious of men. He is a born competitor and could no more think of retiring than could William Paley. Though his life is an open book and there never has been a hint of scandal about him, he remains a rather enigmatic figure. His associates still do not know what really makes him tick. One of his closest friends, Jack Hausman, when asked for anecdotes about Goldenson, could not think of any except to say: "I never met a man who disliked Leonard Goldenson." Either Hausman is so overwhelmed with affection for his friend, or it is an example of even a close friend being unable to capture Goldenson in anecdotal form.

If a person is known by the company he keeps, so can a corporation be said to be known by the leadership it has, the problems it has solved, and the storms it has weathered.

Leonard Goldenson has certainly been ABC's leader. He has helped solve many of the problems. He has weathered all the storms. But in the final sense Leonard Goldenson remains a mystery wrapped within an enigma. Yet one thing is sure: he remains the ultimate survivor.

23

Dilemma of the Tube

PERHAPS IT IS BECAUSE we are not at war. Maybe it is because our democratic system of government has become so complex we can no longer be cohesive as a nation unless we are at war. Whatever the reasons the truth is that Americans have seldom been in such a mood as they are in today.

We are divided. Quarrelsome. Suspicious. It is a querulous mood verging on the ugly. Bitterness, rage, and frustration permeate the atmosphere. There is a sense of helplessness more than hopelessness. Anger more than despair, as though the game plan had broken down, the rules had been tossed out, and the referee had disappeared. It is a feeling of no longer being masters of our national fate or our personal destinies.

We are mired in a quicksand of the spirit. There is a fungus on the American soul. Past precepts of family, honor, institutions, and values have been discarded. It seems impossible to form a consensus on anything. The Presidency has become too big a job for any one person. Bureaucracy reigns supreme in the land. We perceive dimly that our own greed will never permit us to win the battle of inflation. There is a bitterness between generations which is a skeleton in our national closet, a secret we are too embarrassed to talk about.

Timorously we are beginning to look inward—that in itself is a new adventure for Americans. We have never been good at introspection. The realization dawns that we have had too much change, too soon, and we ask ourselves: will there ever again be the orderliness and tranquillity of bygone times?

We retreat further into ourselves and try to sort out personal priorities; such pragmatic concerns as where to go on vacation; fixing up the house or apartment; accumulating things as a hedge against an inflation that obliterates all dreams of future planning.

No question about it, we tell ourselves: the whole business of living in some orderly, systematic way seems to have gone down the drain. But when we look around at the tumult and change going on elsewhere in the world, we see little to make us envy others. So we retreat still further, much as we did in the 'fifties, but without the values we clung to in the 'fifties.

In such a mood we need victims. The ideal scapegoat for our frustration and rage is, of course, television. As the mountains of rhetoric pile up, television has become blamed for nearly all of the ills of mankind. Name a problem, a disease or a condition and you can be sure that there are some people who are convinced that television caused it.

Such a situation, looked at rationally, is so profoundly absurd as to be amusing. But television—meaning the television industry—is not laughing. Its members have developed a case of profit-induced self guilt. Next to the oil industry, broadcast profits are the highest of all, in terms of profit ratios. This quite naturally causes embarrassment and induces a very real sense of paranoia. To make enormous profits, and especially to be so visible in making them, is definitely not "in" these days.

As the cacophony of dissent and accusations grows more shrill, the television industry finds itself like the little boy who cried out in protest against a beating he could not understand; when it was over he said to himself: "It was such a good beating I must have done something very bad!"

When a network (ABC) hears itself castigated as "the sleaziest, most exploitative outfit ever to operate in what probably is America's sleaziest, most exploitative industry," it is bound to cause pain.[1]

When the same critic adds: "We're already beginning to pay for the propagation of such bullheaded attitudes. And the price is bound to escalate as a generation of young people raised on those priceless falsehoods grows into adulthood," it sends industry leaders running for the Maalox bottle.

When the same critic concludes, "the tyranny of youth will have cleared its final hurdle—and a promising mass-audience tool will have surrendered itself to the basest instincts of an increasingly hedonistic and thoughtless subculture," it is bound to have the effect of increasing the industry's already acute jitters.

The finger-pointing can get personal, the protests violent. Gerald Gransville Bishop, of California, pumped 17 shots into his television set. When the police came, Bishop said he had no regrets. "I killed it! Haven't you ever wanted to kill your TV set?"

Television tubes have been punched out, sets have been dropped out windows, and set afire. Tight security has become standard procedure at television stations and networks. Some station managers have been beaten up because of editorials they have spoken on the air. Managers, for the most part, now take a low, not high, profile in their communities. Network executives have been threatened at stockholder meetings. Citizen groups like the National PTA, Action For Children's Television, the National Citizens Committee, and many others, know the pressure points of the industry—and use them.

Television criticism has become so strident and vindictive that Richard Schickel of the *New York Times* says it has assumed proportions of a threat to the national ecology.

"The brightly glowing box in the corner of the living room is perceived by those who write books and Sunday newspaper articles about it as a sort of smoking chimney, spilling God knows what brain-damaging poisons not only into the immediate socio-

---

[1] Gary Deeb, *Chicago Tribune*, 10-23-78.

political environment, but also, it is predicted, loosing agents whose damage may not become apparent to us for decades to come."

Schickel makes the point about how bad the situation has become, but he does not agree with the critics. Put simply, he suggests that television may be no worse for us than Captain Billy's Whiz Bang.

Panaceas to negate the "monster" of the tube are springing up everywhere. Groups are boycotting advertisers, going on periodic "TV Fasts," or banning the tube entirely. Any day we can expect to see "TV Addicts Anonymous" in which angry viewers will sit around and discuss how they have licked the problem of their television addiction. One journalist in *Newsweek* soberly suggested that the government create a real family hour by banning all television broadcasting for sixty to ninety minutes each night. "By using the quiet of the family hours to discuss our problems we might get to know each other better, and to like each other better."

John Camper, a former Chicago television critic, had a quick answer to that. "The opposite would happen. Family members would begin to hate each other more than ever before." One of the few good things Camper could say about television was that, "it keeps members of a family from bugging each other."

And so the debate rolls on . . . And the public continues to watch.

If you want behavioral studies to prove your bias or prejudice there are scores to choose from. The most specious of all are those that question whether television has *any* motivational effect on viewers—this in the face of the fact that television is supported by advertising budgets that increase each year because clients and their agencies report glowingly how effectively television sells products and services!

There are defenders, of course, out there amongst those millions who are caught up in a frenzied love-hate relationship with the tube. The old and infirm love it with scarcely any criticism. Children accept it uncompromisingly. If television is a hypnotic drug reducing children to robot-like acceptance of the status quo, and obeisance to the corporate ikons, Jeff Greenfield wonders why "the first generation of television viewers turned into the most raucous, dissident, anti-corporate generation this nation has ever known."

And, he points out, if television was supposed to turn us into armchair spectators, why does it exist now, "side by side with an unprecedented explosion of physical fitness?"

If television is the latest step in the modern world's separation of man and his sensory gifts, it puzzles Greenfield that our nation is experiencing a widespread rediscovery of everything from backpacking to natural food.

He admits that one can argue that television showed us the Viet Nam war and domestic violence, "but that kind of argument really confuses the messenger with the message."

No one can deny that television has changed the way we live. It has undoubtedly contributed to a sharp decline in reading skills among students, but how does that equate with the fact that more books and magazines are sold today than ever before? Or that most of the books, and many of the magazines, are as trashy as the programs we love to criticize?

Time has a way of making the past loom larger than the present. Neil Hickey, in *TV Guide*, laments the loss of anthology dramas and other traditional forms of adult television fare that used to fill the screen. "The staple now is featherweight comedy and pulp action-adventure fiction, mitigated at intervals by mini-series and other pre-emptive material of uncertain quality overlaid with heavy-handed gobs of sex as extra-added enticement."

But was television really all that good in the good old days? Aram Bakshian, Jr., writing in the *Wall Street Journal*, does not think it was. "Nostalgia fans revel in the memory of Sid Caesar's *Your Show Of Shows, Playhouse 90,* and Ed Murrow's *See It Now,* but they forget the arid hours that were characteristic of early television—the plastic newscasts of John Cameron Swayze, the anaesthetizing antics of Jerry Lester, the drab foreign 'B' films and westerns, the horribly amateurish local programs which consisted of a blowsy hostess or moth-eaten host plugging local tradesmen in between one-reel featurettes provided by the travel, hardware, auto, food, or other publicity-hungry industry."

"The impossible dream of an enlightened mass medium," writes Mr. Bakshian, "spoon-feeding culture and proper political and social ideas to a captive national audience, continues to haunt many critics of television. They remain wed to the notion that if only people like them ran television they could remake society in their own image."

He goes on: "If television has become the sinister electronic babysitter some claim, it is because parents, teachers, church and community have neglected their babysitting and child-rearing responsibilities and have consigned to television a role it cannot play. Human nature being what it is, however, the desire grows to pin the blame for such failings on that most convenient scapegoat, the one-eyed monster."

The debate goes on . . .

What all these polemics fail to deal with, however, is the fact that the television industry is in a dilemma which has no solution.

That dilemma revolves around the system—a system that requires the networks (and stations as well) to reach the largest number of people at all times so that it can sell the greatest number of products and services for advertisers.

Some call it the "LCD Machine," and liken it to a racing car at the Indy 500. The mechanic at Indy who fine-tunes the carburetor of his machine a mite better than his competitors usually wins the race, provided that other factors are equal, such as the quality of the driver, and the benign blessing of Lady Luck.

In television the network that fine-tunes its mass audience to the LCD factor—*lowest common denominator*—wins the mass numbers rating race for that year. Fred Silverman is the master mechanic who has achieved singular fame for fine-tuning the carburetors of both CBS and ABC, although he now declares that the time has come to go in a somewhat different direction.

There are many skeptics who insist that Silverman can not go in a different direction. The system will not permit it. The system cannot be changed. The system is inextricably bound by its own rigid dynamics.

The median age of Americans today is 29.4 years. Of 200 million Americans, 35% are under 21. Another 29% comprise the 21–39 age group. Those middle aged (40–64) make up for 25% of the population, and the elderly (over 65) account for 11% of our population.

Television perceives that the biggest spenders in the U.S. today are those between 18–34 years of age. Advertisers pay $13 per thousand homes to reach this group, and only $6 per thousand homes for those over 50, although the latter group watches more television.

Thus the real target group for those mechanics who fine-tune the "LCD Machine" are those who grew up between 1955–1965. They are now in their mid-thirties. They were weaned on, as Gary Deeb points out, "the early gutbucket rock of Elvis Presley, Fats Domino, and Jerry Lee Lewis; or the later refinements of the Beatles, the Beach Boys, and the Bee Gees; or the acid rock of the Woodstock generation."

"The first politician you cared for," writes Deeb, "was John F. Kennedy, because he was young, handsome, and witty. Chances are you were against the Viet Nam war. And now that you've attained adulthood and ideally have become a responsible citizen and conspicious consumer, the television moguls need you. As a scruffy kid you meant nothing to them; today, however, you represent money in their pocketbooks."

The grownup rock and roll generation is unquestionably the networks' program target, which, of course, explains why so many of television's so-called prime time hits are so mindlessly banal.

But that makes its own scathing statement about just *who* and *what* we are as a nation today!

Adding to the frustration is the fact that a growing number *within* the system would like to extricate themselves from it. Aaron Spelling, a producer who has made millions from the system, asks: "How in hell do we stop this network mania?" He is referring to ratings, of course.

Norman Lear, another eminently successful producer, calls it, "the most destructive force in television today."

Even station managers are joining the protest. Alan Bell, a manager in Philadelphia, declares: "They can't maintain this kind of ratings war. If they stopped worrying about who is number one, and started building some better programing, we'd all be better off."

Fred Silverman, whose actions will be watched more closely than any other television leader, admits it has become a "competitive frenzy" and vows he can do something about it.

Networks have become as hypersensitive about the system as their critics. They know that Americans want something other than the "LCD Machine," and ironically, all of them are concentrating their diversification efforts on publishing, a field in which Americans have welcomed the almost inexhaustively wide range of reading choices that now exist.

But the fact remains the system *cannot* be changed. There will be attempts made to tamper with it, but the essential fundamentals will remain the same.

To add to the dilemma of the tube the networks know that, in the next decade, and certainly by the end of the century, their system will be subject to massive pressures of change in a technological sense. A Pandora's Box of new techniques and inventions will turn the tube into an in-home information and service center. We already have super screen sizes, video cassette recorders, video disc players, video games, cable, and pay television over the air as well as by cable.

Cable today, feeding up to 75 channels, reaches about 15% of the nation's 73 million television homes. A television program beamed from a "superstation" via satellite can reach 282 cable systems. Pay TV cable has 1½ million subscribers on 604 of 4,000 cable systems, and by 1980 will reach 3–4 million subscribers.

As early as 1982 cable penetration may reach some 30% of the nation's television homes and that is the "magic number" at which cable will "explode" and make a national impact—just as black and white television, and color, did when this percentage was reached. By then there will be an estimated one million video cassette recorders at work in U.S. homes, and 1,000 satellite receiving stations.

It is already technically feasible to interface one's home television set with a computer, making it possible to read and receive information from banks, stores, doctors' offices and libraries. An experiment in Columbus, Ohio, called QUBE presently enables subscribers to take part in opinion polls, rate performers on talent, vote on local issues, and other merchandise.

"Superstations" like WTCG, Atlanta, use a satellite to extend their normal signals to 2.3 million cable homes, with an increase to 3.4 million homes projected for 1979. Other major market stations are also becoming "superstations": WOR-TV, New York; WGN-TV, Chicago; KTVU, Oakland; and KTTV, Los Angeles. There will be others.

There is little doubt that the television set of today is beginning a new era: from passive entertainer it will soon become a visual information system for many purposes, of which entertainment as we know it today will be only one small part.

Small part? Not everyone agrees on that. Many think that, despite the onslaught of some truly awesome technical developments, the present network dominated "LCD" system will continue to be "the only game in town" at least till the end of this century.

Merrill Panitt, editorial director of *TV Guide*, flatly declares that "there is not going to be any revolution in the foreseeable future."

There will be an "erosion of audience," he admits. This process, in fact, has already begun, but it will be "gradual" and not devastating to the networks' economy.

FCC Commissioner, Joseph R. Fogarty, is less sanguine. He thinks that the development of fiber optics, broadband programing, and satellite-aided "superstations" could make over-the-air broadcasting "extinct."

Erik Barnouw, a respected chronicler of the broadcast business, thinks that the present system will expand to the extent that it will one day rule every facet of our lives.

"There's grave danger television will eventually take over

most everything—education, business, entertainment, and even
politics. If that happens people will lose their ability to cope with
real life. A child's education will come from a television screen,
and adults will conduct business face-to-face from their homes.
The business office as we know it will be obsolete."

But all these points—the dilemma of the industry, its inability to extricate itself from the system, new threats to the system—
are irrelevant to the real questions we should be asking:

why television is the way it is today.

Three classic questions are usually debated at cocktail parties
where television is always discussed:

1) Should television be the leading edge in societal influence? (Which begs the further question: who is to play God and
determine what that "leading edge" should be? Your leading edge
might be entirely different from mine.)

2) Or should television be a trailing edge?

3) Or should television be no edge at all, but merely a reflecting mirror of our society?

With this come additional questions: are we responsible for
the kind of television we get, or is television responsible for turning us into mediocre zombies? Where should the responsibility
be placed? And what can be done about it?

We get closer to the truth, it seems, when we begin asking
the fundamental question, which is:
Who are we?

Regrettable as it may be, the time has come when we must
point the finger at ourselves, for the incontravertible truth is: *We
are what we do.*

We are what we *think*. What we *drink*. What we *eat*. What
we *wear*. And what we *read*.

And certainly, when it comes to the tube, *we are what we
watch!*

As a nation, it is generally agreed that, yes, we are turning
inward. It's about time. It's not a pleasant experience to ask ourselves questions like: are we becoming another "Decline and Fall
of the Roman Empire?" Have we become the most hedonistic,
gratification-seeking society since Rome?

As Americans, we have never been very good at looking into our own souls. We experience discomfiture when others look too deeply into our eyes. Perhaps that is why so many of us wear those one-way sunglasses.

We do not like to think that television may simply be a reflection of who we are—and who we are *not*. It disturbs us to think that, if there are superior creatures from outer space, and if they came to our planet to investigate us, all they would have to do is rent a room at any Holiday Inn and watch U.S. television for 48 hours! In that short span they would learn everything they need to know about Americans, circa late 20th century.

Perhaps this exercise of introspection will do more to change television than anything else. To call the present "LCD" system imperfect is beside the point. Of course it is imperfect. Our system of government is also imperfect because it is untidy and fragile. Surely we will bring it down one day, just as surely as man has brought down all systems that he creates—not because our systems are imperfect, but because, let's face it, we are a mean-spirited species much more adept at destroying than building. The media may be harbingers of our fate, but they do not cause it. No single medium, even one as powerful as television, can change us from what we essentially are.

Thus we will push, like lemmings to the sea, to whatever fate awaits us. And television will provide us with a giant looking glass as we move in the direction we inexorably must.

But that is *all* that television will do, because in the final analysis, we are nothing more, nothing less than what we watch.

◇ ◇ ◇

If the networks are locked into the present LCD system, as this author believes they are, they must then struggle with a problem which they *can* solve—and that is the problem of seeking new and broader dimensions of leadership beyond the hard facts of profits and dividends.

How refreshing it would be if one, or all, of the three networks would say something like:

We know we are locked into an imperfect system. We know,

for us, there is no escape. But you can escape! We don't expect all of you to watch us all of the time. Indeed, we hope you will not. We know we cannot be all things to all people, so take us for what we are—no more, no less.

We recognize that there is another system out there, an alternative system called public broadcasting. We also know that this system represents for us the greatest safety valve *we could possibly have. We encourage you to watch this system because it can give you things we cannot give.*

What remarkable candor that would be! Because public broadcasting *is* the greatest safety valve the networks have. It *is* a hedge against punitive legislation that may result one day if an angry public gets the support of a responsive Congress and causes drastic changes in the present system.

Here, it seems, lies the networks' greatest opportunity to express "new dimensions of leadership"—not the polite acceptance and tokens of support they have grudgingly given in the past.

As for us, the viewers, 220 million of us who rave and rant over what we see on the tube, it is time for us to concede that yes, unfortunately, we *are* what we watch.

Having accepted this rather dismal premise we will then descend a scale lower in our self-esteem. But only for a time. Having once passed that threshold, the time will come when we can ascend again, because it is a peculiar trait of man that he can transcend himself. He can move from the low of an ignoble plateau to the heights of a noble one. It does not happen often, and the movement is usually cyclical and distressingly short-lived. But the potential is there, and it would be inspiring to see Americans begin another cycle upwards to renewed dignity, higher self-esteem, and honor.

Selective Bibliography

ABC. American Broadcasting Companies, Inc. Library.

Advertising Age. Chicago, 1930—

Allen, Frederick Lewis. *Only Yesterday*. Harper, 1951.

Archer, Gleason L. *Big Business and Radio*. American Historical Company, 1939.

———. *History of Radio*. American Historical Company, 1926.

Appointments To The Regulatory Agencies, 1949–1974. Printed at direction of Honorable Warren G. Magnuson, Chairman, Committee on Congress. U.S. Printing Office, 1976.

Arlene, Michael J. *The Living Room War*. Viking, 1969.

Barnouw, Erik. *The Golden Web: A History of Broadcasting in the United States. 1922–53*. Oxford University Press, 1968.

———. *The Image Empire: A History of Broadcasting in the United States from 1953*. Oxford University Press, 1970.

———. *A Tower in Babel: A History of Broadcasting in the United States to 1933*. Oxford University Press, 1966.

———. *Tube of Plenty! The Evolution of American Television*. Oxford University Press, 1975.

Berkow, Ira. *Maxwell Street*. Doubleday, 1977.

Bliven, Bruce. *How Radio Is Remaking Our World*. Century, 1924.

Bogart, Leo. *The Age of Television.* Ungar, 1958.

Broadcasting & Cable Television, Policies For Diversity and Change—A Statement by the Research and Policy Committee, Committee For Economic Development, 1975.

Broadcasting Magazine. Washington, 1931–

Broadcasting Yearbook. Washington, 1935–

Broadcasting in the United States. Washington. National Association of Broadcasters, 1933.

Brown, Les. *Television: The Business Behind the Box.* Harcourt Brace Jovanovich, 1971.

———. *Encyclopedia of Television.* Times Books, 1978.

Campbell, Robert. *The Golden Years of Broadcasting: A Celebration of the First 50 Years of Radio and Television on NBC.* Rutledge Books/Scribners, 1976.

Chase, Francis, Jr. *Sound and Fury: An Informal History of Broadcasting.* Harper, 1942.

Cole, Barry, and Mal Oettinger. *Reluctant Regulators.* Addison Wesley, 1978.

Cosell, Howard. *Cosell.* Playboy Press, 1973.

Conant, Michael. *Antitrust in the Motion Picture Industry.* Macmillan, 1946.

Davenport, Elaine, and Paul Eddy, with Mark Hurwitz. *The Hughes Papers.* Ballantine Books, 1976.

Davis, Clive, with James Willwerth. *Inside The Record Business.* William Morrow and Company, 1975.

Davis, H. P. *The Early History of Broadcasting in the United States.* A. W. Shaw, 1928.

Dessart, George (ed.). *Television in the Real World: A Case Study* (IRTS). Hastings House, 1978.

Dreher, Carl. *Sarnoff: an American Success.* Quadrangle Press, 1977.

Dunlap, Orrin E. Jr. *The Story of Radio.* Dial Press, 1935.

———. *The Future of Television.* Harper, 1947.

———. *Radio and Television Almanac.* Harper, 1951.

Evans, James F. *Prairie Farmer and WLS.* University of Illinois Press, 1969.

FCC: Docket No. 16828.

Friendly, Fred W. *Due To Circumstances Beyond Our Control.* Random House, 1967.

Gates, Gary Paul. *Air Time: The Inside Story of CBS News.* Harper & Row, 1978.

Goldsen, Rose K. *The Show And Tell Machine.* Dial Press, 1975.

Gordon, George N. *The Communications Revolution: A History of Mass Media in the United States.* Hastings House, 1977.

Greenfield, Jeff. *Television: The First 50 Years.* Abrams, 1977.

Gross, Ben. *I Looked And Listened.* Random House, 1954.

Hinckley, Robert H. *Autobiography.* Brigham Young University Press, 1977.

Hutchinson, Thomas H. *Here Is Television: Your Window on the World.* Hastings House, 1946.

Innis, Harold A. *Empire and Communications.* Oxford, Clarendon Press, 1950.

Johnson, Nicholas. *Test Pattern For Living.* Bantam, 1973.

Kendrick, Alexander. *Prime Time: The Life of Edward R. Murrow.* Little, Brown, 1969.

Landry, Robert J. *This Fascinating Radio Business.* Bobbs-Merrill, 1946.

Lazarsfeld, Paul F. *The People's Choice.* Duell, Sloan & Pearce, 1944.

Levy, David. *The Chameleons.* Dodd, Mead, 1964.

Lichty, Lawrence W. and Malachi C. Topping. *American Broadcasting: A Sourcebook on the History of Radio and Television.* Hastings House, Publishers, 1975.

Lyons, Eugene. *David Sarnoff—A Biography.* Harper, 1966.

MacNeil, Robert. *The People Machine.* Harper & Row, 1968.

Mander, Jerry. *Four Arguments For The Elimination of Television.* Morrow, 1978.

Mankiewicz, Frank, and Joel Swerdlow. *Remote Control.* Times Books, 1978.

Martin, James. *Future Developments In Telecommunications.* Prentice-Hall, 1971.

Mayer, Martin. *Madison Avenue, U.S.A.* Harper, 1958.

———. *About Television.* Harper & Row, 1972.

Media Decisions. New York. 1965.

Meyer, Richard J. *The Blue Book.* Journal of Broadcasting, Summer, 1962.

Metz, Robert. *CBS—Reflections In A Golden Eye.* Playboy Press, 1975.

Minow, Newton N., John Bartlow Martin, and Lee M. Mitchell. *Presidential Television.* Basic Books, 1973.

——— and Lee Mitchell. *Equal Time.* Hawthorn, 1973.

NAEB Journal. National Association of Educational Broadcasters, 1957—

Ogilvy, David. *Confessions Of An Advertising Man.* Atheneum, 1963.

Sampson, Anthony. *The Soverign State of ITT.* Stein & Day, 1973.

Schickel, Richard. *The Disney Version: The Life, Times, Art and Commerce of Walt Disney.* Simon & Schuster, 1968.

Schramm, Wilbur (*ed*). *Mass Communications.* University of Illinois Press, 1954.

————. (*ed*). *The Process and Effects of Mass Communications.* University of Illinois Press, 1954.

————. *Responsibility in Mass Communication.* Harper, 1957.

Schulman, Arthur, and Roger Youman, *The Television Years.* Popular Library, 1973.

Schwartz, Bernard. *The Professor and the Commissions.* Knopf, 1959.

Seldes, Gilbert. *The Public Arts.* Simon & Schuster, 1956.

Shayon, Robert Lewis. *Television and Our Children.* Longmans, Green, 1951.

Quinlan, Sterling. *Merger.* Doubleday, 1958.

————. *The Hundred Million Dollar Lunch.* O'Hara, 1974.

Randolph, Bert. *The Thrill of Victory.* Hawthorn, 1978.

Rather, Dan, with Herskowitcz. *The Camera Never Blinks.* Morrow Press, 1977.

Roe, Yale. *The Television Dilemma: Search for a Solution.* Hastings House, 1962.

Schorr, Daniel. *Clearing The Air.* Houghton Mifflin Co.

Siepmann, Charles A. *Radio, Television and Society.* Oxford University Press, 1950.

Skornia, Harry J. *Television and Society.* McGraw-Hill, 1965.

Sponsor Magazine. New York. 1948—

Stanley, Robert H. (*ed*). *The Broadcast Industry: An Examination of Major Issues* (IRTS). Hastings House, 1975.

————. *The Celluloid Empire: A History of the American Motion Picture Industry.* Hastings House, 1978.

Steinberg, Charles S. (*ed.*). *Broadcasting: The Critical Challenges* (IRTS). Hastings House. 1974.

————. (*ed*). *Mass Media and Communication.* 2nd Edition. Hastings House, 1972.

Television Digest. Washington, 1945—

Television Factbook. Washington, 1948—

Television/Radio Age. New York, 1952—

Television Quarterly, Journal of National Academy of TV Arts and Sciences. Syracuse University. 1962—

Fireman, Judy (*ed*). *TV Book.* Workman, 1977.

TV Guide. Philadelphia, 1948—

Variety. New York. 1905—

Wakeman, Frederic. *The Hucksters*. Rinehart, 1946.

Waller, Judith C. *Radio, the Fifth Estate*. Houghton, Mifflin, 1950.

Wolper, David L. with Quincy Troupe. *The Inside Story of TV's "Roots."* Warner Books, 1978.

Index

ABC, 3-7 *passim,* 16-28 *passim,* 31, 33, 53-77 *passim,* 80, 82, 83, 87-91 *passim,* 132, 138, 143, 145, 153, 154 and *n.,* 155, 159, 160, 165, 171-78 *passim,* 185, 199, 200, 209, 210, 215, 218, 220, 221, 222, 223, 226, 227, 263; and affiliated network stations, number of (1979), 233*n.;* and color television, 88, 145; consolidation and realignment within (1970), 169-70; and corporate raiders, vulnerability to, 88*ff.;* film syndication division of, 136, 142; and Hughes' "takeover machine," 145-52 *passim;* International Division of, 75, 121, 136, 142, 163, 239-40; and ITT, xiii, 92-118 *passim,* 127, 132, 144, 145, 248; leadership by (1976-1979), 222-23, 224-25, 228-34, 237-39, 241-42, 261-63; mavericks in, 68*ff.;* and Monogram Industries, 144; motion picture production by, 122, 178, 179, 196 and *n.,* 197*n.;* "Mr. Broadcasting" title in, 153, 159, 160, 162, 165, 169, 173; and newscasts, 136, 145 and *n.,* 161, 185, 205, 212, 233, 238, 244, 245-55; non-broadcast operations by, 209-11, 233, 239; Olympics covered by, 140, 205, 222; present-day, 237-76 *passim;* profits of, in 'Seventies, 173, 177, 184,

204-05, 213, 215, 222, 228, 234, 237, 240; publishing operations by, 177, 241; radio operations by, 27, 75, 122-32, 179-83, 202, 229, 237 and *n.* (*see also* FM radio stations, ABC's); and ratings, 137, 175, 185, 204, 205, 213, 214, 221, 223, 224, 225, 228; realignment and consolidation within (1970), 169-70; record and tape division of, 75, 122, 177, 183, 187, 206-07, 209, 218, 221, 233, 240; reorganization of (1972), 200-05; and Senate Juvenile Delinquency Subcommittee, 82; as "shirt-sleeve company," 68; in shootout at 66th Corral, 59*ff.;* and Silver Springs, 122, 177, 211, 240; and "Silverman syndrome," 257, 258, 259, 260; and sportscasts, 136, 140, 212, 243; television network of, 76, 133, 136, 139, 142, 154, 155, 157, 158, 159, 162, 166, 169, 170, 173, 184, 185, 201, 202, 211-12, 215, 216, 217, 225, 229, 232, 237 and *n.,* 243; theatre division of, 122, 177, 178, 211, 239; and theatrical films, 88, 89, 145, 186, 187, 196 and *n.,* 197*n.,* 205; of today, 237-76 *passim;* UPT merger with, 28, 29, 30, 32, 35-47 *passim,* 54, 55; VHF franchise acquired by (1947), 5; and Weekee

282

Wachee Spring, 75, 177, 211, 240; and
  Wildlife Preserve, 210, 222
ABC Entertainment, 123, 131n., 204,
  211, 215, 218-19, 240
ABC Leisure Group, 209, 210-11, 215,
  218, 222, 240
ABC Theatre, 205, 213
AB-PT, 48-54 passim, 59, 62, 63, 66, 89n.
Achley, Dana, 188, 189
Action for Children's Television, 267
Agnew, Spiro, 175
Aldrich, Robert, 178
Allen, J. Roy, 9
Alsop, Joseph, 21
American Home Products, 74
Anderson, Earl, 5, 23, 64
Andrews Sisters, 56
Arbitron, 164n.
Arledge, Roone, xii, 76, 140, 172, 212,
  238, 243, 245, 249-55 passim, 257, 258
Aubrey, James, 70, 71, 155, 170
Aug, Stephen M., 108

Baker, Seth, 241, 257
Bakshian, Aram, Jr., 269, 270
Balaban, Barney, xiii, 11-16 passim, 33,
  34, 35, 36, 38
Balaban, John, 16
Bardot, Brigitte, 178
Barnathan, Julie, xii, 69, 78, 81, 82, 83,
  140, 177, 217, 233, 243
Barney Miller, 217
Barnouw, Erik, 273
Barretta, 217, 221
Bartley, Robert T., 46, 99, 101, 105, 110
Bates Agency, 74
Batten, Barton, Durstine & Osborne
  (BBD&O), 77
Baum, Martin, 178
Bautzer, Gregson, 146, 148, 149
Bazelon, David L., 112
Beach, Jim, 77
Beach Boys, 271
Beatles, 271
Beaudin, Ralph, 123-28 passim, 131, 136
Bee Gees, 271
Beebe, John, 77
Beesemyer, Richard, 166, 174
Behn, Hernand, 92
Behn, Sosthenes, 92

Bell, Alan, 272
Benton & Bowles Agency, 74
Bergman, Ingmar, 186
Berkson, Herb, 147
Bionic Woman, The, 222
Bleier, Edward, 140
Blue Network, NBC, 6, 7 and n., 19, 20
Boldt, George C., 9
Bonsal, Dudley B., 148, 149, 150
Brando, Marlon, 178
Breakfast Club, 126, 128n.
"Bridge on the River Kwai" (film), 121
Bristol-Myers, 9, 74
Brittenham, Raymond, 107
Broadband programing, 273
Broadcasting magazine, 174, 175
Brown, Gordon, 32
Burnett, Leo, 76, 77
Burton, Richard, 178
Bus Stop, 82

"Cabaret" (film), 186, 187, 197n.
Cable television, 210, 272
Caesar, Sid, 269
Caine, Michael, 197n.
Campbell, John, xii, 99, 158, 160, 162
  and n., 210, 211
Campbell-Mithun Agency, 77
Camper, John, 268
"Candy" (film), 178
Carlin, Phillips, 20
Carter Country, 259
Casablanca, 51
CBS, 5, 12, 17, 18, 20, 21, 22, 23, 25, 27,
  29, 32, 39-43 passim, 47 and n., 48, 54,
  55, 58n., 62, 65-70 passim, 73, 76, 79,
  83, 87, 88, 95, 100, 116, 124, 131n.,
  154 and n., 155, 163, 165, 166, 173,
  175, 178, 185, 199, 205, 210, 220, 221,
  229, 230, 238, 241; and affiliated network stations, number of (1979), 233n.;
  at "Black Rock," 155, 172, 185, 230;
  diversification of, 243; Goldenson's
  compliments for, 231; and newscasts,
  246, 247, 248, 250, 251, 252; and
  ratings, 176, 214, 224, 225, 228; Silverman at, 218, 219-20; Weinrott's
  view of, 170-71
Chancellor, John, 248, 251, 252
Chapin, Slocum, 58

Charles, Ray, 207
Charlie's Angels, 222, 259
"Charly" (film), 197n.
Cheyenne, 51, 73
Chicago Tribune, 241, 267n.
Chilton Company, 241
Cinemascope, 50
Cinerama, 50
C.I.T. Financial Corporation, 149
Clark, Dick, 73
Clark, Samuel H., 75, 132, 136, 177, 178, 179, 187, 196, 197n., 206, 207, 208, 209; retirement of, 209
Clayton Antitrust Act, 47, 110
"Cleopatra" (film), 178
Clyne, Terry, 78
Cochran, Ron, 246, 248
Cohen, Manny, 148
Cohen, Ralph, 14
Cohn, Marcus, 109
Coleman, John A., 27, 52, 64, 90, 144
Color television, 17, 87, 88, 145
Colt 45, 51
Columbia Pictures, 226n.
Como, Perry, 56
Computer, TV set interfaced with, 273
Congress, and ABC-UPT merger, 44
Conley, James, 154 and n., 158
Connery, Sean, 178
Conte, Silvio, 102, 111
Cosby, Bill, 140
Cosell, Howard, 165, 243
Court of Appeals, U.S., 105, 111, 112, 115, 117, 144, 150, 152
Cousteau, Jacques, 213
Cowles, Sy, 223
Cox, Kenneth, 99, 101, 105, 106, 110
Coyle, Donald W., 163, 164
Craddock, Billy "Crash," 206
Crane, Clarence A., 8, 9
Croce, Jim, 207
Cronkite, Walter, 248, 251
Crosby, Bing, 21, 252
Crosby, John, 39, 40
Cuban missile crisis, 255
Cunningham, James D., 106, 107

Daly, John, 245, 246
Dark Shadows, 187
Dart, Justin, 19

Davis, Erwin, 189, 190
DeBare, Charles A., 131, 229
Deeb, Gary, 241, 242, 267n., 271
D.E.F. (delayed electronic feed), 253
DeSylva, Buddy, 15
Diller, Barry, 213, 215, 217, 223, 226
Disney, Roy, 51
Disney, Walt, 51, 52
Disney Studios, 52
Disneyland, 52, 53, 75
Disneyland (TV program), 52, 53, 62
Doherty, Richard, 184
Donny and Marie, 222
Dreier, Alex, 247
Duffy, James E., xii, 137, 138, 156, 169, 201-05 *passim*, 211, 232, 233, 257
DuMont, Allen B., 12, 13, 33, 41, 47n.
DuMont Laboratories, 12, 31, 33, 41
DuMont network, 5, 12, 13, 29, 31, 33, 37 and n., 41, 43, 45, 47n.
Durell, Thomas P., 7n.

Eastman, Robert, 124-25
Eight Is Enough, 259
Eisenhower, Dwight D., 76, 108, 246
Eisner, Michael D., 215, 217, 223, 226, 227, 258
Eleanor and Franklin, 223
Emmy Awards, 223
Erlick, Everett H., xii, 74, 114, 116, 127, 132, 145, 146, 147, 148, 150, 151, 169, 176-77, 197, 233, 257
Eyewitness News, 185

"F. Scott Fitzgerald and the Last of the Belles" (ABC Theatre), 213
Family, 222, 259
Fantasy Island, 259
Fats Domino, 271
Federal Communications Commission (FCC), xiii, 4, 13, 16, 17, 18, 20, 22, 24, 29-33 *passim*, 35, 36, 38-46 *passim*, 54, 117, 127, 128 and n., 129, 132, 144, 174, 177; ABC radio networks approved by, 129-30; ABC-UPT merger approved by, 46-47; Broadcast Bureau of, 31, 43, 44, 45, 109; and Hughes' "takeover machine," 147-52 *passim*; and prime time access rule, 185; and

proposed ABC-ITT merger, 92, 98-112 *passim*
Feuer, Cy, 186
Fiber optics, 273
Field, Marshall, 7n.
Fitzpatrick, Thomas B., 109
FM radio stations, ABC's, 124, 127, 128, 131 and n., 132n., 179-83 *passim*, 229, 232, 237
Fogarty, Joseph R., 273
"Fonz, The," 223
Football: NCAA, 54, 57, 58n., 59, 64, 76; NFL, 221, 243
"For Love of Ivy" (film), 178, 197n.
Ford, Frederick, 35, 36, 37, 40, 45
Fortune magazine, 231, 237
Freeman, Y. Frank, 15, 50
Friendly, Henry J., 150
Frizzell, Lefty, 206

Galactica, 259
Galane, Morton, 36
Garland, Harvey, 177
Geller, Henry, 150
Geneen, Harold, S., 92, 93, 94, 95, 98, 100, 101, 108, 113, 114, 115, 116, 118, 144, 248
General Foods, 74
General Motors, 17, 57
Gerrity, Ned, 115
Get Christie Love, 214
Giacalone, Richard, ix
Gilbert, John, 137, 138, 156
"Glass Menagerie, The" (ABC Theatre), 213
Goldberg, Leonard, 173
Golden, Jerry, 65
Goldenson, Genise, 72, 73n.
Goldenson, Isabelle, 63, 72, 189, 190, 191
Goldenson, Leonard H., xi, 3-13 *passim*, 16, 17, 22-28 *passim*, 34, 35, 42, 48-56 *passim*, 58-76 *passim*, 79-83 *passim*, 89, 90, 91, 98, 99, 137, 139, 140, 142, 143, 144, 153, 154n., 156, 159, 164, 176, 177, 178, 185-89 *passim*, 195, 196, 197, 203, 208, 213, 214, 215, 222, 230-34 *passim*, 245, 256-57, 258, 262-64; as artist, 190-94; in chairmanship role, 195-96, 199, 208, 247;

Fortune magazine on, 231; heart attack incurred by, 188, 189, 191, 195, 196; and Hughes' "takeover machine," 145, 146, 148, 149, 151; and ITT, 92, 93, 94, 95, 99, 100, 101, 106, 107, 108, 112, 114-18 *passim*, 248; in letter to mother, 191-94; Kintner discharged by, 65; and merger of ABC and UPT, 28, 30, 36, 37, 49; and motion picture production, 122; and reorganization of Paramount, 15; in shootout at 66th Corral, 59*ff.*; Treyz discharged by, 82; tribute to, 263-64
Goldsmith, Alfred N., 19
"Gone with the Wind" (film), 228
Goodman, Julian, 246
Gould, Elliot, 186
Gould, Jack, 41, 138, 139
Grant, W. T., 221
Gray, Joel, 186
Greeley, Bill, 180, 214
Greenfield, Jeff, 269
Greider, William, 226
Griffis, Stanton, 38
"Grissom Gang, The" (film), 186
Gross, Walter, 5, 26, 28

Hagerty, James, xii, 76, 108, 147, 246
Haggerty, Harry, 26-27, 28
Hale, Edward Everett, 213
Haley, Alex, 225, 226 and n.
Happy Days, 222, 223
"Happy Talk" news, 161, 250
Hardy Boys, The, 259
Harry O, 214
Hart, Philip A., 100
Hartman, David, 147, 150
Harvey, Paul, 131n.
Hausman, Jack, 264
Hawaiian Eye, 73
Hearst, Patty, 172
"Hell in the Pacific" (film), 197n.
Hennock, Frieda, 45, 46, 47
Hepburn, Katharine, 213
Hickey, Neil, 269
High Fidelity magazine, 210, 241
Hill and Knowlton, 147
Hinckley, Robert, 4, 5, 18, 39, 64, 65, 66
Hitchcock Publishing Company, 241
Hoffman, Abbie, 180

Hoffman, Dustin, 187
Homes Magazine, 241
Hope, Bob, 180
Hudson, Earl, 24
Hughes, Howard, xiii, 145-52 *passim*
Hughes Tool Company, 146
Hunt Foods, 90
Hunter, David R., 107
Husky, Ferlin, 206
Hutton, Betty, 56
Hyde, Rosel, 45, 100, 101, 105, 106, 150

Indiana Prairie Farmer, 241
International Telephone and Telegraph
   (ITT), xiii, 92-118 *passim*, 122, 127,
   132, 143, 144, 146, 248

Jacobs, Herb, 224, 225
"Jane Goodall's Africa" (ABC Theatre),
   213
Jennings, Peter, 246, 254
Johnson, Lyndon, 143
Johnson, Nicholas, 99, 101, 105, 106,
   109, 110
Jones, Robert, 32
Justice Department, U.S., xiii, 4 and *n.*,
   10, 29, 30, 32, 34, 35, 44, 46, 100-12
   passim, 116-17, 178

KABC-TV (Los Angeles), 133, 156, 158
Kaiser Company, 74
Kaye, Danny, 56
Kenmore, R. H., 107
Kennedy, John F., 271
Kennedy, Joseph, 15
Kennedy, Robert F., 175
Kestenbaum, Lionel, 108, 110
"Killing of Sister George, The" (film), 178
King, B. B., 207
King, Martin Luther, 175
Kings Row, 51
Kintner, Robert E., xi, 8, 21, 22, 24, 26,
   35, 36, 39, 42, 48, 52-66 *passim*, 87, 95,
   117, 165, 245, 246
Klein, Paul, 73, 242
Kobak, Edgar, 20
Kodiak, 213, 214
Kolchak, 213
"Kotch" (film), 186
KTLA-TV (Los Angeles), 12, 16, 31, 34,
   43, 273

KTVU-TV (Oakland), 273
Kung Fu, 213, 214

Laine, Frankie, 56
Langer, William, 44, 46
LaRoche, Chester, 7n.
Lasker, Jay, 207, 218
"Last Valley, The" (film), 186, 197n.
Laverne and Shirley, 222, 259
Lavin, Leonard, 82
Lawman, 51
Lawrence, William, 246
Lazarsfeld, Paul, 53
LCD (lowest common denominator) for-
   mula, 258, 260, 270, 271, 272, 273, 275
Lear, Norman, 272
Lee, Robert E., 101, 105
Lester, Jerry, 269
Levinsohn, Roann, ix
Levinthal, Lou, 207
Levy, Gus, 90
Lewis, Jerry Lee, 271
Lifeline, 259
Liggett and Myers account, 78
Little Ladies of the Night, 223
Loevinger, Lee, 101, 105
Loew's Theatres, 34, 49
"Long Day's Journey into Night" (ABC
   Theatre), 213
Los Angeles Magazine, 241
Louis-Conn fight (1946), 21
Love Boat, 259
"Lovers and Other Strangers" (film), 186,
   197n.
Lower, Elmer W., xii, 108, 136, 172, 205,
   212, 246, 247, 248
Lund, Art, 77, 78
Lundell, L. Walter, 149
Lynch, Kitty, ix

McAndrew, William, 246
McCall Corporation, 90, 91, 92, 99
McCann-Erickson Agency, 78
McClintock, Earl, 3, 5
McDermott, Tom, 74
McGranery, James P., 44, 46
McGraw, James, 7n.
McKenna, James, 42, 109, 117, 147, 148
McLaughlin, Edward F., 131, 229
Mallardi, Michael, xii, 257
"Man Without a Country" (ABC
   Theatre), 213

Mann, Al, 246
Manufacturers Hanover Bank, 145
Margulies, Stan, 227
Marine World, ABC, 177
Martin, Tony, 56
Marvin, Lee, 197n.
Marx, Frank, 5, 18
Maverick, 51, 68, 74
Mayes, Herb, 90
MCA, Inc., 240
Melnick, Dan, 82, 187
Merrick, David, 227
Merrill, Eugene H., 46
Metromedia Corporation, 47n., 180
MGM Pictures, 49, 50, 66
Mickey Mouse Club, The, 53
Mifune, Toshiro, 197n.
Miller, Elam, 19
Miller, Tom, 160
Miller Publishing Company, 241
Minnelli, Liza, 186
Mitchell, John, 60, 61, 62
Modern Photography magazine, 210, 241
Monogram Industries, 144
Moore, Ellis O., 170
Moore, Thomas, xii, 70, 82, 108, 132-42
    passim, 155, 156, 157, 158, 212, 247
Mork and Mindy, 259
Morse, Wayne, 100, 102
Mounds candy account, 81
"Mr. Broadcasting" title, 153, 159, 160,
    162, 165, 169, 173
Murrow, Ed, 269
Mutual Broadcasting System, 21, 41, 45,
    130n., 131n.

Nakia, 213, 214
National Citizens Committee, 267
National Geographic specials (ABC
    Theatre), 213
National PTA, 267
National Theatres, 11, 14
NBC, 5, 6, 7 and n., 12, 19, 20, 21, 27, 29,
    39, 40, 47 and n., 48, 54, 57, 58n., 65-
    70 *passim*, 73, 76, 79, 83, 87, 88, 95,
    116, 117, 124, 131n., 154n., 166, 170,
    173, 175, 185, 199, 205, 221, 229, 238,
    242, 261; and affiliated network sta-
    tions, number of (1979), 233n.; and
    newscasts, 246, 247, 248, 250, 251,
    252; and ratings, 214, 224, 225, 228;

Silverman at, 171, 238, 244, 257,
    258-59, 260, 261; Weinrott's view of,
    171; *see also* RCA
Neal, Harold L., Jr., 124, 126, 131, 181,
    182, 202, 229
Nelson, Gaylord, 100, 102
New Land, The, 214
New Republic magazine, 112
New York Daily News, 4
New York Herald Tribune, 39, 42
New York magazine, 219
New York Post, 4
New York Times, 41, 106, 108, 138, 203,
    267
Newsweek, 268
Nielsen ratings, 137, 175, 185, 214, 221,
    228
Night Stalker, 214
NILS Publishing Company, 241
Noble, Edward J., xi, 3-9 *passim*, 16,
    18-27 *passim*, 37, 39, 42, 48, 52, 54, 55,
    59, 61, 63, 64, 65, 66, 95
Noble Foundation, 61, 90
Northern Group of ABC theatres, 211

O'Brien, Robert H., 5, 6, 13, 16, 17, 23,
    24, 26, 42, 54-59 *passim*, 60, 62, 65, 66,
    165
O'Leary, Richard A., xii, 160, 161, 166,
    170, 185, 212, 229, 257
Olivier, Laurence, 213
Olympic Games, 140, 205, 222
O'Neill, Eugene, 213
Operation Petticoat, 259
Osborne, Jim, 134
Oscar Awards, 223

Paley, William, 17, 19, 20, 21, 22, 25, 48,
    49, 51, 55, 67, 88, 95, 185, 231, 261,
    264
Palm Springs Desert Museum, 190
Palomar Pictures International, Inc.,
    178, 196
Panitt, Merrill, 273
Paper Moon, 214
Papp, Joseph, 213
Paramount Pictures, Inc., xiii, 3, 4, 7,
    11-16 *passim*, 32-38 *passim*, 41, 42, 43,
    44, 47 and n., 50, 66, 215
Pastore, John O., 175
Patrick, Duke, 42

Pauley, Robert, 125
Pay television, 45, 272
Pearson, Drew, 21
Philip Morris Company, 76
Pickford, Mary, 36
Pierce, Fred, xii, 202, 204, 215-20
  passim, 223, 225, 227, 232, 242, 257,
  258, 259
Pival, John, 158 and n.
Playhouse 90, 269
Plitt Theatres, Inc., 239
Plummer, Curtis B., 43
Poitier, Sidney, 178
Pompadur, I. Martin, 157, 158, 169, 181,
  182, 206, 207, 209, 210, 211, 218, 221
Porter, Paul, 13, 32, 34, 42
Prairie Farmer Publishing Company, 75,
  124, 210, 241
Presley, Elvis, 251, 271
Priaulx, Nick, 57, 60
"Primal Man, The" (ABC Theatre), 213
Procter & Gamble, 74, 80

QUBE, 273
Quinlan, Sterling, 57, 154n.

Radio Networks (ABC), 126-32
Raibourn, Paul, 13, 33, 38
Raskob, John J., 17
RCA, xiii, 6, 17, 19, 21, 27, 41, 42, 47, 55,
  87, 88, 117, 171, 241, 257, 259, 261
Reasoner, Harry, 172, 185, 205, 212, 248,
  249
Rebel, The, 51
Red Network, NBC, 20
Resnick, Leo A., 31-35 passim, 37, 38,
  40-46 passim
Reynolds, Frank, 251, 254
Rich Man, Poor Man, 223
Riddell, James, 71, 75
Ridgeway, James, 112
Rifleman, 51
RKO Pictures, 34n.
Roberts, William, 42
Robertson, Cliff, 213
Robinson, Max, 251, 254
Robinson, Spottswood W., 112
Rock and roll generation, 271
Rookies, 221
Roots, 225, 226, 227, 228, 234

Ross, Wilbur, 108
Rubinstein, Jerold H., 218
Rudolph, Lou, 226
Rule, Betty, 134, 135
Rule, Elton, xi, 133-43 passim, 153,
  156-62 passim, 169, 173, 176, 177, 181,
  182, 188, 209, 213, 214, 215, 218, 222,
  234, 252, 256, 257, 258; as President of
  ABC, 195-200 passim, 206, 208, 233;
  reorganization plan by, 200-05

Sacks, David, 154
Safer, Morley, 252
Sarnoff, David, xiii, 6, 7, 19, 20, 48, 49,
  51, 87, 88, 231
Sarnoff, Robert, 95, 171
Satellite transmission, 121, 210, 272, 273
Schenck, Nick, 49, 50
Scherick, Ed, 82
Schickel, Richard, 267, 268
Schiff, Dorothy, 4
Schneider, Jack, 68, 153
Schwann music catalogues, 241
Schwartz, Walter A., 124, 126, 130, 131,
  201, 202, 211, 212, 213, 215, 217
Securities and Exchange Commission
  (SEC), 146, 147, 148
See It Now, 269
Seligman, Selig, 80, 178, 196
Selmur Pictures Corporation, 178, 196
"Seven Seas" tourist attraction, 210
Shaker, Theodore, xii, 133, 135, 136,
  141, 142, 143, 153-66 passim, 169, 212,
  246, 247; resignation of, 164
"Shalako" (film), 178
Shanahan, Eileen, 108
Sharif, Omar, 197n.
Shaw, Allen B., 131, 179, 181, 182, 183,
  229
Shaw, Irwin, 223
Sheehan, William, xii, 246, 248, 249, 253
Sherman Anti-Trust Act, 11
Shore, Dinah, 180
Shriner, Herb, 39
Siegel, Rose, 115
Siegel, Simon B., xii, 57, 60, 61, 65, 71,
  75, 78-82 passim, 91-96 passim, 110,
  114, 115, 116, 117, 123, 125, 126, 127,
  128, 132, 135-45 passim, 148, 153,

154n., 156, 159-64 passim, 169, 176, 188, 195, 198, 200, 245, 246, 247; and resignation of Shaker, 164; retirement of, 196, 197, 199
Sills, Beverly, 207
Silver Springs, 122, 177, 211, 240
Silverman, Fred, xii, 67, 73, 218, 219, 220, 225, 227, 238, 244, 257, 258, 259, 260, 270, 272; at NBC, 171, 238, 244, 257, 258-59, 260, 261
Simon, Norton, 90, 91, 92, 96, 97, 99
Sinatra, Frank, 56
Six Million Dollar Man, 214
Skelton, Red, 56, 180
Sklar, Rick, 182
Skouras, Spyros, 50
Smith, Gene, 42
Smith, Howard K., 185, 205, 212, 248, 254
Smithville, Historic Towne of, 210, 240
Soap, 259
"Song of Norway" (film), 186
Sonny Comedy Revue, 214
Soss, Wilma, 99
Southern Group of ABC theatres, 211
Spelling, Aaron, 271
Stage 67, 137
Stanton, Frank, 170
Starger, Martin, 173, 202, 204, 211, 212, 213, 215, 217, 219
Stark, Howard, 218
Starr, Ringo, 178
Starsky and Hutch, 221
Station Representatives Association (SRA), 129
Sterling, George F., 46
Stoddard, Brandon, 215, 226, 227
Stout, Jed, 108
"Straw Dogs" (film), 186, 187, 197n.
Streets of San Francisco, 214, 221
Studio One, 49
Sugarfoot, 51, 73
Sullivan, Ed, 56
Sunset Strip, 73
"Superstations," 273
Supreme Court, U.S., 11, 20, 35
Surfside Six, 73
S.W.A.T., 217
Swayze, John Cameron, 246, 269
Swertlow, Frank, 219, 220

Tamm, Edward A., 112
Taxi, 259
Television: cable, 210, 272; color, 17, 87, 88, 145; computer interfaced with, 173; criticisms of, 266-68, 269; dilemma of, 270-71, 272, 274; and "LCD Machine," 258, 260, 270, 271, 272, 273, 275; and new dimensions of leadership, 275-76; pay, 45, 272; question about, 274; and ratings war, 271, 272; target group for, 271; violence on, 175
Television Bureau of Advertising (TVB), 60
Telstar, 75
"Texaco Presents the American Heritage" (ABC Theatre), 213
Texas Wheelers, 214
That's My Mama, 214
Three's a Crowd, 259
Ticketron Corporation, 141n.
Time magazine, 72, 229
Tisch, Larry, 92
Tobey, Alton, 189, 190, 192, 193
Tobey, Charles, 44, 45, 46
Tomorrow Entertainment, 141n.
Tony Awards, 223
"Touch, The" (film), 186
Trendle, George, 10
Treyz, Oliver E., xii, 58, 59, 67-83 passim, 108, 137, 141, 155, 177, 217, 219
Turner, Donald F., 101, 102, 104
TV Guide, 269, 273
Twentieth Century Fox, 50, 110, 178
20-20 news special, 254

UHF channels, 40, 109, 111
United Artists, 186
United Cerebral Palsy Foundation, 72, 73n., 186, 262
United Paramount Theatres (UPT), 3, 4, 6, 7, 10, 11, 12, 13, 16, 17, 18, 23-45 passim, 47 and n., 54, 55, 56, 57, 60, 62-66 passim
United States Steel Corporation, 53
Universal Pictures, 223

Vane, Edwin T., 215
Variety magazine, 32, 154, 180, 199, 214
Vegas, 259

Video cassettes, 210, 226, 272, 273
Video games, 272
Vietnam War, 172, 269, 271
Village Voice, 182
Violence, television, 175

WABC-Radio (New York), 124, 130, 132n.
WABC-TV (New York), 165, 166
Wadsworth, James J., 101, 105
Walker, Paul A., 44, 46
Wall Street Journal, 41, 108, 269
Wallace's Farmer, 210, 241
Wallace-Homestead Publishing Company, 241
Walters, Barbara, 249, 254
Warner, Jack, 50, 51
Warner Brothers, 16, 51, 53, 62, 82, 178
Washington Post, 226
Watergate, 255
WBBM-TV (Chicago), 47n.
WBKB-TV (Chicago), 12, 16, 25, 31, 32, 34, 41, 43, 47n., 62, 154n.
Weaver, Sylvester "Pat," 67, 117
Webster, Fred, 46
"Wedding Band" (ABC Theatre), 213
Weekee Wachee Spring, 75, 177, 211, 240
Weinrott, Lester A., ix, 170, 171
Weisl, Ed, 5, 6
Weitman, Robert, 24, 48, 55, 56, 57, 58, 62, 66
Welk, Lawrence, 186, 187
WENR-Radio (Chicago), 7n., 124

Westinghouse Broadcasting Company, 47n., 123
WGN-TV (Chicago), 219, 273
What's Happening, 259
WHDH-TV (Boston), 174
Wide World of Sports, 57, 76, 137, 253
Willkie, Wendell, 9
Wilson, Tug, 57
Winchell, Walter, 21
Winkler, Henry, 223
Winter Olympics, 140, 222
Wisconsin Agriculturist, 210, 241
WLS-Radio (Chicago), 75, 123-24, 132n.
WLS-TV (Chicago), 154n., 161
WMCA-Radio (New York), 19
Wolper, David, 225, 226 and n., 227
Wood, Robert D., 175
Woods, Mark, 7n., 20, 21, 22
Word, Inc., 210, 241
World War II, 21, 92
Worldvision, 239
WOR-TV (New York), 273
WPIX-TV (New York), 219
WTCG-TV (Atlanta), 273
Wussler, Robert, 242
WXYZ-TV (Detroit), 158
Wyatt Earp, 51

Young & Rubicam Agency, 74, 177

Zanuck, Darryl, 50
Zorro, 51
Zukor, Adolph, xiii, 11, 13, 14, 36